Collection Management

Background and Principles

William A. Wortman

American Library Association
Chicago and London
1989

Text and cover designed by
Interface Studio
Composed by Interface Studio in
Garamond on a Compugraphic 9600
Printed on 50-pound Glatfelter B-31,
a pH-neutral stock, and bound in
10 pt. Carolina by Versa Press.

The paper used in this publication meets the minimum
requirements of American National Standard for Information
Sciences—Permanence of Paper for Printed Library Materials,
ANSI Z39.48–1984. ∞

Library of Congress Cataloging-in-Publication Data
Wortman, William A., 1940–
    Collection management / by William A. Wortman.
        p.   cm.
    Bibliography: p.
    Includes index.
    ISBN 0-8389-0515-3 (alk. paper)
    1. Collection development (Libraries)   I. Title.
Z689.W787   1989
025.2′1—dc20   89-6785

Printed in the United States of America.

93 92 91 90 89   5 4 3 2 1

Knowing books and men—knowledge of
the materials and their sources, and
empathy with the patron and his needs—these
are the twin pillars upon which
library service rests.

—Jesse Shera

Contents

Preface   vii

Acknowledgments   ix

The Collection Management Program   1

Collections   15

Quantity, Prices, and Publishers   39

Users, Uses, and Missions   73

Evaluation and Analysis   101

Selection   123

Access and Availability   147

Preservation, Weeding, and Renewal   179

Personnel, Administration, and the Profession   211

Bibliography   227

Index   239

Preface

In this book I have tried to describe the best way to manage library collections. Providing a good and appropriate collection is, I believe, the library's primary mission, and to fulfill this mission librarians must devise and carry out a comprehensive collection management program based on a sound understanding of library materials, of users and their needs, and of the nature of library collections. Librarians should know the basic principles and be aware of the many examples of good practices, both of which I hope I have outlined clearly, but we also must have an enthusiasm for our work, an enthusiasm that I have tried to demonstrate and elicit. Collection management is worthy, challenging, and tremendously rewarding.

A collection management program recognizes that each library's collection is a unique and coherent whole—developed and maintained in a particular time and place, for a particular community, and by a particular group of librarians—and treats the development and maintenance of this collection as interrelated activities requiring professional skill and understanding. Librarians must understand the uses and limitations of the various kinds of library materials, now produced in great variety and nearly endless quantities at often staggering prices (see chapters 2 and 3). Librarians also must identify their community, the range of their users' needs, and the ways these people use library materials (chapter 4). Librarians also must understand how their collections are coherent wholes, assessing their quality and appropriateness and identifying the unique character of each (chapter 5). Selection of new materials is based on our understanding of the character and usefulness of the existing collection—of materials, users, and the evolving relationship between them—and on a clearly defined mission. It also depends on a coherent and realistic collecting policy that considers past achievements as well as future directions and that emphasizes access to materials in our local collections and elsewhere and considers alternatives to purchasing such as interlibrary cooperation (chapter 6).

The collection must be accessible to users, with its materials available and in usable condition. Bibliographic control, circulation management, a storage system, and cooperation with other libraries contribute to effective access and availability (chapter 7). Usability is maintained through a systematic program of repair and replacement, preservation, and weeding (chapter 8). The responsibility for developing an effective collection management program lies with all of us. Library administrators must provide time, resources, and direction; library schools must provide a sound and up-to-date beginning education, followed by appropriate continuing-education opportunities; librarians individually and through their associations must provide an alert and responsible professional cadre (chapter 9). Ultimately, good management depends on good librarians.

This book presents my own understanding of collection management, developed through working in a particular situation but also through reading, teaching, and talking with other librarians. I hope it accurately represents the view of all practicing librarians who must deal with both the trees and the forest of their own collections. These practicing librarians are the primary audience for this book; they will find here a commonality of interest and a strong affirmation of the value of their work. A second audience is the newcomers to the profession, librarians just taking up collection management or even students in library schools, for whom this book could serve as a core text in collection management courses. A third audience is library administrators who, like the practicing librarians, may take this occasion to step back and view their operations broadly.

We work daily with practical realities yet long for the leisure to take a longer and wider view of what we do. The impact of this book, if any, will come from the fact that those who read it will do so because they are interested in collections: this will be not the cause but the occasion for improved collection management. We can talk and think about collections in general, but we all work with a specific collection, and so ultimately we must close this and other books, put aside the professional journals, come home from the conferences, and get down to work. Our collections await our attention.

Acknowledgments

The idea for this book originated in a class I taught at Columbia University's School of Library Service, and I must acknowledge first of all the students who took this course in the spring and summer of the 1983–84 school year and next Dean Richard Darling and the SLS faculty for encouraging me. If the course precipitated this book, my several years of working with the collection at Miami University provided the experience and much of the understanding that underlie it. Donald E. Oehlerts was director for most of my years here, and more recently C. Martin Miller as acting director and Judith Sessions as dean and university Librarian have both supported me in collection management work and have shown me how to do it well. Likewise important have been colleagues here with whom I have worked, thought, and learned as we sought, with some success, to build and maintain a collection appropriate to our university's mission.

Miami University gave me a professional development leave during the summer of 1985 when I was able to read and think without the distractions of the very thing I was planning to write about: work. I have tried to augment my experience by reading widely and sympathetically; library literature is on the whole sound and sensible and I hope I have cited the best of it. Much of this material I could not have found without the help of Sarah Barr, Miami University's interlibrary loan librarian. The book's graphics were produced by Miami University's audiovisual services. Both Herbert Bloom, senior editor at ALA Books, and Sheila Dowd, formerly assistant director for collection development at the University of California, Berkeley, read the manuscript and offered important criticism and suggestions for improvements.

I thank Sue, Emily, and Alice Wortman for their support, and I dedicate this book to my parents Allen and Zelma Wortman and to the memory of Jean Wortman.

Chapter 1

The Collection Management Program

The library's primary service is a good collection. This service is provided for users, actual and potential; the collection is made up of a variety of objects and media. Before libraries existed, there were materials to put in them; after libraries were built people came to them to find these items. The whole array of our profession's accomplishments—the Dewey classes and Sears headings and MARC records and Cutter numbers and Newark systems and Princeton files—and the whole range of our services—children's and young adults and reference and circulation and information and referral (I and R) all these techniques, inventions, and procedures serve collections that exist in a wide range of forms and sizes in a variety of libraries. Even though we do not create the information nor produce the materials in the collections, nor can we even claim to be interpreters of the collections, it is these collections that we gather and protect and make available.

This emphasis on collections begs a number of questions, of course. What is a "good" collection? Of what use is a collection at all if there are no services provided to make it accessible and usable? How can we talk about a collection without taking into consideration its users and their needs, expectations, and interests? Can a collection exist at all without the librarians who select, manage, and make it accessible to users? For that matter, what is a collection? Obviously, these are rhetorical questions designed to lay out the pattern for the discussion that follows. It is important to say now and as plainly as possible what it is I hope to accomplish in the following pages.

I hope to guide thinking toward the essential activities in a comprehensive collection management program and the principles

1

and understanding that underlie these activities. The term *collection management* describes all the activities involved in selecting, acquiring, and maintaining appropriate and usable collections. These activities must be treated as interrelated parts within a comprehensive collection management program. Librarians at all levels and in all areas must think holistically of their collections and recognize connections among the elements of the collection and the management activities. Although selection and acquisition have received considerable attention in the literature, they are only part of the total set of activities involving collections. The time and energy spent dealing with existing collections can dwarf the effort that is spent selecting new materials. Mending, preservation, and weeding decisions; filling gaps, measuring use and evaluating quality; and dealing with confused, irate, and desperate users all require a deep knowledge of collections, good managerial skills, a very clear sense of what the collection is and should become, and strong administrative support. Collection management is hard work based on hard thinking, accurate information, and real understanding. In this book I will try to ask the right questions, point to the key elements of the collection and the key managerial cruxes, and direct librarians and their associates toward effective professional work.

What Is a Collection Management Program?

A Collection Management Program (CMP) explicitly identifies all the aspects of librarianship directly connected with the development and maintenance of library collections, requires that librarians think about these activities as an integrated whole, and asserts that management of the collection is a library's primary mission. A Collection Management Program is not magic; a concept by itself will not produce better practices. Practices do need to be improved, however, and a first step toward improvement is to understand what all is involved. With that step taken, we can see more clearly what must be done and, possibly, how to do it. The Collection Management Program, as it will be presented here, should be helpful to administrators who more than ever need to see their operations as whole entities, but it is equally important for individual librarians who, whether having clear and direct responsibility for some aspect of the collection (such as subject bibliographers), or whether having significant contact with the collection through specialized assignments (such as catalog, circulation, or reference librarians), should think of their work in terms of the whole.

Fragmentation versus Understanding. Although I hesitate to offer yet another acronym, the CMP, I feel that activities involving collections have become so fragmented that librarians must reconceive their work. Because of this fragmentation, which is seen, for example, in our common administrative and position titles—technical and reader services, cataloger, acquisition, reference, circulation, bibliographic instruction, online-services librarians—we fail to recognize how central and all-pervasive the collection and all activities connected to it are. Likewise, our professional lives are fragmented. *Library Literature* and *LISA* do not contain headings for "collection development," "analysis," "management," or "maintenance." Subdivisions of the American Library Association (ALA) serve types of libraries or types of services but fail to provide directly for the collection. Activities connected with the collection occur in all divisions, most clearly perhaps in Resources and Technical Services (despite the strong tendency in academic libraries to have collection development handled by reader-services librarians). Only recently have journals been published that explicitly aim at librarians dealing with their collections. This fragmentation does not mean that good work is not being accomplished; certainly collections have grown and users generally have been able to find what they want on the shelves, but improvements still are necessary. We have reached the point where these improvements cannot occur until we reorganize and reintegrate our thinking.

On the other hand, while fragmentation may be the predominant condition, improvements are under way. The profession seems to be on the verge of recognizing that all the elements of collection management are related and of understanding the implications of this fact in planning. Many libraries have a collection management program, though not quite in name and perhaps not quite fully realized. These libraries can serve as good models for others. More librarians today seem to recognize the importance of the collection than they did a decade ago. Renewed interest within the ALA and other professional groups has led to the Collection Analysis Program and the Collection Management and Development Institutes, for example, while two journals, although not ALA-sponsored, now are providing a regular forum for publication *(Collection Building* and *Collection Management).* Specific aspects of collection management are being studied and acted on, most recently in the area of preservation.

Current Literature. This is not a field in which nothing has been written; a number of useful books are in-print. Annual reviews of the literature on collection management record upwards of 200 items per year.[1] Several textbooks on collection development or selection have received favorable reviews, have served students well, and have provided useful information and viewpoints for experienced librarians. Robert Broadus's *Selecting Materials for Libraries* is particularly helpful with its coverage of the tools and techniques of selection in specific subject areas.[2] Arthur Curley and Dorothy Broderick's *Building Library Collections* (the sixth edition of the now classic text by Mary Duncan Carter and Wallace J. Bonk) also devotes most of its material to selection, primarily as practiced in public libraries, with some discussion of principles and general issues in collection development, weeding and storage, preservation and replacement.[3] G. Edward Evans's *Developing Library and Information Center Collections* contains good material on publishing and distribution, community analysis, and weeding.[4] In addition, Evans's first chapter discusses the "Collection Management Process," taking an explicitly comprehensive view such as I offer here. Richard Gardner's prize-winning *Library Collections: Their Origin, Selection, and Development* offers a number of strengths, chief being its long section on the "origin" (that is, the publication and distribution) of library materials.[5] Sections on resource sharing and collection development policies also are helpful. William Katz's *Collection Development* touches on a great many aspects of selection,[6] and David Spiller's *Book Selection,* a textbook for British library school students, reflects British attitudes and practices.[7]

The closest we have to a comprehensive monograph on collection management is Stueart and Miller's *Collection Development in Libraries: A Treatise,* which, despite its title, is a collection of essays by several leading practitioners and teachers and not really a treatise.[8]

1. Ross Atkinson, "Preparation for Privation: The Year's Work in Collection Management," *Library Resources & Technical Services* 32 (1988): 249–62.

2. Robert N. Broadus, *Selecting Materials for Libraries,* 2nd ed. (New York: Wilson, 1981).

3. Arthur Curley and Dorothy Broderick, *Building Library Collections,* 6th ed. (Metuchen, N.J.: Scarecrow, 1979).

4. G. Edward Evans, *Developing Library and Information Center Collections,* 2nd ed. (Littleton, Colo.: Libraries Unlimited, 1987).

5. Richard K. Gardner, *Library Collections: Their Origin, Selection, and Development* (New York: McGraw-Hill, 1981).

6. William A. Katz, *Collection Development: The Selection of Materials for Libraries* (New York: Holt, Rinehart and Winston, 1980).

7. David Spiller, *Book Selection,* 4th ed. (Chicago: American Library Assn., 1986).

8. Robert D. Stueart and George B. Miller, Jr., eds., *Collection Development in Libraries: A Treatise* (Greenwich, Conn.: JAI Press, 1980).

Several chapters are excellent, although the whole book lacks unity of treatment and a consistently high level of discussion. A number of books deal with specific kinds of materials, activities (such as shelf maintenance, weeding, and preservation), and types of libraries, and these will be mentioned at appropriate points throughout this book. Because acquisition, processing, and cataloging will not be covered here, readers should refer to Magrill and Corbin's *Acquisitions Management and Collection Development in Libraries.*[9] What remains is a need for a comprehensive overview: just as the concept of a Collection Management Program demands comprehensive thinking, so does it demand comprehensive discussion.

Collections and Users

The concept of a Collection Management Program is founded on five assumptions about library collections. First, the collection exists to serve users' needs. The composition of a collection, however, is determined by librarians' understanding of who the users are and what their particular interests and needs are and what these subjects require in information and materials. No collection exists in a vacuum. It is important to recognize the elements involved: users, subjects, materials, and librarians. Librarians should and do make informed judgments based on their understanding of users and subjects, and it is not always true that users' needs and interests match perfectly with the requirements of a subject. Users are not always easily identified, and even when identified they may differ among themselves in range and intensity of needs and interests. To say that a subject has its own requirements helps librarians look at their collections free from the insistent requests of the most importunate users. For example, a library that intends to offer a collection of travel information and literature does not simply acquire what has been asked for but analyzes what kinds of literature and information exist in this field and then selects from this array, with some reference, of course, to the expected use the collection will receive. The librarian, then, responds to users' requests, interprets their needs and the requirements of subjects, and considers how various materials will satisfy these needs and requirements.

Second, a collection must be thought of in the broadest way. It

---

9. Rose Mary Magrill and John Corbin, *Acquisitions Management and Collection Development in Libraries,* 2nd ed. (Chicago: American Library Assn., 1989).

consists not just of printed books and periodicals but also of non-print and computer media; not just materials but also information and the contents of the materials; not just what is owned locally but also what is accessible (or should be) in other libraries. Information exists in some type of physical format, and it is these physical things, in all their variety, beauty, and troublesomeness, that we are most aware of. While we are dealing with the things in the collection, however, we must not overlook the content of these things. While we are managing the things in our own library, we must work cooperatively with other libraries to share what we all have and to ensure that together we collect all that we should to create a comprehensive collection.

Third, every collection is a coherent whole and, as such, has its own unique character and its own particular mix of materials, users, history, and hopes. Each is not merely an assemblage of items nor an abstract of the total, but is a selection that is, we hope, of good quality and appropriate to its users. In managing the collection we should try to improve or maintain its identity, and we should realize the importance of this coherent identity to users and to other collections that it complements.

Fourth, every collection is dynamic. Its materials change; its users and uses change. Growth is the most obvious change. Changes, however, can be deterioration, either in the physical condition of the materials or in the intellectual value of their contents. Changes also can be improvements, as when up-to-date materials are added or access is improved by better maintenance. A book or any other material is never, and never should be expected to be, static in the collection. Reclassification, relocation, rebinding, and replacement are facts of a collection's life; the information in books becomes obsolete, the illustrations out-of-date, the subject of diminished interest to the users. Librarians must be able to manage these changes and must be as alert to changes in the existing collection as they are aware of newly published materials.

Fifth, the library is an arena, a place in which people encounter our collections. The physical location, the arrangement of materials, the facilities and services for access and use, the space and place where the collection, conceived broadly, is used do matter. "Arena" also serves metaphorically: the collection itself is an arena in which users encounter information, knowledge, sensibility, even the physical objects themselves, and are affected. Libraries also have been described as storehouses of the published information and knowledge about and from the past; as sanctuaries where people can go to read on their own, at their own pace, of their own choosing, for their own purposes, and without distracting intrusions; and as gateways into the universe of information and media. But the library is most significant, I believe, when we go into its collection to encounter the past and rethink the present. The sixth-grader who studies Mexico in *World Book,* the parent who reads *A Nation at Risk,* the scholar who seriously undertakes to comprehend Derrida's ideas about philosophy and literary criticism, the business executive who analyzes the latest business data, all these users have encountered something new that has altered, however slightly, the pattern of their lives. For them, the library is the arena in which their ignorance, presuppositions, and carefully built-up understandings are challenged and changed. The collection matters.

Although this arena metaphor might seem excessively dramatic, we must agree that the users who come in to use our collections do not come to sleep. They come because they find something exciting in the library, they find their lives recharged there, whether it is their professional lives, their civic lives, or their personal aesthetic, intellectual, and spiritual lives. These users and their uses fall into a number of categories, from genre reading to scholarly communication, that we can anticipate and prepare for. It is usually the information and the content of the materials, more than the materials themselves, that users encounter. In the library arena, littered and piled high with books and periodicals, computer terminals, and audiovisual cassettes, we engage these materials hoping to subdue them for our users' benefit. The collection matters—to users.

Managing the Collection

The elements of collection management are universal and exist in all libraries, and although the importance of one or another element might vary from library to library and from day to day, a Collection Management Program is necessary in every type of library. Furthermore, what is said about the Collection Management Program in one situation generally will apply in others; therefore, I have not written separate chapters for different types of libraries. At the same time, I do have my own particular set of experiences and understanding. To make these clear, let me give an example that I think presents an accurate view of the ways in which the collection involves one librarian and, by extension, many of the ways in which all librarians are involved.

I am a humanities librarian working on reference and collection management in a medium-sized university library that serves students (undergraduates and graduates up to the Ph.D. level), faculty, and a variety of others—visiting scholars, interlibrary loan librarians in other libraries, local citizens, and the world of academic libraries in general. I find myself dealing almost constantly with matters involving the collection, with colleagues, students, and faculty, and also with publishers and the subjects I am responsible for. Beside my desk is a book truck loaded with books awaiting decisions about whether to mend, rebind, replace, send to storage, or discard. In my in-box are a fresh batch of publishers' catalogs, slips from our approval plan vendor, slips for books newly cataloged, and mail, some of it requests or suggestions from faculty about library materials. The door is open, the telephone is ringing.

The acquisition librarian calls to see whether I have a publisher's address for an item not listed in the usual trade bibliographies; I, in turn, ask for a follow-up on an order declared out of print (OP). A cataloger consults me about an item I had ordered that arrived in 88 separate parts. We have to decide how to process these parts, whether they should be bound or boxed, whether the separate parts should be labeled, whether they should circulate at all, whether we should put them in an acid-free box. I, in turn, want to be sure an expensive new book is targeted for the security system. Another cataloger wonders whether a particular subject tracing wouldn't be more appropriate in our library than the one given in Cataloging in Publication (CIP). The interlibrary loan librarian must verify an outgoing request on which the citation is faulty and also must deal with a request for a currently in-print book not in our collection. Our policy usually is to buy rather than borrow, but this one seems somewhat outside of our collecting range: a decision has to be made.

My office is near the reference desk, so a student whom I had helped yesterday stops by to seek more help: a key book on the subject is checked out on a long-term loan to a faculty member. Another student can't seem to find the specific edition of James's *Daisy Miller* that had been recommended by the instructor, although we certainly have plenty of copies of this novel. Yet another student wants materials on liberation theology, a subject that has not yet appeared in our curriculum. A faculty member who is working on late nineteenth-century British literature and is preparing a new course, as well as advising graduate students working on dissertations, presents a list of materials we will need to add over the next three-to-five years, including microfilms of little-known periodicals, several books now long out of print (but possibly available in reprint), and copies of unpublished typescripts of plays now in the British Library. A new area of our collection is going to be developed, it appears, with materials from a variety of sources. Can we afford this, interesting as the subject and the materials are? Should the library insist that professors work with what we already have or seek grants to buy these new materials? Should we just buy the reprints or should we go to the OP market for these novels (the reprints, not incidentally, are printed on acid-free paper)? How will we process and catalog those copied typescripts? Which of these materials must we buy or seek immediately, which can be put off for a year or more? Which can be bumped to a second or third priority, so that we can accommodate similar requests from other faculty members?

At the same time, I turn to the book truck with its damaged books, knowing at a glance that some are irreplaceable and completely unusable, although still needed. We cannot discard the books, and proper storage facilities do not really exist. Reprints of some are available, but are they really worth the cost, given the actual, immediate needs of the students and faculty who have stopped by? We know from our own analyses that mending is less expensive than rebinding, but that rebound books will stay usable for a longer period of time. Should we decide to patch up a quantity of books or more thoroughly repair a lesser quantity? Looking at these damaged books and thinking about the increasingly fragile humanities collection, about the high use certain parts of it receive year after year, and about the new scholarly editions of primary works and the flood of secondary studies, it becomes frighteningly conceivable that the whole collection will have to be replaced, while at the same time the publishers' catalogs and vendors' slips in my in-box already present far more than we can afford.

I need help. I must call a faculty member to ask her recommendation about a new periodical subscription. I must call my counterpart in a nearby library and try to coordinate some of our selection, weeding, and preservation decisions. I must call my director to urge cooperation among libraries on preservation and on lobbying for budget increases and price restraints. I must call the personnel committee to request travel funds to attend a Resources & Technical Services Division (RTSD) collection management conference.

This example makes several points. The most obvious is that the existing collection takes up the lion's share of librarians' attention, whether developing it by adding new materials or maintaining it in usable condition. There might be glamour and excitement in dealing with the new, in reading *TLS, Choice,* and *PW,* but these alone certainly do not prepare a librarian to answer the bulk of the questions nor deal with the bulk of the issues involving the collection. The interaction among librarians is a delicate process. We know situations where pettiness and ineptitude make cooperation impossible or where heavy-handed administration turns cooperation into a bureaucratic slough, situations where professionalism either died or was stifled. Furthermore, while many reference questions involve the contents of the collection, others concern the materials themselves, including the publishing industry and materials outside our library. The collection, that which is on hand and that which exists beyond the library, clearly is a constant concern of users and librarians. The example also shows many of the elements of collection management that will be discussed in the succeeding chapters:

1. Defining the kinds of materials available for and appropriate to a particular collection, based on librarians' understanding of users, awareness of publishing activity, and knowledge of the subjects.

2. Assessing the existing collection's strengths and appropriateness and developing short- and long-term plans for developing it.

3. Selecting new materials and making decisions about mending, weeding, storage, and preservation in line with policies and guidelines, according to plans, with awareness of and coordination with other accessible collections, and with attention to a reasonable distribution of budget funds.

4. Assuring access to and availability of the collection through efficient shelf management, reasonable circulation policies, and prompt replacement of lost, worn-out, and obsolete materials.

5. Maintaining the physical quality through proper shelving and handling, through a vigilant repair, rebinding, and replacement operation, and through a comprehensive preservation and storage program.

6. Reviewing on a regular schedule the use, availability, physical condition, and intellectual quality of the contents of the materials.

7. Keeping records that will ensure accurate and up-to-date budget figures, accurate projection of growth, and accurate understanding of the actual needs for such things as shelving, additional

acquisitions money, replacement and preservation of existing materials.

8. Providing for the continued professional development of librarians.

Merely creating a concept or coining an acronym will not make a better library. It is reasonable, however, to hope that librarians' professionalism, the library's performance, and the collection's quality will be enhanced when librarians and library administrators realize that all their disparate activities should be arranged to make up a comprehensive program for managing the collection.

Administration and Librarians

The example above described a librarian at the center of a web of collection management activities. It is too easy to talk about principles, guidelines, procedures, and practices and to overlook the people who put these into operation; it is easy to talk about the abstract as if it were actual. At the center of this web, the librarian has a number of responsibilities. Collection management is not a passive activity, not one of waiting for book requests and announcements to arrive on one's desk, for colleagues to call with problems and suggestions, for users to discover the gaps and the books supposedly held but actually unavailable. Good collection management demands aggressive and farsighted activity. We know collections must be relevant to user needs and subject requirements; therefore, we must discover these and anticipate them. We know collections change; therefore, we must anticipate and manage that change. We know that plans are essential to successful management; therefore, we must devise them and see them through to completion. We know that a collection is not just books and periodicals, nor even just materials; therefore, we must seek out the full range of media and information that should be in our collection.

The currently available books on collection development and selection are fine guides to the main tools and techniques of selection, but they are only the beginning. Individual librarians must develop their own repertoire of tools and activities. Library education must teach students the elements of collection management and must provide a coherent curriculum that is a model of concern for a coherent collection management program. Individual librarians must carry these examples and attitudes into their professional lives. The professional organizations must continue in directions that are now being taken to provide continuing education for individuals (such as the RTSD's Collection Management and Development Institutes), to provide management expertise to libraries (such as the CLR's Collection Analysis Projects), and to provide ways to link libraries and clarify the contexts in which they exist, such as the bibliographic utilities' and the Association of Research Libraries' (ARL) compilation of statistics on collections. They must continue to publish practical manuals, such as the recent ALA handbook, *Guide for Writing a Bibliographer's Manual*.[10]

Library administrations must provide a more carefully developed system for supporting the collection management activities of individual librarians. On the one hand, there must be freedom from the simplest kind of control, that of librarians higher in the organizational hierarchy unnecessarily overseeing the individual selection decisions of those lower down the scale. All this assures is that two people do the work of one. On the other hand, more attention needs to be paid to assuring the quality of the collection, the adequacy of its access and availability, and the upkeep of its condition. These activities are meaningful only if performed systemwide; one librarian's particular excellence goes for naught if the rest of the collection is only second-rate. Besides these organizational mechanisms and activities, the library administration must take some responsibility for enhancing and coordinating the work of the individual librarians. Most library departments, such as catalog, acquisition, reference, and circulation, produce manuals listing practices and policies and offering guidance for individuals; they also organize more or less formal programs of continuing education. Similar manuals and support or educational programs must be created for collection management librarians; the University of Texas libraries' *Bibliographer's Manual* is a good example.[11] Then, too, an appropriate scheme for evaluating, recognizing, and rewarding performance must exist. A fully developed Collection Management Program requires institutional and administrative support.

Ultimately, the individual librarian must take on responsibility for a segment of the collection and responsibility for one's own professional performance, and often must do this without a fully developed

10. Carolyn Bucknall, ed., *Guide for Writing a Bibliographer's Manual,* Collection Management and Development Guides, No. 1 (Chicago: American Library Assn., 1987).
11. *Bibliographer's Manual* (Austin: The General Libraries, University of Texas, Austin, 1982).

support structure. What is required? The previous example suggests several things. One must recognize the extent of collection management activities, their integration with activities of other librarians and their nearly all-pervasive character. One must become well informed about the particular collection requirements of one's subjects and about the publishing in that subject to be able to select materials and to answer collection-related reference questions. One must recognize one's role as a manager of this segment of the collection and undertake analyses, record relevant data, and use that data and these analyses to evaluate the quality of one's own work and the adequacy of the library's support for that segment of the collection.

Librarians must become more self-reliant. It has been said that the librarian is the last generalist. If that is true, then we also must recognize that this generalist status is our specialty. Being a generalist does not mean that we are generally ignorant in the presence of specialists, whether these are the local chess club and travel buffs or advanced researchers and senior professors, but that we are able to analyze and understand our specialists' collection needs. Collection management ultimately depends on knowledgeable, responsible, and up-to-date librarians.

Conclusion

The remainder of this book explains in more detail, and less rhetorically, what a collection can consist of, how it is selected, and what must be done to determine and maintain its usefulness. No collection can exist in any usable form without a full array of services working to make it accessible and available to users. Libraries, library schools, library associations, and librarians exist to develop collections and maintain their usefulness. To say that a library has a collection is to say that the library has a dynamic, constantly changing store of information and materials, over which it exercises careful custody through administrative mechanisms and the work of individual librarians, for the benefit of users, users present and future, local and distant. A collection is not a shelf of books, a rack of periodicals, a file of clippings, nor even a bank of data. Without the library the collection would exist in inaccessible form, unknown, unused, increasingly unkempt.

A Collection Management Program is a way of organizing these activities in a library so that what has to be done is done well, by librarians who are provided support, continuing education, and reward. By explicitly identifying the various elements in collection management, by integrating these elements in the most effective way, and by coordinating the work of librarians, the library develops a service without which no collection could continue in its usefulness. The best collections depend, finally, on a library's staff and services.

Chapter 2

Collections

Our primary service is a good collection, but what makes up a collection? A collection is a large number of those physical materials traditionally found in libraries—books, magazines, maps, video-cassettes, and so forth. A collection also is the information in or contents of these things, as well as the information trails into these contents. People come to the library to find a good novel or biography, or they come to find the latest journal; they also come to learn what novels exist that would make good reading, an author's birthdate, or the essential data provided by a graph in an article. As new ways are developed to package and provide access to information, the collection's ingredients become more varied; the information explosion has caused an explosion of collectible items. Yet while libraries increasingly include the information storing and manipulating capabilities of computers, they continue assiduously to acquire, maintain, preserve, and replace the traditional library materials. A librarian of the eighteenth or the nineteenth century, a Leibniz or a Panizzi, would have no trouble recognizing today's library, and an information manager such as John Shaw Billings would see true progress.

Not long ago the prospect of a paperless library terrified or excited librarians; we got hot under the collar debating the likelihood and desirability of such a future. Already, however, library collections provide a complex and dynamic mix of traditional print and nonprint formats, new computer services, and telecommunication links to other libraries. This surely is the model for the immediate and, I believe, long-term future. While computers won't replace books, they will supplement and complement them. Interlibrary cooperation won't turn libraries into dusty, seldom-visited stacks, but it will enable each library to acquire what it needs immediately and retrieve by shuttle, facsimile, or online what may be called for only occasionally. The role of books, crucial for creative literature and for the creation of

15

knowledge from the dynamic mass of information in serials and computer services, will be recognized and appreciated anew. The library still will be a place, the collection in it still will be tangible, and librarians still will worry about reshelving, mending, adding copies, and selecting effectively, only now applying these to compact discs as well as books and magazines. We may, in fact, be more able to think of our collection as a collection—that is, a *selection* from among a number of different materials, services, and arrangements. As *Webster's Third* defines it: "a number of objects . . . collected often according to some unifying principle or orderly arrangement."

The objects in the collection are the media through which authors communicate with readers. In subsequent chapters we will look at ways in which authors and publishers produce the materials and services, then at the range of users and the kinds of uses they make of collections, and finally at ways in which a collection can be defined and assessed. In this chapter, however, we will look at the three broad categories—print, nonprint, and computer media—that make up collections, hoping to understand the ways in which each is useful. The book is unique, but so is the compact disc, the magazine, the map, the videocassette, the loose-leaf service, the microfilm. To build a good collection, librarians cannot simply continue collecting books and ignoring new computer media, but neither can they abandon books and other traditional materials for a battery of computers. By knowing books (that is, the nature of collections) and by knowing people (that is, users and their uses), we can create and maintain good collections.

An incredible variety exists within these three categories. Print includes books and serials, pamphlets, newspapers and newsletters, loose-leaf services and lab manuals, maps, charts, posters, and a range of ephemera, and within these subdivisions is further variety. Books come in hardback or paperback, as monographs or collections, from trade publishers and university presses and small independent publishers, serving general readers or the most specialized of specialists, crammed with text or laced with illustrations, in an almost infinite gradation of sizes. Serials also appear in great variety, including monographic series—books—and annual directories, handbooks, and other book-form compilations as well as periodicals. Newspapers appear daily, weekly, and in between, from independent and not-so-independent publishers, covering narrow areas of interest or international affairs; and newsprint in newspaper format is the medium for a number of periodicals. Nonprint materials range from audiovisuals such as sound and videocassettes, films and filmstrips, records and tapes, realia, and kits, to microforms that usually are reproductions of printed matter. Computer services include hardware and software, CD-ROMs and online links, machine-readable data files, and OPACs, and they provide texts, indexing services, programs for manipulating data, and games. Some replicate traditional print services, while others are entirely new.

Not all materials in the collection have been purchased from publishers or sources outside the library. Librarians themselves produce a considerable quantity of materials, from indexes of local newspapers to detailed guides to collections to a variety of user aids such as bibliographies or pathfinders. Librarians also are resources in the library, informally when patrons ask them to recommend good novels or formally when they produce lists of recommended novels. The public card catalog or OPAC is a source of considerable biblio-graphic information, some of it not otherwise available even in the items cataloged. Librarians' significant knowledge and professional abilities must be considered part of the collection.

Collections are both materials and information, and users want and need both. Although it may be possible to distinguish format and function in some cases, in many others it is not. A novel is a book, a poem has to be printed; each can exist in other formats but neither is at its richest in any other form. "This is no book, Who touches this touches a man," said Whitman; *Leaves of Grass* on record, video, or printout would be absurd.[1] Knowledge, too, seems more likely to endure and to be used when in print than in digital bytes. Information, however, does not so readily depend on format, and data or opinion or pictures can be made available in several different ways, giving libraries the ability to provide them in the form most readily usable. To be successful librarians, we must discover those unifying principles and orderly arrangements that best meet users' needs. Collections, then, consist of three categories of materials, with the balance among them in any particular library determined by the ways these materials can—and will in future permutations—meet users' varying needs.

Print

Print is an integral feature of the modern world. It has had a

---

1. Walt Whitman, "So Long!" in *Walt Whitman: Complete Poetry and Collected Prose* (New York: Library of America, 1982), p. 611.

conservative and a liberalizing influence, providing on one hand a means of standardizing messages and texts to assure their authoritative (or authorized) expression, accurate reproduction, and wide dissemination, and, on the other, enabling individuals to read or publish independent opinion, alternative views of truth and fact, and increased opportunity for private, personal thought. Literacy surely has freed the literate, yet the illiterate have been pushed to the periphery of society, not freed but imprisoned. Life without literacy is unimaginable, yet life with it is complex beyond belief. Libraries existed before print, of course, but have flourished since its invention, as if entailed by it, and serve both to enable its essential virtues to flourish and to circumvent its negatives.

Print is a handy and inexpensive medium readily stored and reproduced, so that printed records, laws, sacred texts or documents, and cultural treasures can be collected into secure repositories and distributed to people at large. Readers can carry books or journals or printed sheets with them, shelve them at home, refer to them readily, and expect libraries to do likewise. Moreover, print has enabled effective integration of text and graphics. The travel book with text, maps, and photos; the scholarly journal with text, tables, and graphs; the Christian Bible with chapter and verse identified, certain sections highlighted by color or typeface; the illustrated children's book; the art history book; the college yearbook—all these integrate words and illustrations as they could not have before printing and in ways that provide a complex intellectual, aesthetic, and emotional experience.

Print is liberating. The reader gains access to an almost infinite range of fact and opinion, of graphic records, or knowledgeable discussion from all over the world and in almost any degree of complexity. There is no frigate like a book (said Emily Dickinson). The author can have virtually any thought printed and disseminated and can reasonably expect to find a sympathetic reader somewhere. Both author and reader are freed to find what truth they can in printed documents, to create or find new combinations of information and opinion, to make and express independent judgments on all matters. Likewise, social groups, from coteries to clubs to associations to communities and nations, can record and publish their messages.

Of course, there is a negative side. The dead weight of authority is heaviest in a pile of books; the chaos of crackpot opinion and misunderstood fact spreads wildly from an overactive press. Pornography, idle tales, slander, and libel flowered along with the elite book. Printers from Gutenberg's time on have done as much job work as book work and, while showing flights of ambition and sublimity, have like the rest of us usually aspired little higher than to keep happily occupied, make a decent living, and avoid incarceration or worse. It is nevertheless true that authority can be loosened and chaos restrained by accurate, conveniently available printed information and opinion. More significantly, an essential characteristic of the modern world—the application of reasoned, experimental, and democratic thought—can be linked to the invention of printing. As Elizabeth Eisenstein argues in her *Printing Press as an Agent of Change,* "As an agent of change, printing altered methods of data collection, storage and retrieval systems and communications networks used by learned communities throughout Europe."[2]

The capability of printed matter to record and store, to permit access and facilitate comparison and analysis, and to communicate and disseminate information, opinion, and knowledge also defines the capability of libraries and library collections. Scribal culture had books and libraries and a literate community, but this community and writing, its essential medium, were transformed by the Gutenberg Revolution. Printing worked in complex ways, however, and some of this complexity, as described by Eisenstein, is operating again today as computer media develop. The immediate effect of printing on books was conservative: old books and books already existing in manuscripts simply were redone in print. The immediate effect in other areas was different: "law books, reference works, maps, charts and tables, calendars, treaties, bills, petitions" were printed in which graphics and texts could be combined, accuracy and wide dissemination achieved, revisions and alterations incorporated, and in general truth promoted over error, scientific observation over imprecise impression.[3] In other words, information handling was affected more drastically than literary texts.

Alternatives to print today are working not to replace print but to replace—or improve—some of the things print had accomplished better than manuscripts. Microforms store and preserve certain kinds of texts more effectively than print; computer indexes often can provide more immediate and more precise access than print indexes; educational media can lead students quickly and clearly into complex concepts or learning situations. But print still has strengths in all these

2. Elizabeth L. Eisenstein, *The Printing Press as an Agent of Change: Communications and Cultural Transformations in Early-Modern Europe,* 2 vols. (Cambridge: Cambridge University Press, 1979), p. xvi.
3. Ibid., p. 30.

areas and in others that should not be sacrificed. Librarians must continue to study and think about what works best for what purposes in what situations.

Our thinking can benefit from the kind of analysis Elizabeth Eisenstein has applied to the communications revolution, as she calls it, that took place from the 1460s to 1500. A marked increase in the output of books and a reduction in labor needed to produce them occurred. A simultaneous development of text, pictures, and numeral printing took place so that pictures, tables, and charts could be reproduced accurately and in large quantities and could be coordinated with texts. Bookselling and related businesses sprang up or, in the case of binders and papermakers, expanded. Printing occupations, such as typefounders, compositors, copperplate makers, pressmen, editors, and proofreaders, developed and "new ways to coordinate the work of brains, eyes, and hands" evolved.[4] The master printer, an entrepreneuer, production manager, marketing expert, and large-scale employer, created a new kind of business and business mentality. Job printing of "commercial advertising, official propaganda, seditious agitation, and bureaucratic red tape" filled out the production schedule of printers and perhaps produced a greater impact than books in creating a print culture.[5] Literacy became crucial and widely, though unevenly, spread (and spread in ways that we do not yet understand: Who could read and to what degree? What was read and by whom? What differences were there in literacy among classes, rural and urban populations, different countries and regions?). Print, Eisenstein reminds us, involved pictures as much as text: "Surely the new vogue for image-packed emblem books was no less a product of sixteenth-century print culture than was the imageless . . . textbook."[6] Finally, the revolution worked broadly and deeply. "The movement of centers of book production from university towns, princely courts, patrician villas and monasteries into commercial centers; the organization of new trade networks and fairs; the new competition over lucrative [printing] privileges and monopolies; the new restraints imposed by censors" were essential in the creation of the modern Western world.[7] Each of these points can be seen happening today as one result of computerized information storage, manipulation, and transfer, and each already has occurred and recurred as print and nonprint media have

---

4. Ibid., p. 56.
5. Ibid., p. 59.
6. Ibid., p. 69.
7. Ibid., p. 58.

evolved. Libraries and their collections likewise have evolved and will continue to do so.

Books. Books come in many formats from many kinds of publishers. Hardbound books, whether in bindings supplied by the publishers or crafted in the library, whether perfect-bound or sewn, are produced by trade, scholarly and academic, religious, educational and juvenile, professional and technical, association and institutional publishers, and paperbacks by scholarly, trade, and mass-market publishers. Most books arrive whole, but some appear in fascicles to be bound when completed; there are books in spiral bindings, rings, or loose-leafs; there are books that include a packet of slides, records, cassettes, computer disks, microfiche, or a packet of removable print matter (maps, blueprints, illustrative plates, tables of data). To add books to our collection is thus to add a wide variety of items that often are not closely related, that must be handled, processed, and shelved in different ways. "Books," clearly, mean more than just books.

Books also offer a variety of contents. There are monographs, discussions of single subjects by single authors; there are collections of chapters on a single or on diverse subjects by a single or by multiple authors, including essays published previously or published here for the first time. These monographs and collections differ from novels and collections of short stories, poems, or plays. A novel is not a monograph, a book of poems not the kind of collective work indexed in *Essay and General Literature Index.* A book of poems, not infrequently, is technically a pamphlet because it contains less than 49 pages, but it seems wrong to describe a book of poems—hardbound, possibly handprinted on fine paper with careful craftsmanship—as an informational pamphlet.

The book is a unique package of text, graphics, and data, with its substantive contents arranged in suitable fashion and indexed. A novel needs no more organization than its story's inherent divisions and can do without graphics other than the basic design of typeface, page layout, title page, headings, and chapter divisions. A treatise on collection management, however, must have an arrangement of chapters and subdivisions that demonstrates the organization of the substantive discussion, must have appropriate graphs or charts, and must have an index. This treatise is, ideally, a coherent whole that is more than simply a collection of information, and as such it plays a specific role in the process of scientific and scholarly communication. While technological developments have enabled printed technical reports, conference proceedings, festschriften, and other collections and monographic series to improve in timeliness, the particular value of the monographic treatise, in which an author can synthesize previous work or theorize about basic patterns within the subject, is enhanced by, if not made possible by, the convenient, portable, and eminently consultable book format.[8] The book in this sense has not been, nor is ever likely to be, superseded.

On the other hand, factual information that traditionally has been collected in almanacs, yearbooks, data handbooks, loose-leaf information services, and directories probably can be presented and accessed more effectively through computer media than through books. The information itself can be updated and corrected continuously, and the whole expensive process of publication can be avoided. No handling of volumes is involved, and access is possible immediately and through multiple points and with Boolean logic. With the right software, the data can be manipulated in the same process as it is accessed, and the computer media thus turns into an entirely new tool than the book compilation.

The book as a medium of deep, satisfying comfort derives not merely from its physical shape or aesthetic conditions, but from its now inherent connection with what is believed or strongly felt to be truth. "To curl up with a good book" can be understood figuratively as well as literally and must be understood profoundly as well as casually. While we might not always curl up, we do isolate ourselves in the presence of a good book and experience profound appreciation of literary style, religious utterance, philosophical analysis, scientific synthesis, or heroic narrative that allows us to transcend the mundane and quotidian.

Those who have access to the book are privileged and find immense satisfaction and support in it. To call the book a medium of information is to understate its effect and to misunderstand readers' hankerings for it. Libraries, thus, have long been the seat of power for ordinary people, for the common reader. For our readers the book is essential as a source of pleasure, whether that is the deep pleasure of, say, *Pride and Prejudice* or the more transient solace of the latest Harlequin romance. Not every book is a good book, but every good

8. Marshall Lee, *Bookmaking: The Illustrated Guide to Design/Production/Editing,* 2nd ed. (New York: Bowker, 1979). *See,* for example, pp. 133–35 on the Cameron belt press.

book has strengths that cannot be duplicated by any other format of library material.

Serials. Serial publications are a complex category, ranging in format from bound books to single sheets of paper. *AACR2* defines them as "a publication in any medium issued in successive parts bearing numerical or chronological designations and intended to be continued indefinitely."[9] Succinct as this definition is, it has not brought absolute clarity to the field. Andrew D. Osborn in his *Serial Publications* devotes a chapter to defining serials and another to tracing their history, and then in the remainder of his book he discusses, among other matters, these kinds of serials: abstracting and indexing services, annual reports, directories, financial reports, government publications, journals, little magazines, monographic series, newsletters, newspapers, proceedings, official catalogs, society publications (from learned, professional, and other associations), technical reports, and yearbooks.[10]

A key element for librarians, often omitted from definitions, is that serials must be ordered on a subscription basis and almost always must be paid in advance or with very limited return privileges. Financially, serials take precedence over books. There are more serials than books, serials cost more and claim their share immediately, serial prices have inflated faster than those of books. There is a cottage industry in check-in, claiming, and binding or microfilming periodicals, and there is constant concern about effective management (as evidenced by Marcia Tuttle's *Introduction to Serials Management* and David Taylor's *Managing the Serials Explosion*).[11] There is also a matter of contents. Serials on the whole carry the most recent, the most specialized, the most innovative information and cater to the most specialized reader interests. Human hunger for news, scholarly and scientific research, and the accelerated pace of development in all fields require serials. While few would argue that serials are any more important than books and although each has a crucial role in collections, it is not inaccurate to say that libraries have become serial-centered.

9. *Anglo-American Cataloguing Rules,* ed. Michael Gorman and Paul W. Winkler, 2nd ed. (Chicago: American Library Assn., 1978), p. 570.

10. Andrew D. Osborn, *Serial Publications: Their Place and Treatment in Libraries,* 3rd ed. (Chicago: American Library Assn., 1980).

11. Marcia Tuttle, *Introduction to Serials Management* (Greenwich, Conn.: JAI, 1983), and David C. Taylor, *Managing the Serials Explosion: The Issues for Publishers and Libraries* (White Plains, N.Y.: Knowledge Industry, 1982).

Periodicals: Magazines and Journals. Although the term *periodical* is not used in *AACR2,* it still is widely used by librarians for magazines and journals, those serial publications that appear at least twice a year, with a consistent range of subjects covered and manner of treatment of these subjects (articles, reviews, editorials, letters to the editor, etc.). Periodicals require specialized handling, including the whole process of checking in, routing, special shelving, binding, and other kinds of maintenance, such as claiming missing issues, replacing lost pages, microfilming for preservation or storage, providing adequate indexing. More to the point, periodicals are used heavily. This category of materials, albeit difficult to define with precision, has become as important in a library as books. According to Charles Osburn, research library collections have become "journal-centered" (the exact meaning and implications of this observation will be examined more thoroughly in chapter 4), but it is just as true that nonresearch library collections make increasing use of magazines.[12] Magazines and journals, which have proliferated in number and increased in specialization, now consume an ever larger share of acquisition budgets.

No useful distinction between magazine and journal is made in the *ALA Glossary, AACR2,* nor by Osborn, yet readers often are expected to distinguish between them. Style manuals, such as the *MLA Handbook* and the *Publication Manual of the American Psychological Association,* give directions for citing them as different kinds of publications. A definition should consider frequency, contents, and format; title is no sure indication, for the *Journal of Accountancy* is a magazine while *American Psychologist* is a journal. Magazines are periodical publications with a variety of contents, including articles that tend to be journalistic in their mix of factual information and analytical opinion, fiction and poetry, regular columns, features such as puzzles and contests, letters to the editor, a large amount of advertising, and illustrations (including cartoons)—all usually aimed at a wide and nonscholarly audience. Frequency of publication is usually at least six times per year (weekly, twice monthly, monthly, or every other month). Journals are periodical publications for scholarly or professional readers, usually specializing in subject matter with articles tending to be factual and analytical. Editorials and columns of opinion are less common, but letters to the editor commenting on previous

---

12. Charles B. Osburn, "New Directions in Collection Development," *Technicalities* 2 (2) (1982): 1, 3–4.

articles can be extremely important, as can book reviews. Some journals include the features of newsletters, and some carry limited amounts of advertising, usually for products of professional interest. Frequency of publication is usually two, three, or four issues per year. Magazines are essential in public and school libraries, journals in academic and research libraries.

Journals play an integral part in scholarly and professional communication. In journals the latest research is published, and published in a form that allows readers not just to hear of it but also to analyze its quality and to take these reports and replicate experiments or analyses, to apply results or methods in their own research, and to compare them very carefully with others. Through the process of peer review, journals have become the medium for communication of authoritative, specialized, current research information. Other media, such as newsletters, personal letters, word of mouth, conferences, and professional meetings, can be more current, but they lack the kind of authority that the refereed journal has. The tremendous variety of journals, which seemingly increases daily, and their preciseness of specialization have made them suspect to some librarians, who view this abundance as a plethora and little more than institutionalized academic vanity and aggrandizement. These librarians are, on the one hand, hard-pressed to keep up with the increase in relevant titles let alone able to take out subscriptions to new ones requested and needed, and, on the other, harassed by title changes, twigging of one journal into two or more, supplements and special issues, price increases, binding, fulfillment, and claiming problems. The exasperation of the serials librarian is understandable, but we must not overlook the essential role that journals now play.

The field of magazine publishing also is changing rapidly, although it may be that this field always has changed rapidly as publishers and audiences shift interests and needs. Today, there are fewer general-interest magazines than in previous generations. General-interest magazines are those magazines that try to appeal to a large audience by providing a broad range of features on a wide spectrum of subjects aimed at a readership catholic but nonscholarly in taste. Possibly the closest thing today to a general-interest magazine is the newsweekly, but even these newsweeklies, despite their frequent use of extended articles on specialized topics, do limit themselves to coverage of newsworthy people, events, and developments in broad fields such as education, arts, and medicine. Of the ten U.S. magazines with the largest subscription lists only one is general interest, *Reader's Digest.*

The other nine are *National Geographic, Modern Maturity, TV Guide, Better Homes and Gardens, McCall's, Time, Ladies Home Journal, Guideposts,* and *Good Housekeeping.*[13]

Special-interest magazines have multiplied as dramatically as specialized scholarly journals. Perhaps the best way for the librarian to realize this is to spend ten minutes browsing through a well-stocked newsstand with its magazines, in multiple titles, on such subjects as health, fitness, sports, apartment living, science, computers, fashion, wrestling, hunting, motorcycles and motorcycling, cars, guns, homemaking, a variety of women's concerns, career living, states and cities, cooking and eating, travel, games, antiques, local or regional history, hobbies and crafts, social, political, and intellectual issues—and more. The audience for these magazines varies according to such different factors as income, education, age, and geography, so librarians must be aware of local demographics and interests as well as nationwide trends.[14]

Newspapers. Since the first newssheets appeared in the seventeenth century, newspapers have maintained a remarkably consistent format and character. First, their main concern is news, a record of recent events of interest to the intended audience, usually news of political, military, economic, and some social and cultural affairs, generally directly related to a community, state, or nation. Second, the use of newsprint and of folded but not bound or fixed sheets has long been standard format. Third, the regularity of publication, whether daily, twice-weekly, weekly, or less often, along with the regularity of certain features such as weather reports and forecasts, advertising, calendars of local events, in addition to news, has made the newspaper an integral part of the commercial and social community. Fourth, the role of the newspaper as a segment of the political body, as indicated by the common phrase "fourth estate" and as implied in the U.S. Constitution and established in English common law, has given it a multiple identity—at once booster and critic, disseminator of useful information and investigator or discoverer of information not otherwise readily available. Finally, because the newspaper reports news and advertises products and services, it is a record of human activity.

---

13. *Folio 400, 1984: The Magazine for Magazine Management* (New Canaan, Conn.: Folio, 1984), pp. 49–73.

14. On the problems of trying to balance "women's" and "men's" magazines in the public library *see* Gail Pool, "Magazines," *Wilson Library Bulletin* 59 (1985): 348–49.

In the United States, newspaper ownership has tended to be local and independent of both government and large commercial interests. Yet recently, the corporate nature of the ownership of many papers has called into question their independence and objectivity, and much of the contents of newspapers now is purchased from centralized services, such as the Associated Press or King Features Syndicate. An inherent conflict may exist between the need to operate at a profit sufficient to attract and reward investors and the need to appear—to actually be—independent of any kind of controlling ideology. There are many newspapers because they are profitable businesses and because readers want the variety of news represented in several papers.

For libraries, newspapers are an important information medium and must be treated with care and in a carefully worked-out program. Selection, access, indexing, preservation, and storage all present unique problems and require specialized knowledge on the part of librarians. Newspapers have historical as well as current usefulness; the extent to which they are a record, often the only record, of local events and local reaction to events elsewhere requires that they be preserved yet stored accessibly. The need of local people for news of or from other communities requires careful consideration of the range and number of newspapers to subscribe to. These and other matters are treated by Osborn, in Geoffrey Whatmore's *Modern News Library,* and in Richard Schwarzlose's *Newspapers: A Research Guide.*[15]

Newsletters. Despite the similarity of name, newsletters and newspapers are quite different publications. Newsletters are almost always the disseminator of information produced by some organization or association. They are occasional, more-or-less regular publications from associations, organizations, institutions (such as the library itself), and other bodies containing mainly news about the doings or interests of the members or employees. Although frequently of very short-lived and very specialized interest in appropriately inexpensive format, these can contain significant news or authoritative opinion for which subscribers are willing to pay expensive rates. Some develop into more substantial magazines or journals. See Brigette Darnay and John Nimchuk on the "newsletter phenomenon" in *Newsletters Directory.*[16]

---

15. Geoffrey Whatmore, *The Modern News Library* (Syracuse, N.Y.: Gaylord, 1978), and Richard A. Schwarzlose, *Newspapers: A Research Guide* (Westport, Conn.: Greenwood, 1987).

16. *Newsletters Directory,* ed. Brigette T. Darnay and John Nimchuk, 3rd ed. (Detroit: Gale, 1987), pp. 9–11.

Popular Culture Materials. A number of advocates, notably Frank Hoffmann in his *Popular Culture and Libraries*, have made a persuasive case for the historical and intellectual value of popular culture materials, even though libraries have not commonly collected them. To the extent that libraries consider themselves agents for collecting and preserving a record of human culture, then to that extent they should include popular culture materials. To the extent that they seek to collect and make available cultural materials of interest to a significant share of their actual or potential users, for scholarly or recreational purposes, they should collect popular culture. Popular culture includes such materials as genre fiction (science fiction, mysteries, romances, westerns); popular biographies; works about movie, television, sports, and entertainment personalities; religious and self-help works. For juveniles there are comic books, fanzines, series and genre fiction, an increasing number of magazines, and more-or-less educational nonfiction. For adults, in addition to the forms just mentioned, there are also a number of works about current events and issues that even if they do not contribute to a reasoned and informed analysis of the particular issue or event do record the response of a significant share of our population.

Purely local items belong here, of course, as part of our local history collections, and local history collections should also include in some measure printed ephemera, a subgenre within popular culture. Political fliers, posters, programs, and advertising sheets tell us about prices, attitudes, controversies, and fads of the past. The scale of ephemeral materials is so vast that it almost has to be limited to localities, but at this level collecting ought to be conscientious and purposeful, if necessarily constricted because of the great quantity of material involved. See Chris Makepeace's *Ephemera: A Book on Its Collection, Conservation and Use.*[17]

It has been pointed out that we are all influenced by popular culture whether we are devotees of it or not. The juxtaposition, for example, of news of real wars with the fictional treatment of wars in movies, on television, in comic books, toys, and popular music recordings cannot help but produce attitudes and feelings not accounted for by rational thought about the significance and merits, if any, of war. Popular culture can to some extent be thought of as a "fictional realm" that coexists with a "factual realm," commenting

17. Chris E. Makepeace, *Ephemera: A Book on Its Collection, Conservation and Use* (Brookfield, Vt.: Gower/Grafton, 1985).

on it, reinforcing or undercutting it, and in general augmenting it.[18] At the very least popular culture provides an underlining of events in the factual realm recorded by news media.

Nonprint Material

Nonprint varies in format and uses, from popular entertainment (movies and television, for example) to educational filmstrips and teaching materials to great collections of primary historical material crucial to scholars but usable by all. Pearce Grove in *Nonprint Media in Academic Libraries* lists 18 general and 73 specific designations of nonprint media, all distinguished by format or means of production.[19] Rather than enumerate all these, however, we can split off computer data files, which actually have developed into a separate media, and then arrange the remaining into three broad categories. There are nonprint media whose primary function is preservation and research; these are mainly microforms. There are educational nonprint media, the traditional audiovisual materials. And there are cultural media, such as videocassettes and music and spoken-word recordings.

Preservation and Research. Microforms are the primary form for preservation and a significant form for research materials. They are used to preserve individual titles of books, newspapers, periodicals, and other originally printed material, and they are used similarly for such unprinted matter as manuscripts, financial ledgers, and correspondence. These materials usually have research value (as does just about everything) but often they are also important cultural records that should be preserved. The antislavery pamphlet material collected at Oberlin College and published in microformat by Lost Cause Press, for example, is an invaluable piece of our cultural heritage.[20] The entire record of English language books (including pamphlets and many broadsides) published before 1701, much of those of the eighteenth century, and a large share of the newspapers and magazines of the eighteenth century to the present have been or are likely to be filmed, preserving a mine of information for historians, genealogists, general readers, and scholarly critics.

---

18. C. Lee Cooper, "Introduction," in Frank W. Hoffmann, *Popular Culture and Libraries* (Hamden, Conn.: Shoe String, 1984), pp. viii–xv.
19. Pearce Grove, ed., *Nonprint Media in Academic Libraries* (Chicago: American Library Assn., 1975), pp. 48–50.
20. Suzanne C. Dodson, *Microform Research Collections: A Guide*, 2nd ed. (Westport, Conn.: Meckler, 1984).

Preservation microfilming is newly recognized as an important library function, one that must be put on an organized and long-term basis. We have long collected microfilm volumes of periodicals and newspapers to save storage space and preserve obviously deteriorating newsprint, but with our realization of the enormous problems with acidic paper we have renewed and expanded our preservation work. Additional ambitious projects, such as that undertaken cooperatively by the American Philological Association and the Research Libraries Group, no doubt will develop. This subject is explored more fully in chapter 8.

Microforms have, in addition, led not only to the preservation but also the creation of research collections, largely through the efforts of entrepreneurial publishers. Certain materials, such as doctoral dissertations and a mass of unprinted educational reports that would not have been published nor even given adequate bibliographic control, have been made accessible and usable in microform. Other materials, from rare printed books existing in only a few libraries to uncollected materials such as publishers' business archives, have been located, filmed, and then sold as a microform collection. Both the conception and the media are the result.

Microforms also have been developed as library tools, such as the *National Union Catalog* now in fiche. Many publications routinely combine print and fiche, and this combination holds promise of economical publication of heretofore prohibitively expensive research materials (for example, a microform collection of a person's correspondence and other unpublished material along with a printed index). Microforms play an even greater role in the business sector where they are used to store records and for such access tools as fiche catalogs. Alan Meckler estimates that these uses surpass scholarly uses by more than five times.[21]

Users claim to dislike using microforms, but this objection mainly applies to reel films of periodicals, newspapers, and books. Microforms are not a quick medium, nor are they easy to index or access. The various microfiche tools meet with less resistance. Whether digital laser-disc technology will replace microfilm remains to be seen—or, more accurately, the ways in which computer media supplant and complement microforms remain to be seen. The many microfilm projects already completed or well under way will not be duplicated

---

21. Alan M. Meckler, *Micropublishing: A History of Scholarly Micropublishing in America* (Westport, Conn.: Greenwood, 1982), p. xiii.

or replaced by digital disks, but in the future many similar projects could be performed with this new technology, provided that it has a suitable degree of permanency. For the moment, however, the National Archives has ruled out computer media as a preservation tool.[22] No doubt microforms will continue to occupy a valuable place in libraries.

Educational Media. Educational media, those nonprint materials such as audiocassettes and videocassettes, films, filmstrips, slides, kits, games, puzzles, and models, are highly purposeful and sharply focused on a distinct user group. They clarify and highlight themes and details and thus direct students toward what is to be learned. They motivate and reinforce, drawing students into the learning experience and rewarding their attention. Ultimately, however, they refer outward, often to print that can present information and knowledge of greater complexity. School libraries are the primary location for their use, while academic libraries vary in their degree of use. The use of these materials in schools and school libraries is discussed thoroughly in Prostano and Prostano's *The School Library Media Center*.[23] Print material seems to have regained a larger share of user interest here; certainly the audiovisual share of academic library budgets has decreased steadily in recent years.[24] Public libraries can use some documentary-type educational media and can use more overtly educational media in their public programming. Corporate libraries may well be major users, at least in those firms with active employee-training programs.

Cultural Media. Nonprint media have a particularly effective place in modern cultural life, having taken over some of the functions that books and sheet music once had. Some people regret this, but libraries do not deal with regrets, only with the realities of our cultural life. Box-office films, televisions shows, recorded radio broadcasts, music records and cassettes, and even video games are a sizable business and clearly occupy a large, as well as effective, place in our lives. The part they play has to be described as cultural and is comparable to that of books, serious magazines, the fine arts. The current popularity of videocassettes may pass, but if it does it will be replaced by some

22. Alan Calmes, "New Confidence in Microfilm," *Library Journal* 111 (Sept. 15, 1986): 38–42.

23. Emmanuel T. Prostano and Joyce S. Prostano, *The School Library Media Center*, 3rd ed. (Littleton, Colo.: Libraries Unlimited, 1982).

24. *Bowker Annual*, 16th ed. (New York: Bowker, 1970–), reports public and academic acquisitions of audiovisuals as well as books and periodicals.

other visual media. Among the first and most popular books were elaborately illustrated works: people want and need pictures as much as words.

The videocassette industry is still forming and the continued popularity and ultimate value of videocassettes remain to be seen. Rental of feature-length movies is popular with the public and profitable for stores; production and sales of them may not be so profitable. Videocassettes overcome some of the problems of film rentals, because they are easy to use, less liable to be damaged, inexpensive to purchase and maintain, and playable on users' own home equipment. Public libraries report very high use of these videos, but these libraries in the future probably will buy and circulate more nontheatrical videos, those dealing with health and physical fitness, sports, educational subjects, culture and the performing arts, science and nature, and children's subjects.[25] The existence of a lively retail market in bookstores, supermarkets, and specialty stores also reduces some of the public library's selection anxiety; by providing nontheatrical videocassettes or less-popular theatrical videos such as foreign films and black-and-white classics, libraries can perform a distinct service.

Computer Media

If media, in whatever form, are the instruments between author and reader, then the word is appropriate here. Computer media in libraries include, most recognizably, CD-ROMs, machine-readable data files (MRDFs), and a variety of software from video games to highly sophisticated analytical tools; they also include our online public access catalogs (OPACs) and telecommunication links with bibliographic utilities, online databases, and other libraries that can be used just as we formerly used printed indexes, bibliographies, and catalogs. Computer media in libraries replicate many of the functions of traditional print and audiovisual media (albeit with enhanced speed and usefulness) and perform new functions, but they do not replace all the traditional features and functions. Libraries are just beginning to learn what computer media do; we have a long way to go before we can distinguish what it is they do best.

This is an experimental time in an experimental field. Librarians are not devising new software or circuitry, but are evaluating and developing the ways in which computer media can be most useful.

---

25. *Library Hotline* 14 (34) (1985): 2–3.

There is much that computers do well, but at too great a cost. There is much that they do that is unique and so valuable as to justify the cost. There is much that they could do if used effectively and in conjunction with other library resources, if only we knew how. And there are many things they do not do so well as print or nonprint media. We are in the incunabulum period during which media, industry, user, and library are evolving, and the library is the arena where this experiment and development are taking place.

In this experimental period there are four large issues still undecided but about which lively debate and hard thinking continue:

1. Selection. We must choose from among the computer media and also between these and print and nonprint media. Written selection policies are needed.
2. Maintenance. Just as we have developed an elaborate maintenance operation for books, periodicals, and audiovisuals, so must we develop one for computer media. A bank of CD-ROMs, no less than a table of indexes and loose-leaf services, requires personnel and procedures, in this case to keep printers in ink and paper, install software updates, and manage the exchange of compact discs.
3. Costs. Computer media, in addition to being fearsomely expensive, present a new, additional cost. Purchase and subscription, hardware and software, service and repair, new personnel and retraining existing staff—these are entirely new costs to our budget.
4. Payment. Because these costs are new, ideally we should receive new, additional money to cover them; but reality in libraries is, sadly, that there is seldom an adequate budget for existing costs. To what extent should we draw from the materials budget, user fees, and transfers from other parts of the budget or rely on soft money while we try to win additions to our budget? To what extent should we replace print and nonprint media and their costs with computer media and their costs?

To repeat, if we can think of our situation as an experiment and then isolate, record, and analyze the factors, we should be able in time to establish an effective collection management program that includes computer media with print and nonprint. To deal with selection, we must analyze uses and users and allow ourselves enough time for the factors to sort themselves out. What is new is not necessarily better; what the new is designed for now is not necessarily what it will be best for later; current limitations and annoyances may be resolved as technology improves.

Many of today's problems are analogous to problems that we once experienced with print and nonprint as we and manufacturers learned what the physical requirements for library use are and how best to meet them. Already we can see that a battery of CD-ROM indexes requires personnel to maintain and service printers and to clean disks and drives, and we certainly have had set-up problems integrating hardware and software. The former, which will likely continue to occur, are similar to the basic maintenance of books and periodicals, that is, reshelving, binding, and mending. The latter may continue and may be similar to needing an acquisition department to order and receive books. These kinds of need are not new, but they are as yet undefined and unanalyzed. As the experiment continues, we must define, analyze, and provide.

To charge fees for certain services, such as online searches of bibliographic databases, seems to violate the principle that libraries should provide access to information equally to all, yet fiscal realities virtually demand user fees.[26] If fees are charged, then only users who can afford or who choose to pay the fee can receive the information, yet there is a cost to libraries that is directly related to a specific use and to a specific user. Unlike costs for printed indexes, the cost of an online search can be accurately assessed against a specific user and the search does not result in material being added to the collection or library's capital base. Librarians who oppose such fees argue that besides the conflict with the principle of equal access, these services are identical in effect, and sometimes superior in practice, to the services provided by the printed indexes we traditionally have subscribed to. To some extent the debate has been overtaken by technology. CD-ROM indexes replace or at least provide a reasonable, if not perfect, alternative to online searching and enable us to offer this valuable service to all users. Costs are not based on length or complexity of use, except perhaps for the paper used in printouts, and therefore cannot be assessed against individual users. Subscriptions to discs and updates could be considered capital purchases.

---

26. Jay Martin Poole and Glorianna St. Clair, "Funding Online Services from the Materials Budget," *College & Research Libraries* 47 (1986): 225–29, and Sheila Dowd, Marcia Pankake, and John H. Whaley, Jr., "Reactions to 'Funding Online Services from the Materials Budget,' " *College & Research Libraries* 47 (1986): 230–47.

There is no question, however, that these are new, additional costs in the library budget: rarely have new technologies simply replaced printed materials. Whether we deal with CD-ROMs or online searches, our thinking about the costs must be flexible; we must be able to experiment with new ways of calculating, assessing, and paying costs. We need to make initial outlays on a short-term basis, scrambling to pull money from wherever we can and not worrying about its long-term continuation (grants, one-time gifts, garnering unused funds from elsewhere in our own or our institution's budget), and to plan for long-term shifts in funding. Our collections cannot be separated from the services needed to make them usable.

CD-ROMs. CD-ROMs may be the fastest-growing of the library computer media, as well as the most important computer applications after automated systems. Compared with automated systems, they are inexpensive, so one or more can be bought by a library to experiment with. The whole industry is in an experimental stage as it and libraries try to discover what is needed and what is luxury. *CD-ROMs in Print* lists five types:[27]

1. Data files containing popular, business and finance, and scientific/technical data that can be displayed and, in varying degrees, manipulated.
2. Text files that contain the texts of printed matter that can be accessed, displayed, printed out, and in some cases manipulated. Grolier's *Electronic Encyclopedia* is simply a text to access and display but the *Thesaurus Linguae Graecae* can, with proper software, be analyzed linguistically and lexically, as well as displayed for reading.
3. Graphics files ranging from the pictures in encyclopedias to charts and graphs displaying information.
4. Indexes and bibliographies that in most cases replicate print, but add the virtues of computer access—multiple-access points and Boolean searching. *PAIS, PsychLit,* and *Readers' Guide* are examples.
5. Directories and data files that store information compactly, allow multiple-access searching, or in some cases, such as *Compact Disclosure,* bring together and organize information simply not otherwise available.

---

27. *CD-ROMs in Print,* ed. Nancy Melin Nelson (Westport, Conn.: Meckler, 1987–).

CD-ROMs offer tremendous potential, although even now we can see that they complement as well as replace other media. Indexes still must have online counterparts for the most up-to-date searches; printed bibliographies, indexes, and directories combined with a photocopier often can produce faster results; backfiles of printed indexes retain their value and usefulness; full text files are seldom aesthetically preferable over corresponding printed texts, but can be manipulated and accessed usefully on CD-ROMs. CD-ROMs are potentially very user-friendly (several are already), but perhaps what they gain in ease they also lose in subtlety. It is difficult, at present, to combine large databases and sophisticated operating programs. CD-ROMs may free librarians by allowing end-user searching, but they require a variety of maintenance services and additional reference assistance.

Machine-Readable Data Files. Machine- or computer-readable data files—MRDFs—have become a major research resource in the sciences and social sciences. They are a medium for the storage of vast amounts of information and a tool to manipulate that information. Defined by *AACR2* as "any information encoded by methods that require the use of a machine (typically, but not always, a computer) for translation," these files can consist of texts, numeric data, or computer programs.[28] Physically, MRDFs are computer tapes, cassettes, or hard or floppy disks, including CD-ROMs; some, but not all, are accessible online. Examples of data files in the social sciences are collections of results of surveys and questionnaries, census data, election returns, and legislative voting records.

This information, often in massive quantities, must be stored, and computer files are the best way to do so. The unique value of the MRDF, however, is that the data in them can be accessed online and manipulated by scientists and scholars in different ways and for different purposes than the original collectors intended. Valuable time is not wasted collecting data all over again. As new uses are made of collected data, those who gather it can rethink and revise their own methods and the kinds of data they collect, and the data can be analyzed with various statistical programs or compared with data from other files and thus yield new understanding.

A special issue of *Library Trends* has been devoted to data files in the social sciences and the articles deal with such matters as

---

28. *Anglo-American Cataloguing Rules,* 2nd ed., p. 202, and Sue A. Dodd, *Cataloging Machine-Readable Data Files: An Interpretive Manual* (Chicago: American Library Assn., 1982).

reference work with the files, the problems of cataloging, descriptions of some particularly well-developed MRDF libraries, uses of numeric files, evidence from citation analysis of their use in research, problems of security, and training librarians to work with them.[29] This special issue concludes, however, with an article that takes a less positive look at the place of data files in libraries and argues that these files have not received sufficient use, that librarians do not possess the skills necessary to work with them, that financial problems will make files vulnerable to cancellation, and that organizational structures have in many cases already established the files in places other than libraries. Whether the library collects actual MRDFs or limits itself to providing access and analytical software, printed handbooks and operating manuals, and access terminals, it must recognize the scholarly importance of MRDFs.

Software. Programs on disk and cassette are another form of computer media. Public and school libraries have purchased and circulated educational programs and some computer games, particularly ones in the public domain; academic libraries have been more hesitant to add software unless they are clearly related to academic programs. An example of a useful program would be any statistical analysis package that users could check out and then run on their own office or home computers, with their own collections of data. If libraries collect MRDFs, then they also must collect the necessary software along with user manuals. There may be security problems and potential for copyright violation, but *AACR2* provides cataloging rules so that libraries can manage bibliographic control of software packages just as they do with other media.

OPACs and Online Links. I will give only passing mention to this large and important area of library operations by asserting that the various new ways we have of connecting users (including librarians) with the information in a remote database or bibliographic file do qualify as media. Thus, the online link with OCLC and RLIN (and their subfiles), the modem link between users and databases in BRS or Dialog, and interlibrary links such as the LCS system in Illinois that provide access to holdings, cataloging details, and circulation functions all are part of a library's collection. They are not peripheral or luxury services nor are they merely library operations; they can provide often crucial information to users.

29. "Data Libraries for the Social Sciences," ed. Kathleen M. Heim, *Library Trends* 30 (1982): 319–509.

Conclusion

The *ALA Glossary's* definition of a library collection as "The total accumulation of materials . . . for the target group" has to be broadened.[30] While we do deal in materials, we can best understand what materials best meet our users' needs if we first distinguish content from medium and then try to understand how the different media provide different content. Even though all media are physical objects or material, the term *media* helps to focus on the purpose of these physical things in the collection. This is a complex issue, partly because of the great variety of media and partly because these media do different things well.

It is also a dynamic issue. As new media are created and old media reworked and their usefulness rethought, our understanding of the uses of each and of the possible effective interrelations among them improves. This is an issue about which we cannot prescribe: each library has to experiment and develop its own collection on the basis of its own understanding of the ability of the media it has collected to transmit to its users the messages they need to receive. As a further aid to our understanding of the effect of our collections, we must learn about their production and distribution. Chapter 3 covers these subjects.

---

30. *The ALA Glossary of Library and Information Science,* ed. Heartsill Young, (Chicago: American Library Assn., 1983), p. 135.

Chapter 3

Quantity, Prices, and Publishers

At the back of all printed Literature lie the conditions of its transliteration into type.   —Edward Arber.[1]

Each library has a unique collection, selected and maintained for its own community of users and with its own character. Librarians are not, however, free to acquire whatever users want and need. The variety, quantity, and cost of materials and the nature of their production combine in a number of ways to create constraints on what can be added to the collection and also to provide choices that will be made differently by different libraries. It helps to deal with these constraints and make these choices if we have a basic understanding of the production of library materials, in particular the explosive increase in quantities and costs in recent years, the budgetary austerity in libraries, the nature of decision making in publishing, and the decentralization and internationalization of publishing worldwide simultaneous with the centralization of corporate management in this country, Great Britain, and Europe. Libraries participate in a number of communities, from civic to academic to institutional, and they also exist as one part of the publishing industry: librarians must understand this industry and the place they and libraries occupy within it.

Quantity and Price

The quantity of publication is as remarkable as the variety. Fairly reliable figures from several sources provide an impressive picture.

---

1. Edward Arber, *A Transcript of the Registers of the Company of Stationers of London 1554–1640 A.D.*, vol. 1 (London: privately printed, 1875), p. xv.

Prices also are impressive and, in recent years, distressing. Both prices and quantities have increased steadily, but within the past 25 years, price and quantity have burst forward as if they were out of control. We must be approaching the upper limit of how many books and periodicals can be produced in this country, yet in other countries there is plenty of room for continued growth. Publishing costs in general rise along with inflation but also vary by types of materials; the prices each library pays are affected by its own procedures, the particular mix of materials it selects, and such factors as international exchange rates.

Quantity. Various attempts have been made to count publications, but for a number of reasons all understate the total. So much is being published in so many formats by so many publishers in so many places that it simply is impossible to count everything. Moreover, no one has tried to count everything. Each different attempt to record publications has set itself clear limits. Thus, the count of book publication in the United States derived from the *Weekly Record* omits pamphlets, some professional law books, government documents, most textbooks and classroom materials, and book club and subscription books, and until recently seriously undercounted paperbacks. In other countries the count might omit association publications or subsequent editions or paperbacks, or might include government documents and textbooks. These inconsistencies prevent accurate counting of present publication and also prevent accurate historical overviews. Furthermore, no standardization of methods and definitions exists among the various counting agents. Despite these problems, a number of useful and interesting statistics do describe reasonably accurately the universe of publications with which librarians must deal.

Today's yearly worldwide publication of books must approach one million titles, with "book" defined as a nonserial publication of more than 49 pages. The UN *Statistical Yearbook* counts nearly 700,000 books published in 1980, 1981, or 1982, but the counts for some countries exclude paperbacks, children's books, government publications, pamphlets, and subsequent editions, and figures do not seem to be available for book output (likely sizable) in Egypt, the Republic of China, South Africa, or Iran. Interestingly, figures published in the UNESCO *Statistical Yearbook* are slightly different.[2] If it were possible to count book publications consistently and accurately, the

---

2. *Statistical Yearbook,* 34th ed. (New York: United Nations, 1986), table 61, pp. 441–46, and *Statistical Yearbook* (Paris: UNESCO, 1982), table 8.2, pp. VIII/22–VIII/29.

Africa	3,290
North America	106,728
South America	19,748
Asia	135,922
Europe	337,193
Oceania	5,101
U.S.S.R	91,836
TOTAL	696,818

Source: UN *Statistical Yearbook,* 34th ed., 1986.

FIGURE 1.
Worldwide Book Publishing, 1980

total figure surely would approach, if not exceed, one million. Figure 1 lists the total recorded book publishing output by continent.

It is not just the high total quantity that we are seeing but also the spread of publishing into virtually every country of the world. Where there are people, there are presses—and where there are people, there are likely to be useful scientific and technical research, meaningful social statistics and patterns, and imaginative literature. The world truly has become one. No American librarian can assume that simply because a book is published in a developing country that it is irrelevant. In any number of fields, foreign publications have become as important as domestic ones.

Worldwide publication is remarkable, but so is publication in the United States and the United Kingdom, two countries for which very reliable data are available. In 1987, more than 50,000 books (as defined by Bowker) were published in both this country and the United Kingdom (although possibly 30 percent of these are duplicates). Additional English-language titles are produced in countries such as Canada and Australia, of course, but also in nearly 50 others, so that the total English-language book publication now is approximately 150,000.[3] If we assume that American libraries are potentially interested in anything in English, we acknowledge the problem of quantity, a

3. "British Book Production 1987" in *Bowker Annual,* 33rd ed. (New York: Bowker, 1988), p. 420; Chandler B. Grannis, "Book Title Output and Average Prices: 1987 Preliminary Figures," and "British Book Production 1987" in *Bowker Annual,* 33rd ed. (New York: Bowker, 1988), pp. 401–12 and 420–22; *Books in Print Plus* (New York: Bowker, 1988).

problem only exacerbated when we recognize that many libraries, not only university and special research libraries, need non-English materials.

Book publication in the United States is more relevant and fairly accurate figures for it date from 1880, although even these need some qualification. Until 1912, pamphlets were counted as books; they no longer are. Until 1967, volumes rather than titles were counted, thus overstating the quantity. Paperbacks, especially mass-market paperbacks, were not completely recorded until only recently. Government publications, many professional law publications, elementary and high-school textbooks and some other educational books such as lab manuals, and book club and subscription books continue to be excluded.

Yet among these excluded materials will be many that libraries will want to know about and consider. Many books of poetry, for example, are technically pamphlets, at less than 49 pages, yet are part of the universe of books from which librarians must select for literature collections. Government publications, as another example, are invaluable resources on many subjects, in addition to their role in disseminating official information such as laws and agency regulations, and libraries that do not automatically receive these must identify and select them. Because the methods of collecting data have improved, recent figures are more accurate than earlier ones. What the total figures show, allowing for error and exceptions, are a gradual increase of book publication paralleling that of the population growth year by year from the 1880s to the 1960s and then an explosion of the publication rate.

Growth in serials has been similar to that of books, also having increased slowly but steadily, until the 1960s when it burst and then outdistanced the growth of books. As with books, so with serials: counting has been inconsistent and definitions and methods unstandardized until recent years. We do not as yet have accurate figures for total worldwide publication of serials. Osborn estimates 500,000 worldwide serials (200,000 in the United States), including periodicals (magazines and journals), newsletters, annuals and yearbooks, newspapers, and others. Osborn also estimates that 15,000 to 20,000 new titles are issued each year in North America, but that hundreds also cease each year; he projects that a total of one and a half million serial titles will have been published by the year 2000.[4]

---

4. Andrew D. Osborn, *Serial Publications: Their Place and Treatment in Libraries,* 3rd ed. (Chicago: American Library Assn., 1980), pp. 25 and 45.

The UN *Statistical Yearbook* does not count serials, although occasionally it does try to count newspapers. *Ulrich's International Periodicals Directory* limits itself to periodicals—serials published at least twice a year—and excludes most newsletters and periodicals that it does not consider significant. Formerly, it focused on North America and Western Europe, but now is truly international. Other directories do not so much supplement as overlap *Ulrich's*, so we cannot simply total everything listed in all of them. It is not possible to chart accurately the history of growth in serial publication; on the other hand, a chart of the growth of periodical listings in *Ulrich's* is informative and quite likely reflects the growth of serials in general (see fig. 2). The most recent data from the most common directories in the United States, among which is considerable overlap, are as follows:[5]

Ulrich's International Periodicals Directory, 1987: 70,800 international periodicals.
Irregular Serials and Annuals, 13th ed, 1987: 35,900.
Standard Periodical Directory, 1985: 65,000 U.S. and Canadian periodicals.
Gale Directory of Publications, 1985: 12,309 North American periodicals and 11,077 newspapers.
International Directory of Little Magazines and Small Presses, 22nd ed., 1986: 3,600.
Newsletters Directory, 3rd ed., 1987: 8,000.

The absolute number, large as it is, is even more remarkable when compared to previous years. The graph of the growth in quantity of international periodicals and U.S. books should be sobering.

The number of articles in all these publications is staggering, and is perhaps the statistic to note. Serials are not usually meant to be read cover to cover: the significant unit in a serial, at least for users, is the article. The library, on the other hand, must know the number of serial titles and, particularly, the number of bound volumes coming into the library each year. The total number of articles has not been

---

5. *Ulrich's International Periodicals Directory,* 26th ed. (New York: Bowker, 1987), p. vi; *Irregular Serials and Annuals: An International Directory,* 13th ed. (New York: Bowker, 1987), p. vi; *Standard Periodical Directory,* 9th ed. (New York; Oxbridge, 1985), n.p.; *Gale Directory of Publications,* 120th ed. (Detroit: Gale, 1988), p. ix; *International Directory of Little Magazines and Small Presses,* 22nd ed. (Paradise, Calif.: Dustbooks, 1986); *Newsletters Directory,* 3rd ed. (Detroit: Gale, 1987), p. 9.

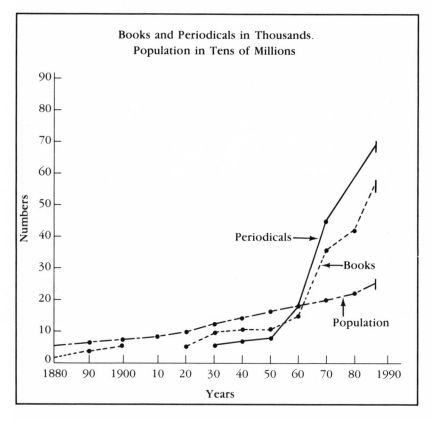

Books and Periodicals in Thousands.
Population in Tens of Millions

FIGURE 2.
Growth in Books, Periodicals, and Population
1880–1987

This graph shows by decade the number of books published annually in the United States, the number of international periodicals (1930–   ), and the U.S. residential population. The book count included pamphlets until 1912, and the figures for 1910 are not graphed because they were anomalous. Sources: Dorothy B. Hokkanen, "U.S. Book Title Output: A One Hundred-Year Overview," *Bowker Annual*, 26th ed., 1981; Chandler B. Grannis, "Book Title Output and Average Prices," *Bowker Annual*, 27th ed., 1982, and 33rd ed., 1988; Chandler B. Grannis, "Final 1987 Figures: Book Title Output and Prices," *Publisher's Weekly*, October 7, 1988; *Ulrich's International Periodicals Directory*, 1932–87; *Statistical Abstract of the United States*, 108th ed., 1988.

tallied and probably cannot be. We do have some hard figures, however. The Institute of Scientific Information's *Journal Citation Reports* estimates that in 1987 the 7,000 titles they processed contained one million articles. A closer look at the data in the reports indicates that there are three times as many science journals as social-science journals and that the science journals contain ten times as many articles as those in the social sciences. No figures are available for humanities journals.[6] Given this disparity, it would be difficult to extrapolate meaningfully other than to suggest that a university library will have well over one million, possibly several million, bibliographic units—journal articles—coming in each year. Other libraries will have less, depending on their size and mission.

Prices. Not only must libraries deal with an enormously enlarged pool of publications, they must pay enormously higher prices for them. Because inflation has been a way of life for nearly a generation of Americans, we may be inured to its ravages. "May be," unless we are librarians, in which case we still are struggling to recover from its effects and now (1989) watching with horror a new outbreak of periodical price inflation. One effect has been to remind us that austerity almost always has been the common lot of libraries. Only for a brief moment in our history was there more money than we knew what to do with, during the last half of the 1960s, when college and university enrollments increased and the federal government distributed money to their libraries as well as to public and school libraries. Even then, however, most libraries continued as they always had, selecting carefully, weighing demand against need, need against resources, resources for new materials against need to maintain old materials. The gross inflation of the 1970s and early 1980s exacerbated but did not radically change the conditions under which most libraries traditionally have operated.

Actually, the growth in prices of books and periodicals paralleled the growth in quantity, rising gradually through the century, but roughly in line with the Consumer Price Index (CPI), and then zooming upward in the 1960s and particularly the 1970s. Figure 3 shows the inflation of book and periodical prices compared to the growth in the CPI for the past 30 years. These book prices are for hardbound books published in the United States. The periodical prices also are for American publications and are based on the more general and popular titles rather than on specialized scholarly and research titles. Prices that university and research libraries paid have been higher. Only energy costs inflated more than prices of books and periodicals during this time.

6. *SSCI Journal Citation Reports: A Bibliometric Analysis of Social Sciences Journals in the ISI Data Base,* ed. Eugene Garfield (Philadelphia: Institute for Scientific Information, 1988), p. 6A.

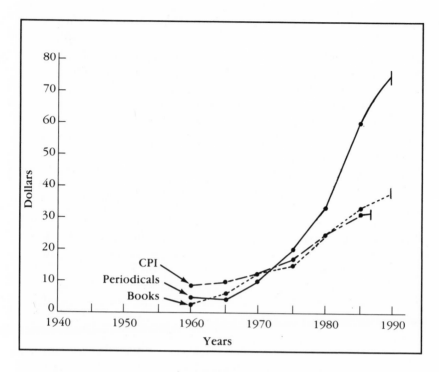

FIGURE 3.
Prices of Books and Periodicals
Consumer Price Index, 1960–1987

CPI in tens of dollars. Base 100, 1967.
Sources: Chandler B. Grannis, "Book Title Output and Prices," *Bowker Annual*, 1963–88; Rebecca T. Lenzini, "Prices of U.S. and Foreign Published Materials," *Bowker Annual*, 1988; *Statistical Abstract of the U.S.*, 1988.

Prices of scholarly journals have increased tremendously during the 1980s, particularly prices of European publications. Two developments have occurred simultaneously. These journals—especially those in science, technology, and medicine—achieved prominence in their fields, drawing the best and the most research articles and becoming crucial to American research as a source of information and as an outlet for our scholars' work, and their prices rose disproportionately, taking an increasingly large share of library budgets. One serials librarian estimates that 10 percent of the journals account for 50 percent of the budget.[7] The price increases seem to have been the result of classic

7. Charles Hamaker, " 'The Least Reading for the Smallest Number at the Highest Price,' " *American Libraries* (October 1988): 764–68.

market forces: as demand for the product increased, its seller raised the price, and as currency values fluctuated, journal prices did as well. The fall of the dollar against European currencies added a price increase to the increases implemented by the journals' publishers.[8] That most of these journals are produced by commercial publishers adds a third factor that pushes prices up: the profit motive.

Commercial publishers argue that they need profit to repay their investors for entrepreneurial risk and to build enough capital to finance new, untried journals. They also suggest that information or at least the process of printing this information has been underpriced and point out that the cost per item is not out of line. Librarians, on the other hand, who may suspect price gouging, certainly have felt like helpless victims of rampaging inflation, commercial opportunism, and shortsighted economic policies. We would like to have figures, as yet unavailable, on publishers' net profits in order to judge whether their profits are fair or exploitative.

Commercial publishers enjoy profit, nonprofit publishers build capital, scholars gain status and in some cases income, while librarians struggle to maintain periodical subscriptions to valuable journals without sacrificing monographic and humanities budgets. Librarians' recent vigorous and cooperative protests may have had a moderating effect on price increases and may have brought a clearer recognition by everyone involved—scholar and researcher, institutional administrator, professional society, publisher—of some of the consequences of putting a price on information. These efforts, however, have not rolled back prices.

Collection Growth. What is not shown in figure 3 is the relative decline in purchasing value of the library dollar and the actual decline in library acquisition budgets during the 1970s and 1980s. A triple whammy hit libraries: price inflation, devalued dollar, and declining budgets. For those needs that libraries exist to satisfy—informational, cultural, intellectual—more and more materials have been published, costing more and more each year. In the face of this growth, libraries have not been able to hold their own. The number of titles that *could* have been added has increased while the number of titles *actually added* has decreased. If we assume that each library buys a certain percentage of the total universe of materials, that percentage can only have gone down in all but the most well-endowed libraries. The

---

8. John Tagler, "Counterpoint: A Publisher's Perspective," *American Libraries* (October 1988): 767.

immediate result was decreased accessibility of materials. Users could not get, handily, what their libraries did not have.

Figures on library holdings are unwieldy and difficult to interpret meaningfully. The size of a collection is seldom by itself a useful figure, although it is usually worse to be too small than too big. Big and small, though, really have to be defined in terms of each library's needs and character. With this caution in mind, we can look at figures showing the growth in size of library collections during this era of growth in publications. Simply put, the growth of library collections has not kept up with the growth of library materials. In individual cases growth may have kept up, and no doubt in many cases the addition of essential materials has been maintained even if absolute growth has not. Growth here is a measure of volumes, not of titles; librarians are not yet able to determine whether the aggregate of all titles has grown. We can count number of volumes added, but not the number of unique titles. Of the world's nearly one million new titles, how many are being added to libraries? We don't know.

What we do know, however, is displayed in figure 4, which shows the growth in collections of ARL university libraries since 1965. We know both the total volumes added per year by these libraries and the median number of volumes added. During these two decades the number of ARL libraries increased 68 percent, from 63 to 106. Total collections increased from 4.9 million to 8.6 million, but these are net figures that include the results of loss and weeding as well as of new and replacement acquisitions, and so do not provide real insight into the libraries' ability to maintain their purchasing levels. The

Year	Total Vols. Added	Av. Vols. Added	Serials Subscriptions	No. Libraries
1964/65	4,861,669	77,169	NA	63
1969/70	7,947,029	94,138	NA	76
1974/75	7,753,746	77,960	18,758	88
1979/80	7,691,761	67,742	19,568	99
1984/85	8,583,542	81,748	27,727	106

FIGURE 4.
Growth of ARL Collections

Sources: *ARL Statistics* (Washington D.C., 1975–86) and *Cumulated ARL Statistics,* comp. by Kendon Stubbs and David Buxton (Washington, D.C., 1981).

more useful figures, for my purposes, are total and average volumes added per year in ARL libraries. As shown in figure 4, during the last half of the 1960s, the total and average additions per library increased by 63.5 percent and 22 percent, while the number of libraries increased just more than 20 percent. More volumes were being added in total and, presumably, more in most of the libraries. Then during the 1970s, however, the number of volumes added dropped precipitately in absolute terms and even more so relatively, considering that the number of libraries had increased. During the 1970s, ARL libraries increased by 30 percent, total volumes added decreased by three percent, and the average volumes added per year decreased by 39 percent. The last figure may be accounted for if the newer ARL libraries were smaller than the original members, although we might have expected them to have added a disproportionately larger number of volumes in an attempt to grow faster. The fact is, however, that 30 percent more libraries purchased 3 percent fewer volumes.

During the 1980s, collection growth has recovered and increased, while the growth of new member libraries has leveled off. What is not yet revealed in statistics is whether the renewed growth is a matter of books and also serials or whether the growth in serials—41 percent—accounts for most of the growth in total volumes. These ARL university libraries may not be typical of all libraries, but their financial condition probably has been no worse than that of any other set of libraries. Net volumes added is a more useful figure for libraries who must determine shelf and floor space needs, but here we are trying to see what, if any, inroads are being made into the gross quantity of newly published materials.

Differentials. The enormous growth in quantity and price is, in itself, an enormous problem for most libraries. This growth is complicated, however, by a variety of differentials. Different materials, different subjects, and different sources have different growth rates and different costs, and these differences affect different kinds of libraries in different ways. It is not enough to note that the average price of a hardbound book in 1987 was $36. If one's library was collecting mainly art books, the average price was $38; if it was collecting mainly technology, the average price was $60.[9] During the past three decades, the quantity of science and technology publications has increased far more than the quantity of art publications. Depending

---

9. Chandler B. Grannis, "Final 1987 Figures: Book Title Output and Prices," *Publishers Weekly* (October 7, 1988): 68–72, Table A.

on their own character and needs, libraries will be affected differently by these factors, and librarians must look at specific areas of their collection, not just at the overall picture.

Figure 3 on page 46 shows the differing inflation rates for books and periodicals. That difference has been particularly difficult for university and research libraries that depend heavily on periodical literature. As explained previously, classic market forces are working to the detriment of libraries' ability to provide equally for all users. It is impossible to continue these subscriptions without forgoing books or journals in other areas, yet to cancel these offending but important journals would penalize their users. It is becoming increasingly difficult to maintain the same level of quality for all areas of the collection.

Libraries differ in their needs for different kinds of materials. Public libraries primarily are book collections, while academic libraries are collections more evenly made up of books and periodicals. The reasons for this difference were mentioned briefly in chapter 2 and will be explained further in chapter 4, but for the moment it is the consequences of this difference that matter. Data from *Bowker Annual's* reports on library acquisitions, as graphed in figure 5, show, first, the difference between public and academic library collections and, second, the gradual growth in size of the periodical part of the acquisition budget. In academic libraries as periodical costs increased, these costs were apparently taken from the book allocation, but more recently the book area has been restored somewhat and costs appear to have been taken from microforms, audiovisuals, and binding. Public libraries maintained their book budgets while increasing their periodical budgets slightly, at the expense of microforms, audiovisuals, and binding. Figures for preservation and computer media costs have just begun to be recorded.

Publication rates and price increases have varied by subject as well as by material. It is not surprising to most of us that publications in the sciences and social sciences have increased. We have long known how hard it has been to fit these books into the nineteenth-century classification schemes of Dewey and the Library of Congress, and we certainly have felt how hard it is to fit the actual books into our libraries. Figure 6 confirms this differential and shows the number of titles published in certain fields and the average prices for books and periodicals in 1987. These figures are found by conflating several fields in the compilation; the total number of books in each is accurate, a matter of simple addition, but the average prices are not accurate

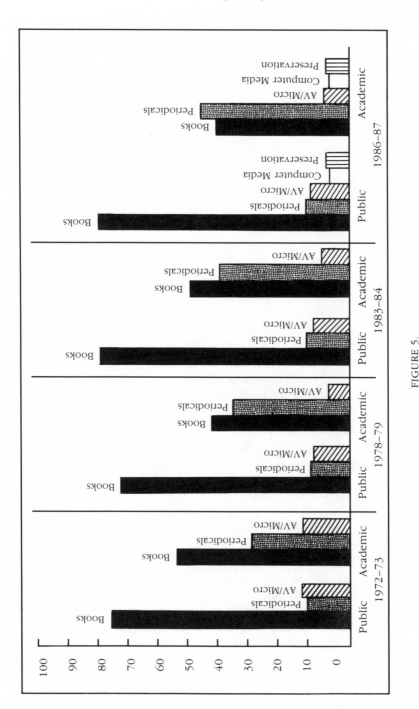

FIGURE 5.

Acquisitions Expenditures for Books, Periodicals, Audiovisuals/Microforms: Percentages 1970–1990

Source: Reports on public and academic library expenditures in *Bowker Annual*, 1975, 1981, 1985, and 1988.

Subject	Hardcover Number	Books Price	Periodicals Price
Sci/Tech/Ag/Med	9,945	$59.23	$129.67
Soc/Econ/Educ	13,775	34.36	44.68
Lit/Fiction	13,568	19.32	20.70
Philos/Rel	4,123	28.66	25.60
Hist/Travel	7,650	33.32	27.72
Fine Arts/Music	1,909	37.37	30.58
Total	34,774	$36.28	$54.97

FIGURE 6.
Subject Differentials, 1987

Sources: Chandler B. Grannis, "Final 1987 Figures: Book Title Output and Prices," *Publishers Weekly,* October 7, 1988, and Rebecca T. Lenzini, "Prices of U.S. and Foreign Published Materials," *Bowker Annual,* 1988.

because they do not include a weighting for the different number of books in each of the conflated categories. This chart is indicative, not authoritative.

To view the overall picture of differential growth by subject, see figure 7. The statistics in figure 7 are for U.S. publications. UNESCO statistics on worldwide publication by subject show an instructive similarity, as seen in figure 8.

Before considering some of the implications of this enormous and increasing quantity and costliness, it may be instructive to look at where it all comes from—that is, the publishing industry.

Publishing

Publishing is an industry with several parts, one of which is the traditional publisher. Other elements in the industry include authors, editors and agents who select and prepare texts for publication, the printing and binding trades who produce books and periodicals (not to mention electronic books and journals, computer programs, the variety of audio, visual, and computer cassettes and discs), the channels and points of distribution (warehouses, mailers and shippers, wholesalers, booksellers), advertising and marketing, reviewing, bibliographic control, and the entrepreneurial skills and resources to bring this all together successfully so that the books that are published find readers

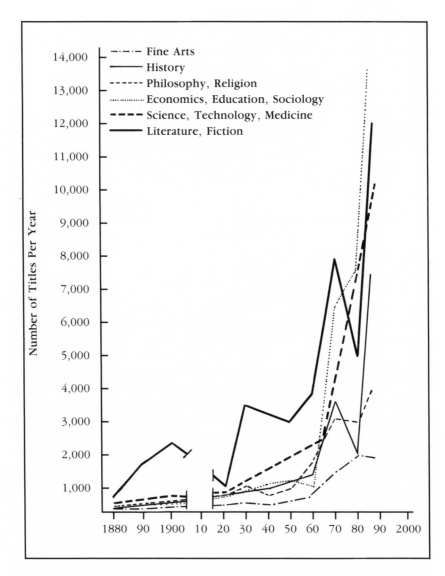

FIGURE 7.

Book Publication by Subject, 1880–1987

Sources: Chandler B. Grannis, "Title Output and Average Prices," *Bowker Annual*, 1982, and "Final 1987 Figures: Book Title Output and Prices," *Publishers Weekly*, October 7, 1988; Dorothy B. Hokkanen, "U.S. Book Title Output—A One Hundred-Year Overview," *Bowker Annual*, 1981.

There have been variations over the years in the subject categories, and, in addition, I have made the following groupings: Economics, Education, Sociology includes law, home economics, sports and recreation; Literature, Fiction includes juveniles, poetry, drama, and language; Philosophy, Religion includes psychology; and History, Travel includes biography, travel, and general works.

	1950	1960	1970	1980
Generalities	4,059	11,269	17,021	25,893
Religion/Phil	11,766	20,163	29,409	43,722
Social Science	24,047	102,116	106,662	153,171
Language/Lit	39,115	88,646	111,114	146,354
Science/Tech	27,071	95,251	130,903	172,346
Fine Arts	10,414	17,318	28,873	45,595
History	12,400	23,024	33,224	39,420
Total	127,919	331,619	501,826	684,444

FIGURE 8.
Worldwide Publication by Subject

Source: UN *Statistical Yearbook* for 1952, 1962, 1972, 1982.

and so that readers find books that they need. Publishers themselves are gatekeepers, with a responsibility for the materials they issue, both the content of these materials as well as their format.

Librarians play a crucial role in the publishing industry, even though we do not deliberately serve its interests. We are interested in new books and periodicals and certainly try to provide best-sellers, the latest scholarly journals, and the first issues of new periodicals. We are even more important to publishing's midlists and backlists, however, and certainly are concerned about the continued availability of older important books and about important but less popular—and less commercially attractive—books and periodicals. Perhaps, too, we, more than any other element in the industry, are concerned with the quality and relevancy of what is published.

Librarians voice a number of complaints about publishers, perhaps because librarians have a largely passive relationship with publishing, receiving the output but not being able to induce or produce that output themselves. They are caught in the middle between users who need publications or information and publishers who provide this material. Librarians can read off a list of problems: good books that go out of print too quickly, nonexistent backlists (necessary for replacement copies), mediocre books hyped at the expense of good books, inadequate physical quality of paper and binding, title changes and erratic numbering of serials, high prices of books and, especially, of periodicals. Publishing, however, is far from monolithic, consisting of several elements not always in perfect synchronization, and is itself affected by a number of external forces. Simply to improve our understanding of publishing is not going to correct the problems, but with understanding we may feel less passive and may be more able to see clearly those points we can affect. As mentioned previously, librarians did succeed in moderating the price increases of periodicals once they acted vigorously and cooperatively and once they identified exactly where to direct their actions. The point of this section, however, is to gain an understanding of the publishing industry, not in order to become tougher adversaries, but so we can be more effective participants within it.

Publishers. Central to the publishing industry is the publisher. There is tremendous variety among publishers, and there are sectors within the world of publishers that are in many cases quite different from others. Publishers serve a number of roles, and they all perform a number of operations. Over the past three centuries, publishers have undergone considerable change, and this change continues, pushed by changing technologies in printing and distribution, by changing economic conditions, and by changes in the human culture they are central to.

Publishers are agents who produce the printed media of communication in aesthetic, intellectual, scientific, political, economic fields— the music performed, the novels read, the research described, the laws and regulations promulgated, the financial data reported, the textbooks studied, the comic books pored over. They produce the nonprint media and provide the electronic channels through which raw and packaged data is exchanged. In this role they are driven simultaneously by commercial interests, by cultural or social interests, and by very personal interests.

Publishers in all categories serve a gatekeeping function, responsible for what gets published and, therefore, play a significant role in determining which ideas, information, knowledge, and literature come before the public. There are publishers who downplay or deny this role and there certainly are many who simply produce and throw out into the market what they believe will sell—bodice-ripper romances and lurid crime novels; diet books and books about how to improve one's golf, sex, memory, and children; books about the latest political scandal or royal wedding; books about cats. With these books it may well be that the packaging is more important than the contents. This kind of publishing, however, is shotgunning, not gatekeeping.

There is also an inherent tension within the publishing house between the desires for profit and for quality. To produce more books while controlling costs, manuscripts are pushed through production as efficiently as possible; editors, however, want to refine the clarity and enhance the validity of their books even if doing so holds up production and increases costs. How the conflict is resolved affects the publisher's marketplace image. Nevertheless, overt gatekeeping is a crucial function and is performed as the publisher selects titles, edits, designs, and distributes them: the publisher is responsible for both the intellectual credibility and the aesthetic design of the book.

Successful publishers are defined in large part by their financial reports; the bankrupt publisher serves no one at all, while the profitable publisher has clearly produced and distributed something that many have wanted enough to pay for. Publishers publish what they hope will sell, but they also publish books they know will not sell enough (nor can be priced high enough) to recover their costs, let alone make a profit. They publish these kinds of books out of a sincere interest in fulfilling a traditional social and cultural role, that of disseminating information, knowledge, and literary art. Publishing is a risky business, sales being uncertain and far from predictable (at least in trade publishing), so there has to be a motivation apart from either the purely economic or the altruistic: "We're in a business of passion," says Howard Kaminsky, executive at Random House.[10] Risk certainly is a condition in trade publishing. More specialized publishers perhaps take less risk, working as they do in a more specialized and more predictable market, but they must have just as much passion. Publishers, then, are entrepreneurs, gatekeepers in the social and cultural worlds of information and ideas, and they are producers (not merely purveyors) of information and ideas.

Categories. There are several categories of publishers, classified according to business organization and operation, the kinds of books published, the ways of marketing and distributing, the audience, and the size and focus of the publisher. Angele Gilroy in a 1980 article in *Printing and Publishing* lists 11 categories:[11]

1. Trade publishers of adult and juvenile books in most subject areas, usually sold through bookstores.

---

10. Howard Kaminsky, "Will Books Survive?" *Harper's* (August 1985): 44.
11. Angele A. Gilroy, "An Economic Analysis of the U.S. Domestic Book Publishing Industry," *Printing and Publishing* 21 (4) (1980): 8–12.

2. Mass-market paperback publishers producing originals as well as reprints, selling through newsstands, supermarkets, and other similar outlets.
3. Religious publishers specializing in bibles, prayer books, inspirational reading, and theological and religious-education materials.
4. Professional publishers in such areas as medicine, law, engineering, and business.
5. Mail-order publishers selling by direct mail.
6. Book clubs that handle their own editions of books as well as others' editions.
7. Publishers of elementary and high-school textbooks, workbooks, and laboratory manuals.
8. Publishers of similar materials for the college level.
9. University press publishers, usually dealing with regional or scholarly subjects and also publishing for institutions such as museums and research foundations.
10. Publishers of subscription reference books, primarily encyclopedias.
11. Publishers of standardized tests.

To these ought to be added:
12. Small-press publishers.
13. Association publishers.

Small-press publishers are a self-defined category, with "small" strictly a relative term. They can publish highly specialized or fairly comprehensive lists. Although poetry and fiction titles are the largest categories of small-press books, nonliterary titles are clearly the main business of the small presses, as is shown in the following breakdown of the subject categories for 2,365 books announced in the September, 1986, issue of *Small Press.*[12]

Poetry	14.5%	Literature	3.5%
Fiction	13.0	Cooking/Nutrition	3.5
Politics/Soc Sci	6.5	Fine Arts	3.5
Psychology	5.5	Sports/Outdoors	3.5
Philos/Religion	5.0	Travel	3.0
History	5.0	Business	2.5

12. Michael Coffey, "Editorial," *Small Press* 4 (1) (September/October 1986): 2.

Bio/Autobiog	4.5	Performance Art	1.5
How-To	4.5	Humor	1.5
Reference	4.5	Science	1.5
Children	4.0	Computers	1.5
Health and Family	4.0	Astrology/Occult	1.0

Small-press literature titles are important because they traditionally have been of high quality and have had considerable influence
on literary quality and trends, as Sally Dennison has argued in her
Alternative Literary Publishing.[13] Although it may be that this
influence is indirect, their role is significant. Small-press publishing
gives untried authors their first opportunity to publish and grooms
them for trade publishers in a sense; these publishers also maintain
in print important, if lesser-known, writers whose impact is on literary
colleagues more than on commercial markets. In nonliterary subjects,
small-press titles often are labeled independent or alternative press
books, frequently devoted to a single subject and offering a discussion
that is different, perhaps radically so, from that found in books from
trade or university presses. Neither literary nor nonliterary small-press
books receive consistently adequate reviewing and the publishers are
seldom able to advertise widely or market aggressively, so librarians
must seek them out (*see* Danky and Shore's *Alternative Materials in
Libraries*).[14]

Association publishers include organizations and institutions that
as part of their regular activities publish a variety of materials, such
as yearbooks and annuals, membership or product directories, informational materials for members, and scholarly or specialized works
by or of interest to their members. *Associations' Publications in Print*
is an attempt to extend bibliographic control to this category, and
the 1984/85 edition includes 104,000 titles from 3,900 associations,
with a total of 19,900 associations in its database.[15]

The three broadest categories are trade, educational, and academic
or scholarly publishers. The first is marked by organization, the second
by audience, and the third by kind of book. John Dessauer in his *Book
Publishing: What It Is, What It Does* and Coser, Kadushin, and Powell

13. Sally Dennison, *Alternative Literary Publishing: Five Modern Histories* (Iowa
City: University of Iowa Press, 1984).
14. James P. Danky and Elliott Shore, eds., *Alternative Materials in Libraries*
(Metuchen, N. J.: Scarecrow, 1982).
15. *Associations' Publications in Print 1984–1985*, 3 vols. (New York: Bowker,
1984), p. vii.

in their *Books: The Culture and Commerce of Publishing* provide an up-to-date description of the publishing industry and focus on these three categories of publishing.[16] Trade publishers try to produce books for a wide range of readers and they market them nationally; their audience is wide, general, mainly adult, and fluid. They produce fiction and nonfiction, how-to-do-it books and poetry, literature and science, social science and technology, books for adults and also for children, hardbacks and paperbacks, all sold primarily through bookstores (rather than by mail, subscription, or book club). The educational publisher produces textbooks and educational materials (workbooks, tests) for all levels of the market, from first grade through college; in some cases this publisher is a subsidiary of a trade publisher, but there are many publishers whose exclusive business is in textbooks. Scholarly publishers produce books for scholars and other seriously interested people who differ from hobbyists on the one hand and from professionals in medicine, law, business, technology, and other areas on the other. They can be independent houses, university presses, or scholarly associations. There is some overlap among these categories, of course. Scholarly publishers, such as university presses, often release popular books of regional interest, books of poetry and fiction, and popular treatments of scholarly subjects. Educational publishers can produce scholarly monographs that do not get used as textbooks. Trade publishers often own subsidiaries who are academic and scholarly publishers and they do on occasion produce scholarly books, especially reference books that might have a fairly sure and secure place in the market.

It is important to realize the extent to which publishers are segmented, that is, confined within their categories. Coser, Kadushin, and Powell in *Books: The Culture and Commerce of Publishing,* a sociological study of publishing, note that there often is more communication between the editors in similar segments of different companies than between editors in different segments of the same large company. Certainly, there are more points of similarity when determining what in a particular segment defines success, constitutes standard practice in acquiring and editing manuscripts, and determines design, production, and marketing. A book that sells 10,000 copies in a year might be considered a failure if it had been intended for

---

16. John Dessauer, *Book Publishing: What It Is, What It Does,* 2nd ed. (New York: Bowker, 1981), and Lewis A. Coser, Charles Kadushin, and Walter W. Powell, *Books: The Culture and Commerce of Publishing* (New York: Basic Books, 1982).

the mass, popular market and 25,000 copies of it had been printed, while another book that sells 500 copies in a year might be considered a success simply because it sold exactly what was planned for, and because it garnered positive reviews that enhanced the publisher's reputation in its subject area.

Process of Publication. From the librarians' point of view, the key functions of publishing are to select good manuscripts, edit them responsibly, design effective books for them, produce a sufficient number of books, at a reasonable price, with a large stock perpetually available, readily obtained through standard jobbers, and advertised or reviewed widely enough to be known to our users. Publishers have the same aim, with the additional one of making enough profit to stay in business and so continue to turn manuscripts into books. The process of publishing, then, seems straightforward, although most observers of the industry seem to agree that there is a "tension between culture and commerce."[17]

In addition to the publishing process, however, librarians must understand "operating behavior," that is, the reasons why publishers make the choices they do. Perhaps the clearest insight into publishers' operating behavior is provided in *One Book/Five Ways,* which describes how one manuscript given to five different publishers was treated.[18] We are shown the factors in the decision to publish, the kind of copy editing, the design elements (illustrations, typeface and page layout), format (paperback, spiral bound, oversize, standard octavo), the actual costs of manufacture, the projected sales and income, and the prices, which differed by up to 50 percent.

The first step in the process is the writing of a manuscript, followed by its acquisition by a publisher. There must be an author (whether individual or joint), and the author must bring the manuscript to the publisher's attention. The majority of manuscripts that finally are published seem not to arrive unbidden, but come through some sort of intermediary, such as an author's agent, acquaintances of the author who have some influence with the publisher (possibly previously published authors, scholarly colleagues, social acquaintances), or even, on occasion, at the publisher's invitation. An important point is that the gatekeeping—or selection—role of the publisher is a complex one that is influenced at many points by many people and factors. The

17. Coser, Kadushin, and Powell, p. 363.
18. *One Book/Five Ways: The Publishing Procedure of Five University Presses* (Los Altos, Calif: William Kaufmann, 1977).

author can submit a finished manuscript or only an idea for one; that manuscript, if finished, can be previewed by an agent or by someone the author engaged, or it can arrive still needing considerable editing at the hands of the publisher's editor. The publisher could have contacted a likely author and asked for a manuscript (or manuscript proposal) or could have established a series whose existence put the idea for a manuscript into an author's mind.

The process of selecting a manuscript is complex, and the relative significance of the various factors in it differ from publisher to publisher, from segment to segment, and from book to book. In *One Book/Five Ways*, we can see clearly the full range of factual data about costs and sales receipts that has to be considered, and we can see how different editors interpret and weigh this data. There are costs for copy editing and proofreading, for design and artwork, for materials and labor in production, for advertising and distribution. Receipts are only potential, of course, but an editor can calculate how many copies would have to be sold to cover the costs and make a profit and can suggest what could be done in editing, design, production, and marketing to improve sales (or reduce costs). The bottom line is perfectly clear. Interestingly, though, the decision to accept or reject a manuscript seldom seems based solely on this line. As Powell notes in his analysis of the publisher's selection process, *Getting into Print,* "The rational elements in the formal decision process often turn out to be more symbolic than real. . . ."[19]

In trade publishing where markets seem less assured, publishers not only take considerable risk with each title but seem to have less concrete and specific grounds on which to base the selection of their titles. In scholarly publishing where one might expect the market to be more predictable, that market—the world of scholarship—is constantly evolving: "The system [of scholarship] is constantly splitting and reorganizing existing fields of research into more specialized subfields."[20] In a sense, each new book (each good new book) alters the scholarly field that it enters, in a way that each new novel or trade nonfiction book does not. Scholarly publishers, therefore, are in the position of publishing for a market that does not exist until their book enters it; their business, like that of the trade publishers, contains its risks and uncertainties.

---

19. Walter W. Powell, *Getting into Print: The Decision-Making Process in Scholarly Publishing* (Chicago: University of Chicago Press, 1985), p. xi.
20. Coser, Kadushin, and Powell, p. 367.

There are, of course, trade and academic publishers who work with minimal risk, if also minimal distinction. Commercial concerns predominate. Few publishers set out to produce and sell useless books, but many do deal with unexciting and unexceptional books of only adequate merit. These are at best useful books; the key factor for publisher and librarian alike is utility. In this case publishers are not taking aesthetic or intellectual risks, nor are librarians evaluating literary works: publishers are producing and librarians are selecting books that fill a particular niche in the collection.

Powell's study of the decision-making process in scholarly publishing seeks to discover what the criteria and the steps are by which the decision to accept and publish a manuscript is made. The matter is not a simple one. There are financial elements: the editor must be concerned for the publisher's profitability, but beyond that an individual title's anticipated contribution to profitability can be anywhere from negative to massively positive. There are reputation elements: publishers do publish books that lose money but enhance their reputation or perhaps reinforce their image. There are strategic elements: a publisher might decide to publish a manuscript because doing so might help keep a particular author with the house, might attract other manuscripts, or might fill out a series. A publisher might accept a weak manuscript while rejecting good ones because the weak one fills a gap in the list while the good ones all cover the same general subject. Also of importance is the fact that each publisher's list is distinctive. Of two science publishers, one might handle only "normal science" and the other only groundbreaking or controversial books; what one rejects the other might accept. Neither absolute quality nor guaranteed profitability is necessarily the main criterion; certainly neither is the sole criterion. If this kind of editorial practice happens in the relatively controlled world of scholarly publishing, then surely the trade publishers' selection decisions must be even more complex.

Once the manuscript arrives at the publisher, it will be edited. Its content might need changing (to make it more up to date, more rigorously reasoned, or more or less scholarly or popular); its style might need significant rewriting to improve clarity and effectiveness. In all cases the manuscript will have to be nested in a particular book and it is the publisher's responsiblilty to design a book that is appropriate to that manuscript. Among the elements of design are such things as title page, table of contents, illustrations, graphs, tables, the addition of appendixes, bibliography, and indexes, as well as choice of typeface, page size and layout, binding, and dust jacket. Design affects the book's contents and its aesthetics, its usefulness and its appeal, and certainly in the case of scholarly books design is an integral part of the finished book. Fiction, poetry, and popular nonfiction all can be enhanced by design; a scholarly book, a textbook, or a professional book relies on the design of its contents. The publisher's gatekeeping role, then, goes beyond simply selecting a manuscript. The publisher must effectively present that manuscript.

Librarians are concerned about the physical quality of books, whether they are printed on alkaline paper by a process that produces legible text and illustrations with a library-quality binding, and also with the quantity of the books printed in the run and warehoused, with plates kept ready for additional printings. Publishers will continue to publish, even if not in familiar formats, but whether libraries will be able to get and keep their wares is a different question. On the one hand, scholarly publishing increasingly works with smaller and smaller print runs, so that a printing of only 500 copies of a scholarly book is common, and once these copies are sold the book is effectively gone. On the other hand, trade publishers often deal only with print runs in the tens of thousands and ignore (that is, refuse to publish) books that they know will not sell more than, say, 5,000 copies. Short-run scholarly books can be profitable to their publishers; large-run popular books can be profitable to theirs; but intermediate-run books, whether scholarly or popular, fiction or nonfiction, topical or timeless, seem to have a difficult time finding publishers who can deal appropriately with them. This is an evolving area, however. Where there is a niche to fill in the market, someone will fill it.

Books have a fixed cost based on the materials and process of their manufacture, on authorship and editorial expenses (author's royalty, agent's fee, editor's salary, contracts for copy editing, indexing, and graphic work), and on advertising and distribution costs. The publisher's problem is not just to predict these costs, but to predict the mix that will be profitable. Advertising and promotion might increase sales, but the publisher has to predict this with enough accuracy so as not to overspend for advertising; in any case the advertising cost has to be added to the book's price. Authors flattered to see their books widely advertised must realize that the resulting higher prices reduce the number of people who can afford to buy their books, and librarians who are happy to receive advertising fliers in the mail and to note ads in a periodical have to realize that the cost of this convenience is found in the books' price.

Production costs do vary from book to book; even editorial costs do. A book with intricate graphics, whether full-color illustrations, elaborate graphs, or detailed tables on foldout leaves, will cost more to produce than one containing only text. Publishers must keep current with the latest developments in printing technology and must be willing to apply them when necessary; using camera-ready copy or copy typed onto a disk and fed directly into the publisher's computer, for example, can so reduce costs as to make an otherwise impossible scholarly book profitable. The danger exists, however, that the publisher will skimp not only on production but also on editing and not give sufficient attention to the quality of the book's contents. The use of outside readers, an editor's critique of the manuscript's ideas and emphases, and copy editing for factual and bibliographic accuracy as well as grammatical correctness are all essential elements in traditional scholarly publishing, unaffected by technological changes. To forgo them will reduce costs but may also reduce quality.

If scholarly publishers are tempted to cut editorial corners, and thus sacrifice quality, trade publishers are tempted to put more effort and expense into designing and marketing a book than into ensuring the quality of its contents. Coser, Kadushin, and Powell argue: "The extraordinary attention paid to promotion can mean that the quality of the package, the meticulously designed jacket plus advertising and promotional materials, is often superior to the merits of the book."[21] A publisher is in business to publish and, not surprisingly, sometimes will have to produce a book even when one isn't truly ready, just as librarians will sometimes buy a weak book simply because it is the only one on the subject. These problems are inherent, but probably not frequent, in publishing.

Not only is the decision to publish complex but so are the subsequent decisions about how to publish and promote the book. The fact of segmentation within a large publishing house can mean that the editor, production manager, and marketing manager do not necessarily consult adequately on each and every title they handle. Conceivably, an editor accepts a manuscript with one thing in mind for it, but the production manager puts more, or less, attention into it, and the marketing manager promotes it differently than the editor (or author) intended. The conditions existing when the book finally enters the market may be different from those existing when the manuscript was accepted. The publication of similar rival books, the

---

21. Coser, Kadushin, and Powell, p. 143.

accidents of current events, the interests of the public all could affect that book's marketing in ways not anticipated by author and editor several months earlier when the manuscript entered the publication process.

Books that are not sold must be either remaindered (producing some slight income), warehoused in hopes of slow but steady sales in the future, or pulped. Warehousing incurs two costs: the warehouse and its operation and the tax liability of the unsold inventory. The Thor Power Tool ruling, an Internal Revenue Service application of a 1979 Supreme Court decision, required publishers to declare their inventories at full price value.[22] Inventory is an asset that appears in a profit-and-loss statement as a cost of sales. As a result of the ruling, publishers could not reduce prices on their books without damaging their margin of income. The effect was to reduce print runs of the books to be published and to write off as tax losses the slow sellers. Direst fears about the ruling's immediate consequences—that small-press and reference-books publishers, as small-run producers, would go bankrupt and that all inventories would be summarily pulped—have not proved true. Since the ruling, the industry has made several positive adjustments, such as developing a viable short-run printing capability and improving its ability to predict the market for individual titles.

Significant, negative long-term consequences also have occurred: print runs are shorter by 20 percent or more; books go out of print sooner than before, and publishers are reluctant to issue second printings; prices have gone up, especially for short-run and scholarly books. Libraries have responded to shorter runs and higher prices on the one hand, by implementing more automatic buying plans in order to ensure immediate receipt of books they need and, on the other, reducing replacement and duplication purchases. In general, they are anticipating shortages of copies while at the same time dealing with an abundance of titles. Publishers meanwhile must include this new factor of inventory value in their acquisition, production, and marketing decisions.[23]

Distribution. The life of a book after it has been produced is

---

22. *Bowker Annual,* 26th ed. (New York: Bowker, 1981), pp. 136 and 145.
23. Leonard Schrift, "After Thor, What Next? The Thor Power Tool Decision (U.S. Supreme Court) and Its Impact on Scholarly Publishing," *Library Acquisitions: Practice and Theory* 9 (1985): 61–63, and Mary H. Loe, "Thor Tax Ruling after 5 Years: Its Effect on Publishing and Libraries, *Library Acqusitions: Practice and Theory* 10 (1986): 203–18.

as important as its prepublication life; a book in the reader's hand is worth any number in the warehouse. Books must be promoted and distributed. The lives of books after they have been published are, however, to some extent out of the publishers' control. Leonard Shatzkin in his book *In Cold Type: Overcoming the Book Crisis* argues forcefully that failure to control distribution is the major flaw in the publishing system.[24] Although his point has not received universal acceptance, both Dessauer and Powell agree: "The most persistent and unresolved problem has been distribution—how to get books into the hands of interested consumers."[25] Shatzkin blames publishers themselves; others criticize booksellers, especially chains that seek to handle not the best but the most salable. Even libraries have been criticized for buying books that no one reads or books that are widely read but only for a short time, after which they simply gather dust and clog the shelves. Publishers do, in fact, work hard to promote their books. Large houses have separate marketing, advertising, and sales departments, while small houses, if they want to succeed, must perform these functions. Figures are difficult to find, but possibly 10 percent to 15 percent of total sales is spent on promotion of midlist books.[26]

The process of distribution includes the publishers' own efforts to promote their books through advertisements in newspapers and magazines, direct-mail announcements, review copies, promotional author tours, and special packages for booksellers (such as cardboard display racks for paperbacks). The process also involves the reviewing media, book wholesalers or jobbers, bookstores, libraries, and even readers. Clearly, publishers do try to market their books. The trick is to make this advertising and promotion effective, to get people to notice new books and buy them before supplies are exhausted or are destroyed, and to do so within a realistic budget. The publisher must invest sufficiently in marketing to increase sales but must not over-invest.

If publishers are doing a reasonably good job of making their wares known, then what do the other elements in distribution do? Reviewing is a continuing problem. First, far from every newly published

---

24. Leonard Shatzkin, *In Cold Type: Overcoming the Book Crisis* (Boston: Houghton Mifflin, 1982).

25. Powell, p. xvii.

26. See various chapters in *One Book/Five Ways* and Gary Facente, "An Overview of American Publishing for Librarians," *Library Resources & Technical Services* 30 (1986): 57–67.

book gets reviewed. Although figures for reviews seem impressive—
Book Review Index covered 68,000 titles in 1987 and *Bowker Annual's*
1986–87 report on American reviewing media showed 42,824
reviews—these do not show exactly how many of the 56,000 new
American books are reviewed.[27] *BRI* covers foreign as well as American
titles and books from previous years as well as new books, and the
Bowker Annual figures do not indicate how many separate titles are
reviewed. Second, even when a book does get reviewed, that review
is not necessarily timely. Third, subsequent editions, often very
important for scholarly works, seldom are reviewed at all.

Increasingly, we buy from vendors (also called jobbers and
wholesalers) rather than directly from publishers, partly because
publishers (certainly the major trade publishers) do not like to deal
with individual orders and so themselves rely on vendors for distribution and sales, and partly because librarians find it easier and more
economical to select from a vendor who typically has on hand the
new works of hundreds of publishers, offers a discount, provides
simplified and economical billing, and can provide useful statistical
reports about the number, price, subjects, and other aspects of the
books handled by them and bought by libraries. At their best vendors
are not merely passive recipients of what publishers happen to send
them, but actually do seek out publishers' production.

Vendors compensate for some of the apparently inherent problems
in distribution, including those of limited supply resulting from short
publishing runs, short shelf life in publishers' warehouses, and the
sometimes obscure publishers. They do develop specializations, with
some emphasizing trade publishers, others academic presses; some
serve school libraries, others public libraries; some ignore small and
alternative publishers, others deal almost exclusively with them; some
with huge warehouses have little interest in searching out titles not
held, while others are particularly good at locating the virtually
unobtainable title. They vary, too, in speed, accuracy, reporting
services, and actual costs, so we must monitor and evaluate vendor
performance and must be willing if necessary to go directly to publishers (especially to alternative, independent, and society publishers)
and to bookstores. Vendors make our lives much easier than they
would otherwise be, but we must not fail to look beyond them.

---

27. *Book Review Index* (Detroit: Gale, 1987), title page, and "Book Review Media
Statistics," in *Bowker Annual,* 33rd ed. (New York: Bowker, 1988), p. 424.

Periodical Publishing. Publishing of periodicals differs in a number of respects from book publishing, but the publisher, with commercial interests foremost in mind, retains the central role. Most large circulation popular magazines are published by magazine publishers, a specialized branch of publishing that is as entrepreneurial as that of book publishing. Profit is the first goal, and library subscriptions probably contribute little to profitability. Commercial magazines, whether tending toward the general or the specialist interests, rely on individuals more than libraries.

Scholarly journals, on the other hand, do rely on library subscriptions for both their subscription income and their fullest distribution. One subscription serves many readers. In the process of scholarly communication, journals and libraries are essential participants, although the essential interests of each differ. Journals must meet their production costs, if not, in fact, make a profit; libraries, however, wish to provide free and ready access to as much scholarly information as possible. Many scholarly journals are published by university presses, learned societies, or professional associations, where there is a continuing staff devoted to production, but a great many are independent publications with the editing and publishing done by staff who have no connection with any other publishing activities and who are more knowledgeable about the contents than about the production. Their ability to produce efficiently, with an adequate degree of regularity, and to market effectively is often learned on the job, if at all.

Increasingly, however, commercial publishers are producing scholarly journals. These have professional editorial and production staffs and well-paid management, along with a need to make significant profits. As a result, commercially published scholarly titles generally cost more than those produced by universities, societies, and independent editors. Moreover, these commercially produced scholarly journals are becoming as important as the university press or independent journals. Dissemination of scholarly information, particularly in the science, technology, and medical fields, has become a major business, and prices of these journals have put library budgets under tremendous pressure, as described previously. This cash nexus in scholarly publishing is a relatively new factor. Costs have always existed, but now one element in the complex stands to profit nicely at the apparent expense of another element—the library—that neither profits nor finds itself properly funded. Neither librarians nor the scholarly world understands all that is entailed as information increasingly becomes a commodity affected as much by market as by intellectual forces.

Information Industry. The information industry started in the 1960s as use of computers and telecommunications became more widespread in business and scientific and technical research.[28] At first the term applied to this fairly coherent and compact segment, but as traditional publishers move into the field and as information rather than the package or media becomes the commodity, then its range of application enlarges. We may be moving toward a time when publishing will be thought of as one part of the information industry. The information industry has developed in ways strikingly similar to the development of the printing industry, as Elizabeth Eisenstein described it (summarized in chapter 2): new occupations, new business centers, new trade relations, and new subsidiary industries supplying parts and machinery have developed. The industry has had a direct economic impact through its own operations that is significant, if not as great as the impact its technology has had on its users. Joshua Smith has described the industry succinctly:[29]

> Producers: Acquire, edit, and process information, then deliver it in the form of electronically accessible data bases, journals, books, and microform collections.
>
> Distributors: Provide value-added information based on their own data bases or those of others, using delivery services such as on-line, videotex, and teletext.
>
> Retailers: Provide customized access to information services, both traditional and electronic.
>
> Managers: Operate clearinghouse or management-information services.
>
> Processors: Provide users with computer-processing and communications capabilities that facilitate the delivery of private and public data and information sources.

Libraries make heavy use of online and CD-ROM technology for bibliographic utilities such as OCLC and RLIN, information data bases such as directories, encyclopedias, and business and financial files, and of bibliographic search and indexing services such as BRS,

---

28. Herbert R. Brinberg, "Information Industry," in *ALA Yearbook 1981: A Review of Library Events of 1980* (Chicago: American Library Assn., 1981), p. 152.

29. Joshua Smith, "Information Industry," in *ALA Yearbook 1983: A Review of Library Events of 1982* (Chicago: American Library Assn., 1983), p. 145.

Wilsonline, and Dialog. How do we include these in our collections? Many libraries already have acquired computer software, whether game, educational, or operational (such as statistical analysis packages) programs; some have subscribed to electronic journals; others have been trying to decide whether to fund access rights to data bases from materials budgets; all have been buying a variety of printed documentation for programs and services, as well as a range of newsletters, magazines, journals, and books having to do with information-industry concerns or with information communication within various subject fields.

Libraries play a role in the information industry just as they do in the publishing industry, even though our central concerns are to serve our users rather than the producers from whom we purchase materials. Relations between us and the publishing and information industries are evolving, sometimes for the better, and our ability to affect this evolution positively will continue to depend on our understanding of their particular commercial and intellectual dynamics as well as on our willingness to speak out for our own interests and principles.

Conclusion

Libraries and publishing are an integrated whole, despite the many differences between their purposes and values. Reading and information have long been treated as a common good. New thinking about information as a commodity, however, raises basic questions of principle and presents new management problems, and these questions and problems can be dealt with only if we understand the nature of the industry that produces library materials. If information and materials are going to be priced according to a new system that gives them higher value, then librarians must participate as equals in the setting of these prices and realigning resources to pay for them, with full recognition by all concerned of the immediate and long-term consequences of this shift in our thinking.

The publishing and information industries and all their elements—author and scholar, avid reader, institutional administrator demanding tenure-winning scholarship, stockholder and corporate management, citizen and government, librarian—must agree to strengthen libraries' bargaining position within the industry and to set an industrywide agenda regarding pricing, production standards, and selection of what needs to be published. Market forces working by themselves without consideration for public good, and libraries' role in providing for it, may well destroy libraries and subvert the public's interests. To pursue our own goals and to carry out our mission we in libraries must recognize our place in the industry, participate in its exciting developments, and yet not ignore its problems nor deny our responsibility to work to correct them.

More immediately, and more within the themes of this book, individual libraries must become more selective. The quantity, variety, and cost of materials force us more than ever before to define our mission and develop a collection that directly serves it: able to buy, but less and less of the more and more that is being produced, we must ensure that what we do acquire is exactly what we need. Furthermore, libraries as a whole must cooperate to ensure the development of an adequate composite collection, as Paul Mosher calls it.[30] This composite collection is the cumulated unique titles of all cooperating libraries. Libraries always have relied on each other's collections, but this reliance will become more important as the gap between what is published and what one library can acquire grows. Truly coordinated management depends in turn on each individual library having identified its mission and having set suitable collection management policies. We cannot cooperate as a whole if we do not know what we need as individuals. Each collection must develop its own unique character, its own particular mix of materials, developed in response to users and the ways they use materials.

Thus, to think about our collections locally and collectively turns us ultimately toward our users. Despite all that has been written here and elsewhere about quantity and costs of materials and despite all the emphasis put on counting what is published and what is acquired by libraries, it is not how much we own or buy but how much our collections are used and what our users manage to accomplish with them that ultimately define and justify our collections. Nor is it the number of citations users find, how much data they record, how many books they check out, or interlibrary loans they receive. We must renew our concern for coherence and order, for understanding and knowledge, or, more simply, for appropriateness. Within the individual library, selection and other collection management decisions must be based on a clear understanding of users' needs and of which materials will best satisfy these needs. From the vast and expanding

---

30. Paul Mosher, "The Nature and Uses of the RLG Verification Studies," *CRL News* 46 (1985): 336–38.

sea of publications we must select exactly what is needed by our users. We must direct our collection management to the actual reading and information needs of our users. To alter Whitman, to have great libraries, there must be great readers, too.[31]

---

31. Walt Whitman, "Notes Left Over," in *Walt Whitman: Complete Poetry and Collected Prose* (New York: Library of America, 1982), p. 1058.

Chapter 4

Users, Uses, and Missions

The library's mission is to build and maintain a good collection suitable to its users' reading and information needs. To manage our collections effectively we must anticipate our users' demands and understand their needs, which means, of course, that we must identify who our users are and then record or measure their demands and analyze their apparent needs, needs that they themselves may not always recognize. Users, indeed, are many and varied. They are individuals and yet are also members of a number of categories, and they make up a community of users. The library itself is an institution or organization within one or more larger communities—civic, academic, school, corporate, or other—and as such has a specific role or set of responsibilities within those communities. Its mission, then, is to meet the reading and information needs of its actual users but also to meet reading and information needs within its particular community. In the following discussion the concept of need, a working definition of user categories and communities, and the library's place in scholarly communication will be presented to help librarians understand how best to define the mission of their own particular libraries and collections.

Need and Demand

Demand is what users ask for; need is what they should use to satisfy their demands. Need and demand are not necessarily different, and often users demand exactly what they need. Many users, however, underutilize a library, seemingly unaware of the depth of information resources and the range of available reading materials. Nonusers may well need something even though they demand nothing. Both need and demand vary in intensity and immediacy, by kind of material, by subject, by kind of library, and from individual to individual. Librarians must first understand their users' needs before they can respond effectively to their actual demands.

Need and demand often are different. We demand chocolate but need carrots, watch the evening news but need to read the newspaper, are influenced by glossy ads with beautiful women and virile men but need to read product reviews. Demand is often a creation of the mass media, advertising, talk shows, newspaper columns, car-pool gossip, even of education and upbringing. Demand often seems to be for a rather limited range of materials. In academic libraries students demand to (or are commanded to) read assigned material, much of it kept in reserve collections. When they write so-called research papers, their ambition too often seems minimal. Professors can be out-of-date or can overestimate their students' abilities. In public libraries even avid readers demand old favorites and shun the new, while users with serious information needs seem willing to take anything that comes to hand. The book hyped on a talk show is not necessarily authoritative nor even, as is sometimes the case of fiction, appropriate for the tastes of the actual readers we know. In short, our users often do in fact need more or other than what they ask for.

The term *need,* on the other hand, perhaps is not the most accurate. It already has been used with more precision by scientists to describe certain physiological and psychological requirements. We know the body needs water, the heart needs love, the mind needs variety, but these needs may be different than a reader's need for a book or a user's need for information. Certainly there have been cases where information has been crucial in saving a life or maintaining health, but it was not information that was needed, rather the condition that information enabled. Information need is not a force coming from or drawing to an individual. It is, instead, the result of a relationship among individuals and the materials and information within a library. The term *information purpose* has been suggested by Richard Derr as an alternative to "need" to describe this relationship. Books, periodicals, and other materials are the source of the information, while the information is the means through which to accomplish a purpose. Derr adds that information purpose usually is described more accurately and meaningfully by the librarian than by the user.[1]

---

1. Richard L. Derr, "A Conceptual Analysis of Information Need," *Information Processing and Management* 19 (1983): 273–78.

Users' demands and needs vary in intensity and immediacy. "I want the number-one best-selling novel, now!" demands one. "Please put me on the waiting list for the latest best-seller," asks another. A high-school student seeks information about possible careers; an unemployed steelworker asks for information about retraining programs or for the Help Wanted section of the newspaper from a different city. User demands vary in quality. "Do you have a copy of *Huckleberry Finn,*" asks a student, but an English professor wants specifically the California edition. Demands vary by kind of library. The same question asked in a public and an academic library could result in a different kind of answer. In an academic library a business-school student will ask for information about a company's financial performance; the information does not have to be the latest, nor is it needed immediately. In a public library, however, the same question is likely to come from someone who does need the information immediately and needs it to be the most recent and authoritative. Demand varies by kind of material. People demand fiction but seldom need a particular novel, at least not immediately—although certainly a student required to read *Moby Dick* must get it and probably must get it in a suitable edition. Nonfiction may be needed immediately by someone, seriously, because of the information it contains.

Need is subject-based. Someone asks for information about nutrition, and this is a demand; but the need is for up-to-date, authoritative information appropriate to the user's ability to comprehend. In some cases the user knows what is needed to satisfy demand and comes to the library knowing (or expecting) it to be there; in other cases the user relies on the librarian. In either case the librarian must have already independently acquired the information and materials that are needed. Need is also use-based. Different kinds of use have different needs: scholarly research, professional application, and popular interest in a subject each require different materials on that subject. With nonfiction the librarian has a distinct professional responsibility to identify and select the best and most appropriate materials to meet users' needs. With fiction, on the other hand, the issue of need and demand is less clear. Some librarians have been accused of elitism for buying only what they consider "best" or "suitable" and ignoring demands for genre fiction or popular biography. Elitism may exist, but it should not be confused with the responsibility of librarians to determine a collection's needs and provide for them. Exercise of this responsibility is not elitism. When a library decides to collect fiction, it also must decide what kind of a collection to develop and maintain. It could, conceivably, decide on an inappropriate collection, one that no one will use or that does not contain what users want. If, however, it decides on an appropriate collection, then it still must provide what is needed by that kind of collection. To develop a collection of genre fiction—mysteries, romances, Westerns, juveniles—does not absolve the librarian of determining what is needed within the particular category.

When determining need, librarians are not trying to dictate but to interpret. Dealing with subjects, they must learn what kinds of information and materials are necessary in their particular collections, be sure these are authoritative and up-to-date, and distinguish appropriate from inappropriate, usable from unusable. They must analyze subject requirements and make use of various data, such as reference statistics, usage counts from circulation systems, and interlibrary loan records. When dealing with users, they must record and then weigh demand. They must consider potential as well as actual users, future as well as present, wider as well as local concerns, the less frequent as well as the avid readers, the recreational readers as well as those with a serious information purpose. They must look at those users actually in the library but they also must look out at the community in which they and their users live.

Users and Communities

Users are individuals; however, we look at categories and communities of users in order to see more clearly how libraries are used, what requests or demands to expect, and what needs to provide for. Each library must identify the categories of users that it is most likely to deal with, must set about building and maintaining a collection suitable to these categories, and must know where to send individuals who need, or would be better served by, materials in another library. There are probably as many categories as there are categorizers: I see seven user categories, each of which places unique demands on the library— juvenile, genre reader, student, common reader, concerned citizen, scholar or researcher, and professional. An individual could be in all the categories serially or in several simultaneously. We must remember that each user is a complex individual who breaks the bounds of any type.

Take two hypothetical examples. A 25-year-old graduate student in economics, buying her first car, seeking a scholarship to study abroad, with an avid interest in realistic, politically committed fiction, and an accomplished amateur violinist will challenge the resources of an academic library and a public library while seeking consumer and education information, scholarly resources in economics, and serious fiction, not to mention violin music for solo and small groups. A small-town insurance agent with local political ambitions will want general financial news, good newspapers reporting on county and state affairs, selected government publications, books on improving his golf game, and a general sense of developments in literature and arts, specifically the latest best-sellers. Each individual shares interests with others and so falls into several categories. If we have prepared for the general, then we have gone far toward preparing for the individuals.

To a degree, however, these examples are a pleasant fantasy, for there is no certainty that either person will actually use a library. The graduate student probably will have to use the university library as part of her study, but for fiction she can go to a bookstore and for information about cars she can ask friends. The insurance agent could make do with the Book of the Month Club, *Time*, and the local golf pro. Although each needs the resources of a good library, neither will necessarily demand them. Even individuals who actually do use a library may ask for a quite limited range of materials and minimal information: they might need much but demand little. A potential gap exists between need as we conceive it and demands actually made by users; nevertheless, we must consider the types of users.

Juvenile. Juveniles range from prereaders to adolescents; often their reading is selected for them by parents, teachers, or librarians, and often they are discouraged from reading adult materials, at least in the library. They are malleable in taste, and it could be argued that it does not matter so much what they read as that they read. Juveniles do favor certain fiction and nonfiction reading and librarians should respond to their demands (most do). At the same time, we recognize that much of what we provide them with is explicitly or implicitly educational, material that they need in order to master their school-work or that we think they need in order to develop intellectually, emotionally, and socially. They are an extremely important group. As heavy users of libraries they deserve an appropriate share of the collection and of collection managers' serious attention, and they can be led to develop strong library habits, with high expectations of the collection and considerable ease in using it.

Genre Reader. The genre reader has predictable, but not necessarily simple, interests. While some genre readers might be served adequately by mass-market paperbacks, many others will depend on the librarian to find not only the latest but the best fiction or nonfiction genre reading. Not every avid romance reader wants Harlequins nor will be happy with just any romance. Although some might be willing to read whatever is put into their hands, most do have their own personal preferences, whether that preference is a matter of literary quality, plot, setting, or character development, or in the case of popular biography and history, of a particular time, place, or culture. Betty Rosenberg's bibliographic guide to genre fiction, *Genreflecting*, can help us to understand the range of such fiction and prepare us to meet genre readers' needs: the field is rich and complex.[2]

The distinction between need and demand applies less clearly in the case of these juvenile and genre readers, who often ask for specific titles or authors, than in the remaining categories where users ask for materials or information about subjects. Librarians must respond to demand as if it were need and try to supply what is asked for. Yet they know that juvenile taste is developing and therefore can be challenged; they recognize the power of books to mold character and to guide thinking and sensitivities and, therefore, they can urge their juvenile readers to read certain efficacious books. Librarians also recognize that genre readers are in part seeking pleasureful books; their need is for good reading such as found in genre books but that could be found in other books, too. In neither case is the concept of need a license to impose our taste on others; in both cases the concept of need introduces an obligation of librarians to understand their users and the materials they are likely to want.

Student. We all, at one time or another, are formally and informally students—the new Nobel laureate trying to learn a little Swedish suitable for the trip to Stockholm no less than the auto mechanic in a dealership that has just taken on a new line or the family transferred to a different state wanting to learn about its history. The role public libraries once had of supporting widespread and serious self-education by adults, many of them recent immigrants, has diminished, but there still are many users who go to the library seeking information and texts with which they can learn to improve their lives, and who expect the library to have selected appropriate materials for them to use.

Adult education today might be seen as preparation for "intentional

2. Betty Rosenberg, *Genreflecting: A Guide to Reading Interests in Genre Fiction,* 2nd ed. (Littleton, Colo.: Libraries Unlimited, 1986).

change," as this concept has been defined by Allen Tough. Areas in which adults regularly find themselves making deliberate change are, in descending order of frequency: (1) careers, jobs, and training; (2) human relationships, emotions, and self-perception; (3) enjoyable activities; (4) residence; (5) maintenance of home and finances; (6) physical health; (7) religion; and (8) basic competencies such as reading, decision making, or driving.[3] Tough's analysis of so-called intentional changes in our lives shows the importance of being able to choose, plan, and implement so we can control the process of change. The complex array of information that people need for this control can be provided by the public library, and a recent study of public library use confirms his view of what is needed: there is heavy use of nonfiction, informational materials, especially by men and the unemployed, and a sizable minority of adult users have no more than a high-school education (presumably they are using information sources as much as recreational reading matter).[4] A significant proportion of all adults, and a significant proportion of public-library users, need information. Our users may have grown more diverse and may no longer need explicitly educational materials, in the sense of graded or progressive textbooks, but many of them still are students.

In academic libraries education is the primary concern, even in universities and colleges with a strong emphasis on faculty research. The facile distinction between teaching and research is difficult to maintain in the library. It is difficult today to provide high-quality undergraduate education where the faculty is not active in research and scholarship, and in universities where faculty are educators as well as researchers, research is more likely to have a historical component than it would in a private research laboratory or other institution. Faculty must read widely in the current literature of their field in order to select material suitable for their students' reading; graduate students at even the most advanced levels are sent to the older as well as the current literature to gain an understanding of their subject and discipline; undergraduates regularly use sophisticated and specialized materials.

Realistically, though, undergraduate needs differ from faculty needs. Students make heavier use than faculty of secondary literature, and they need that secondary literature in manageable and authoritative

---

3. Allen Tough, *Intentional Change: A Fresh Approach to Helping People Change* (Chicago: Follett, 1982), p. 26.
4. Richard Rubin, *In-House Use of Materials in Public Libraries* (Champaign: Graduate School of Library and Information Science, University of Illinois, 1986).

doses. While they must read widely, it is not their responsibility nor within their competency to distinguish good from bad. Faculty on the other hand need primary literature and use the secondary literature not so much to answer questions as to discover new questions or lines of inquiry. For the undergraduate we must select carefully; for the faculty we must gather widely. The collection in a good academic library, then, must serve both ends of the continuum and provide for every member of the university community from freshman through senior scholar or researcher.

Common Reader. *Common reader* is a term from Samuel Johnson by way of Virginia Woolf's *The Common Reader*:[5]

> There is a sentence in Dr. Johnson's Life of Gray which might well be written up in all those rooms, too humble to be called libraries, yet full of books, where the pursuit of reading is carried on by private people. ". . . I rejoice to concur with the common reader; for by the common sense of readers, uncorrupted by literary prejudices, after all the refinements of subtlety and the dogmatism of learning, must be finally decided all claim to poetical honours." It defines their qualities; it dignifies their aims; it bestows upon a pursuit which devours a great deal of time, and is yet apt to leave behind it nothing very substantial, the sanction of the great man's approval. . . . Above all, [the common reader] is guided by an instinct to create for himself, out of whatever odds and ends he can come by, some kind of whole. . . .

We might today call this the educated reader, but I prefer the older term because this common reader exists in all communities, not just those with a particular demographic character, and is unusually independent. Reading is not simply recreational nor strictly educational; reading is the primary mode of gaining information and is deeply satisfying to the mind and emotions. The common reader is not an elitist, seeking out only the best that is and ever was while completely unaware of contemporary currents, reviews, and best-sellers. Like Emerson, however, who never wanted to read a book less than two years old, the common reader seeks something not readily available in bookstores and on newsstands.

If the genre reader demands more of the same, challenging us to discover exactly what appeals to each one, the common reader demands more of the unique. It is the common reader to whom Helen Haines in *Living with Books* addresses her praise of books and reading: ". . . Only through books does the mind itself enrich, deepen,

---

5. Virginia Woolf, *The Common Reader* (New York: Harcourt Brace, 1925), p. 11.

apply, modify, and develop those patterns [learned in formal education] in individual life fulfillment."[6] The common reader's search for this kind of fulfillment through books, particularly in this age of proliferating information, glossy magazines, insistent television, and hundreds of distractions, challenges us to provide a rich, high-quality collection.

Concerned Citizen. The concerned citizen, unlike the common reader, might not find reading so essential to his or her life, might prefer to play softball after supper to reading another chapter, might read only best-sellers, might be more intrigued by the possibilities of computer retrieval of information than interested in reading the best book on the subject. The concerned citizen as defined here is someone who needs information of a certain sort on certain subjects at a certain time. The concerned citizen like the adult student wants to become sufficiently informed so as to act effectively, but differs by focusing on social issues rather than on matters of personal welfare or development. Some issues are predictably recurring: each election season brings the need for materials on agricultural policies, tax reform, international trade, or the records of incumbent candidates. Because all of these can be predicted, the library has a responsibility to anticipate both demand and need. Even though tax reform, for example, might not be an issue of the moment, we must be sure to acquire a just-published book on the subject, if it is a good one, and in so doing anticipate demand by collecting for need.

The more difficult thing, however, is to identify and collect for those specific, local crises and issues. A rural library in a town suddenly threatened with a toxic-waste dump; the public library in a city that has just lost its major employer; the academic library in a college whose faculty has moved toward collective bargaining: each of these libraries could conceivably have had some materials about these issues, but none could have predicted nor built an extensive collection on them. Suddenly each will need multiple copies, the latest information (not necessarily readily available), information representing a variety of points of view and opinion—and, of course, the best information. Where there is controversy and heightened concern, there can be confusion, rumor, misinformation, and demagoguery.

Newspapers have been championed as essential for an informed

---

6. Helen Haines, *Living with Books: The Art of Book Selection,* 2nd ed. (New York: Columbia University Press, 1950), p. 3.

citizenry. They might be understood better, however, as an alerting service, while the library should be where citizens become adequately informed. Through the newspaper, magazine, and television, we hear of issues and persons that affect us, and we find out some of the details of the issues, the opinions or actions of the persons, and the immediate past events and future prospects. On the other hand, we can learn facts, interpretations, and lines of reasoning and argument that can enable us to act effectively. We can gather facts about toxic wastes with which to influence legislators or officials, can find similar examples of citizen action and techniques of action in other communities, can develop more effective arguments and lobbying techniques, and can take courage from this knowledge. An informed citizenry, thus, becomes an empowered citizenry. The library should be the place where that informed citizenry is forged.

Scholars and Researchers. Scholars and researchers probably place the heaviest demands on a library's collection of any of these types of users. As they analyze existing information, create new information, revise current knowledge, and develop new syntheses (or test old ones), they require the accumulated information and knowledge of the past, yet are constantly revising it, working it into new relationships, and adding to it. For them the library truly is an arena. Scholarship, whether scientific or humanistic, is more exploratory than research and pores through libraries in search of questions and problems; research, on the other hand, is more focused on specific problems, projects, or experiments. Scholarship and research in universities make more use of historical information and materials than they do in research institutes or independent laboratories because they include educating students as part of their mission, instilling both correct methodologies and a basic knowledge of predecessors' work.

The distinction is not crucial here, but it helps us to understand that different kinds of collections are called for. The researchers' collection must hold or provide immediate access to the latest, most up-to-date materials; it should be technologically advanced, making use of networks, bibliographic utilities, electronic books and journals, data archives, online search services, and so forth. The scholar's library can forgo speed and immediacy of access in favor of an extensive, even exhaustive, range of materials, preserved and weeded conservatively. Libraries, scholars, and researchers participate in the system of scholarly and scientific communication, which will be discussed later.

Professional. The professional—lawyer, physician, executive, teacher, librarian, journalist, government official, nurse, technologist—

is a problem solver who needs at hand the records of previous solutions to similar problems as well as the latest information that could be used to solve problems not yet dealt with. Unlike the researcher the professional is not trying to find a new synthesis or develop a new analysis but is using existing information or knowledge in a specific situation. This new use may well contribute to a new synthesis or a new version of the previously known, but that is not the intention. Because professionals have very specialized library needs, there are many specialized libraries to serve them, from law and medical libraries to libraries in government agencies and business firms. At the same time professionals need convenient access to the comprehensive resources of a research library.

Communities. Libraries and their users exist within a community. The public library is part of a civic, sociopolitical community; the academic library is part of a college or university; the special library is part of a business, professional association, or some kind of agency or institution; academic and research libraries are part of a community of learning; libraries themselves make up a community of libraries. There are place communities and interest communities.[7] Cities and counties are place communities, as to a lesser degree are colleges and universities and even in some ways businesses, professional offices, and certain institutions. Institutions and corporations, however, also are interest communities, as is the community of libraries. Interests can be shared goals (colleges educating youth, businesses seeking profits), shared operating principles and practices (the community of libraries), and similar vocational or avocational activities. Individuals are members of both place and interest communities: they live in civic communities and share interests with others; those who use libraries are members of the community of users.

The library serves its users—members of its user community—but it also has a role or responsibility within the larger community of which it is a part. The public library, the academic library, and the special library each has a role in its community to provide reading matter and related information services. To perform these responsibilities it must understand the makeup of its community, and for public libraries this requires, initially at least, demographic analysis. Census data describes age, race, and ethnic groups, educational level, socioeconomic status and aspiration, occupations and professions, immigrant

---

7. Ralph Blasingame and Mary Jo Lynch, "Design for Diversity: Alternatives to Standards for Public Libraries," *Studies in Library Management* 3 (1976): 121–35.

and citizenship status of the community's citizens; with it we can map neighborhoods, transportation routes, population density and distribution, and we can chart changes in the data over several decades. Some communities are stable and homogeneous; others are varied and fast-changing. Use of this data is demonstrated in several of the public-library policies collected by Elizabeth Futas in *Library Acquisitions Policies and Procedures*. See, for instance, the policy of the Evanston, Illinois, public library that describes residential character, educational levels and interests, age, race, and income level.[8] Large systems must be sure to collect data from neighborhood communities served by branches.

Academic communities also have distinct demographic makeups revealed by data about students, faculty, and curricula: the number of students, their socioeconomic background, sex, broad academic and vocational interests, and their abilities as indicated by test scores of entering freshmen; the courses and programs listed in the institution's catalog, the institution's stated educational mission and the emphasis on teaching, faculty research, and preparation for advanced study and professional work; the number of faculty, the percentage with Ph.D.s, and the quantity of their publications. Two institutions of the same size could have considerably different demographic and educational characters—and, consequently, quite different definitions of the library's role. It is exactly because of the crucial relationship between the institution's teaching and research functions and the library's purpose to support these that we must analyze the academic community.[9]

Such community analysis is important, but does not directly identify those needs that the library should meet. Community analysis must go beyond a description of who lives in the community and who uses public libraries to determine what their demands and needs actually are. Edward Evans's textbook, *Developing Library and Information Center Collections,* devotes an excellent chapter to information-needs assessment—that is, analysis not simply of who lives in the community but, more, of what these citizens' information or library needs are.[10] In addition to definitions, practical advice, and

8. Elizabeth Futas, ed., *Library Acquisitions Policies and Procedures* (Phoenix: Oryx, 1977), p. 43; *see also* the 2nd ed. (Phoenix: Oryx, 1984).

9. James F. Gowan, "Community Analysis in an Academic Environment," *Library Trends* 24 (1976): 541–56.

10. G. Edward Evans, *Developing Library and Information Center Collections,* 2nd ed. (Littleton, Colo.: Libraries Unlimited, 1987), 26–64.

examples of assessments and useful forms, he provides a basic bibliography on community analysis in public and several other kinds of libraries. Several techniques can be used in community analysis, each appropriate for particular purposes.[11] Within the larger community the library as one public institution or agency has specific responsibilities. Provision of reading matter and information services related to material in the collection are different, obviously, from the responsibilities of police and fire departments, social-service agencies, transportation and utilities, and schools, but just as certainly are an integral part of the community. Ours is a print and information community and the library plays a central role in it. Libraries have a set of responsibilities that must be defined in terms of both actual individual users and the community's known needs.

Attention to the larger community, however, must not divert us from those who use libraries frequently and intensively. This user community is, of course, smaller than the larger whole community and also seems more homogeneous. A 1978 Gallup Poll commissioned by the ALA described the situation nationwide. About 53 percent of a typical community uses the public library. Of this group about half are light users, one-third moderate users, and 17 percent heavy users, with the majority college-educated, 18- to 34-year-olds. Easterners seem to use libraries more than people in other regions.[12] The most frequent users are children, and after them are women with some college education seeking fiction.[13] This description probably surprised no one in public libraries, but we should remember that it is a partial description and that there is still a sizable group of library users who do not fit it. A recent study of selected public libraries (not a representative sample) discovered, for instance, that a significant percentage of users were unemployed, had no more than a high-school education, and were men seeking nonfiction.[14] The user community is fairly homogeneous, but not monolithic. Furthermore, while there is a difference between the broad community and the smaller user community,

---

11. For an overview, *see* Larry Earl Bone, ed., "Community Analysis and Libraries," *Library Trends* 24 (1976): 429–643; for practical advice, *see* Ruth Warnke, "Analyzing Your Community: Basis for Building Library Service," *Illinois Libraries* 57 (1975): 64–76.

12. Michael Harris and James Sodt, "Libraries, Users, and Librarians: Continuing Efforts to Define the Nature and Extent of Public Library Use," *Advances in Librarianship* 11 (1981): 109–33.

13. Douglas Zweizig and Brenda Dervin, "Public Library Use, Users, Uses: Advances in Knowledge of the Characteristics and Needs of the Adult Clientele in American Public Libraries," *Advances in Librarianship* 7 (1977): 231–55.

14. Rubin, *In-House Use of Materials in Public Libraries.*

we also must recognize that there are connections between users and nonusers. Pauline Wilson's study, *A Community Elite and the Public Library: The Users of Information in Leadership,* tries to sort out one example of this indirect but important influence.[15] The public library must serve both the whole community of which it is a part and the smaller user community with whom it has more frequent dealings.

In academic communities, too, we must look beneath the surface of descriptive data to discover actual performance. Even more than the courses listed in the catalog and the numbers of students in each major, we want to know which courses actually are taught, their enrollments, and the kind of work students must do in them (reserve readings, independent study, research papers, oral reports; read widely or do close analysis; demonstrate initiative or persevere doggedly). Do graduate courses serve academic or professional programs and do they enroll more master's or doctoral students? Similar questions can be asked about institutional priorities. What are promotion and tenure critera? Do faculty publish frequently, in the best journals, and with the best presses? Are there trends toward more interdisciplinary courses or econometric research? Does local faculty research mirror national research? What is the institution's pattern of budget support for the various programs? What percentage of the budget goes to humanities programs or comes from enrollments in the business school?

A further refinement of this descriptive data is shown in the research conducted by Paul Metz and reported in *Landscape of Literatures,* 1983.[16] By analyzing circulation data in a university library he was able to chart in considerable detail the relationship between student and faculty users in specific departments and the use of books and journals. He thus found in this particular institution the degree of support that materials in one subject provided for users at various levels in various departments and, conversely, the degree of reliance of users in a department on materials in their own and other subjects. Although his study has national implications about the use of library materials, it is also a community analysis of a specific institution. Metz's study is an example of use analysis, which will be discussed more

---

15. Pauline Wilson, *A Community Elite and the Public Library: The Uses of Information in Leadership* (Westport, Conn.: Greenwood, 1977).

16. Paul Metz, *Landscape of Literatures: Use of Subject Collections in a University Library* (Chicago: American Library Association, 1983).

thoroughly in chapter five. Use analysis generally measures demand, not need; but to understand need we must identify our users and understand their communities. One particular community is the community of learning, and the scientific and scholarly communication within it requires further examination.

Scientific and Scholarly Communication

Scholarly and scientific communication within the community of learning is both the *process* through which scholars and scientists find information necessary to their work and pass on information about, or produced by, their work to others, and the *system* within which scientific and scholarly information and knowledge are produced, evaluated, and made available to those who need it. Libraries—particularly university and research libraries—play an active role in the process and are a significant participant in the system. Both process and system involve scientists and scholars, their ideas and the information or knowledge they create or interpret, the various publication media and computer and communication technologies, scholarly societies and institutions, foundations, and government agencies, and libraries. Despite this wooden definition, which too easily lumps science and scholarship without explaining ways in which they differ, the issue is itself very interesting, complex, important, and, for librarians in academic and special libraries, absolutely crucial to understand. The role of libraries is certainly not new, as John Cole has explained: in the late nineteenth century "American scholarship and scientific activity. . . reorganized itself around the university and its library."[17] Library collections and services now face difficult problems and, because libraries are a crucial element in scholarly and scientific communication, the continued operation of the process and system is threatened. To understand the problems and to devise solutions librarians must examine the process and system of which we are a part.

Communication is an essential element of science and scholarship, for it is in the process of communication that scholarship and science are tested, verified, and formulated or articulated meaningfully.

---

17. John Y. Cole, "Storehouses and Workshops: American Libraries and the Uses of Knowledge," in *The Organization of Knowledge in Modern America, 1860–1920,* eds. Alexandra Oleson and John Voss (Baltimore: John Hopkins University Press, 1979), pp. 364–85.

Scientific and scholarly communication is interactive, and through
its process the initiator elicits criticism, support, and information for
the research while offering particular information from it. Without
this kind of communication there can be no science; it is information
exchange and, equally important, social process. Scientific communication also is crucial in the evaluation of research, and an essential
function of scientific publication is that it is in itself a statement of
validity and significance, not simply a record of research. Communication is not merely one scientist telling another that she or he has
been working on a subject or has just finished an interesting experiment or piece of research; rather, it is telling in such a way that the
listener can evaluate the significance of the subject and the quality
of the research or experiment. This complex and essential process
is the subject of William Garvey's 1979 book, *Communication: The
Essence of Science,* in which he summarizes the results of two decades
of study of the nature and importance of communication among
scientists, and which I summarize here.[18]

Scientific communication is interactive and thus is also highly
personal. From the moment a scientist or scholar conceives an idea
(which more than likely has been suggested directly or indirectly by
something read or heard), through the stages of research and
experimentation, to overt communication in a variety of ways including ultimately publication in a refereed journal, through all the postpublication media, to the idea's final form and accepted relevance,
he or she must be constantly describing the work, gathering additional
information, refining and revising its form, and arguing for its
relevance. This work is personal, for the individual scientist's own
personality, experience, knowledge, and goals affect how he or she
recognizes and uses information. This work is social for it requires
information exchange: the scientist asks for information and usually
gives some in return simply in the process of describing what he or
she is doing or trying to do, and the scientist asks for feedback opinion
about quality and relevancy of the particular research and its experimental procedures. This feedback from other scientists is, of course,
their acknowledgment of the work and of its actual or potential
value.

This interactive communication takes place in two domains, the

18. William Garvey, *Communication: The Essence of Science. Facilitating Information Exchange among Librarians, Scientists, Engineers and Students* (New York:
Pergamon, 1979).

formal and the informal. Librarians encounter it most commonly in the formal domain of scientific journals, indexing and abstracting services, review journals and annuals, monographs, textbooks, and reference books, but for the most active scientists the informal domain is more important. By the time a scientist has published results in a journal, the ideas and evidence already have been presented, often several times. In the prepublication (informal) stage there has been considerable interchange with other scientists through which the research has been reviewed, revised, and thoroughly challenged so that journal publication presents it in its most relevant and usable form. Postpublication communication disseminates it to a wider audience, allows additional judgment of its quality, and establishes the ways or extent to which it is relevant. One could say that in this postpublication, formal domain scientific information becomes scientific knowledge.

The informal domain encompasses all the communication prior to journal publication. Although much of the communication here is oral or ephemeral, scarcely indexed and difficult to access, it is very important to the active scientist, for it contains information often not found in subsequent publication, and follows a regular pattern. This pattern, which involves progressively more formalized forums, might typically consist of the following steps. Once the scientist has begun work (whether actual laboratory processes or only the preliminary development of an idea and preliminary gathering of literature), he or she will make local oral presentations (as in an academic department colloquium) and regional, national, or international presentations also. Frequently the scientist, especially when working in an independent research laboratory, will have to write annual reports on the year's work. If the work is funded with grants, particularly federal grant money, the scientist probably must provide annual reports on the progress of the research. Once the research has been written, submitted, and accepted as an article in a journal, but not yet published, then it may be available as a preprint. During all this progression from idea to article, the scientist may well have been corresponding with others, and these letters could contain useful information.

This informal domain is, to a considerable extent, described by the concept of an "invisible college," in which personal communication is the primary mode of disseminating scientific information. Leading figures in a research area, particularly during the early stages of its formation, both disseminate information about their work and its implications and define the appropriate research subjects and methods (even, in some situations, defining or establishing the appropriate paradigms). The social process of communication, as described by Diana Crane in her *Invisible Colleges,* involves "informal discussions of research, published collaborations, relationships with teachers, and the influence of colleagues," and seems as crucial to the development of scientific knowledge as more cognitive and overt factors.[19]

As research passes through the stages in the informal domain, it is not widely known or accessible. Active scientists in the field will hear about it and may correspond with the researcher; they also might attend meetings and conferences and hear papers; they might be consulted by the editor of the journal to which an article has been submitted. Others on the periphery of the research field, including librarians, will have a more difficult time. Fortunately, there are some forms of prejournal publication that are, or can be, widely disseminated, some of which are considerably useful. An institutional laboratory's annual report could contain summaries of important research that is being conducted. Research undertaken by graduate students could be written in theses and dissertations and could be accessible through standard indexing. Technical reports are common, especially for work funded by federal grants; these often contain more detail than the final journal article—more textual discussion, figures, tables, diagrams of equipment, photographs of operations, specimens, specifications, and other details omitted from articles, as well as longer bibliographies. Published proceedings, which contain the texts or abstracts of papers delivered at conferences, are of course books and therefore easily accessible on library shelves and in indexes. In addition, it is possible to develop a file of upcoming meetings and conferences, many with schedules of the papers to be read, through which one can identify scientists working in specific areas. The informal domain, then, is significant for the active scientist and its usable formats, in some libraries, will be an important part of the collection.

A scientist's research culminates in the journal article, at which point it enters the formal domain where it mixes with a wider group of research and researchers and where it may be cited, reviewed, worked into others' research, and given wide acceptance. The journal article is the keystone of scientific research in several ways: it is an

---

19. Diana Crane, *Invisible Colleges: Diffusion of Knowledge in Scientific Communities* (Chicago: University of Chicago Press, 1972), p. 41.

abstract of the previous research, referring back to papers, technical reports, or other media; it is proof that that research has been carried out to its most flawless and usable point (at least as judged by the scientist and the editors of the journal); it is the document to which later researchers refer. However valuable the prejournal steps are in the development and formulation of the research, they are still the steps taken toward this point. Even though the scientist may have already started other research, this particular research has reached its crucial point in the journal article.

The journal article, then, is the center of a web of communication in which research is wrapped. The article refers to other work in its bibliography, and in turn it is cited: most subsequent reference to the research that it reports will cite the article rather than any of the various prejournal publications. Its audience really is not the peers of the scientist who writes it, most of whom would have been following along with the earlier papers and publications in the informal domain, but is a wider community of scientists and scholars with somewhat different interests over a longer period of time. As Diana Crane notes, "The function of the scientific paper that has been refereed and published in a journal is only secondarily to convey information. Its primary function is to serve as a statement of knowledge that has been evaluated and declared acceptable by the scientist's peers."[20]

It is important, therefore, to note the postjournal career of the article. Presumably the quality and accuracy of the research is verified by journal publication, although certainly there will be further attempts to test it by replication and modification. Only time and continued work, however, can demonstrate its significance; only as it is integrated with the work of others can it become relevant and be considered knowledge. Once published, the article is then picked up in the standard abstracting and indexing services. Annual reviews can cite it, and within a few years it could be cited in one or more critical reviews. The critical review provides far more than a housekeeping function and is more than merely a mechanical sorter of previous indexing and abstracting: it is a synthesis that tries to evaluate previous work, show relationships within it, and create an intellectual framework that can accommodate this new information and make it usable. The critical review is but one step from the monograph that synthesizes earlier research and develops theories. Subsequent reference to the research in handbooks, dictionaries, encyclopedias, and textbooks

20. Crane, p. 122.

marks further steps in the communication process and the development of information into knowledge.

Garvey, like Crane, emphasizes the sociology of scientific work, and urges librarians to discover how scientific information is produced by scientists with whom they work and also to keep up-to-date on their activities and research projects (typically such interests change every two years). Through this and their understanding of scientific communication librarians could

> become part of the scientific process itself—to anticipate scientists' information needs; to disseminate information created by scientists in the community being served to other scientists outside the community on whom it would be predicted to have significant impact; and even to generate information such as synthesis as a result of analyzing information flow and use.[21]

Much of what Garvey says applies equally to humanistic scholarship. Published in the same year as Garvey's book, *Scholarly Communication,* the report of the National Enquiry into Scholarly Communication (funded by the American Council of Learned Societies) chooses instead to examine the *system* of scholarly communication, and in doing so provides a different and important perspective on both scholarly and scientific communication.[22] This system involves scholars and their work, of course, and also the media (journals and books, editors and publishers), scholarly societies, foundations and government agencies, technologists in computing, printing, and communications, and research libraries. It operates for the disciplines of anthropology, the classics, English, foreign languages and literatures, history, philosophy, religion, and sociology. When effective the system benefits scholars and also the publication media and libraries, ensuring coordination of their efforts and a reasonable financial situation. The parties in the system—scholars, publishers, librarians—want only the best work produced, disseminated, collected, and made accessible.

The effective system of scholarly communication has the following characteristics:[23]

---

21. Garvey, p. 120.

22. *Scholarly Communication: The Report of the National Enquiry* (Baltimore: Johns Hopkins University Press, 1979).

23. *Scholarly Communication,* p. 7.

Access. Readers should have access to a comprehensive bibliographic system that allows them to identify and locate material and to obtain it at a reasonable cost and without excessive delay.

Entry. Authors should find a variety of book publishers and journal editors willing to give a manuscript a fair reading and committed to a decision based on scholarly merit.

Quality control. The system should have the capacity to differentiate between works of greater and lesser quality, of greater or lesser importance, and to match the form of publication to these differences.

Timeliness. Manuscripts should be accepted or rejected promptly, and works should be published on schedule. Advance announcements should keep scholars apprised of forthcoming books and articles, and distribution systems should make completed work available rapidly.

Coordination. The participants in the communications venture . . . should be mindful of their obligations and their interdependence, and pursue their goals in light of the effects their actions have on others and on the entire system.

Adaptability. Since the needs of scholars, the tools of scholarship, the uses of knowledge, and the economic and social environment are constantly changing, the scholarly community should maintain a responsive attitude toward the elimination of obsolete methods and materials and toward possibilities of productive innovation.

Financial viability. Financing arrangements should ensure the economic viability of each function essential to the system of scholarly communication.

What gave rise to the National Enquiry was a perceived crisis in the early to mid-1970s affecting the continued operation of the system. Several university presses and journals ceased publishing and libraries canceled journal subscriptions and reduced book purchasing. In investigating the extent and implications of these problems the authors of the report became convinced that a system did exist and that the best way to deal with problems of individual participants was in terms of the whole. Simply increasing the money in library acquisitions budgets, aside from being unrealistic, would not correct the system, and problems that libraries were facing could best be understood in light of the whole system of scholarly communication.

Closer examination of libraries uncovered a more complex problem. Scholars, particulary junior faculty and faculty in less-developed institutions, were making increased demands on the library for materials and reference and bibliographic service; libraries seemed less able to satisfy their demands. Within libraries funds were shifted from books to serials to the point where book collecting was threatened and funds also shifted from materials to salaries, supplies, and services. Library budgets increased less than institutional budgets; cost reductions affected periodicals and books (and, thus, publishers). New problems appeared, such as paper deterioration. Use of interlibrary loans increased and so did costs and delays. Externally, higher education suffered a period of depressed growth and income so that institutions and libraries continued to endure financial austerity. Technology, which had been able to help contain costs but not reduce them, offered no hope of easy solution to the problems. Inflation in materials prices endangered the library as a whole and the humanities in particular.

Specific suggestions for improving the libraries' situation mainly urged new forms of cooperation and new means for developing solutions within the system. Proposals for a national periodicals center, a national bibliographic system, and a national library agency that would plan and coordinate cooperation among research libraries on relevant matters all emphasized the whole rather than individual libraries. Ten years later none of the proposals in the National Enquiry has been realized, at least not through a centralized national authority. Austerity continues: book and subscription prices rise faster than the Consumer Price Index (CPI); institutional budgets outpace library budgets; cooperation is devoutly to be wished but devilishly hard to achieve; scholars' (and their students') needs and demands increase; a new round of price increases savaged serial budgets (as described previously). Yet the system has not collapsed; librarians have cobbled together a means of survival that has preserved the system.

Garvey's analysis of the process of scientific communication (which applies also to scholarly communication) shows how individual scientists typically go about acquiring necessary information, interacting with other scientists, and introducing their work into the stream of scientific knowledge. What he does not show is how scientists go about selecting their areas of research and their approaches to the area or their selection of the kinds of problems or issues they will investigate. Scientists and scholars do not work in a vacuum, nor, objective as they might be once research is under way, do they rely solely on their own inspiration when selecting research lines. A number of forces affect the overall pattern of scientific and scholarly research in this country, and Charles Osburn in another 1979 book, *Academic Research and Library Resources: Changing Patterns in America*, presents the results of his analysis of developments in the research community since World War II, especially in American universities.[24]

Osburn examined in particular the link between government and academic interests in research and found, of course, a close relationship, one in which there was considerable and varied support for and use of academic research by the government. Rather than set up research institutions of its own, the government has contracted out that research through the use of grant money and through the well-publicized concern about certain types of problems or issues. The government has supported basic research, but more significantly it has supported, encouraged, even demanded applied research, and it has expanded the range of areas in which it wants this research conducted. From strictly technological areas, such as military materiel and a variety of engineering problems, to medical, physiological, and biological areas, to social and behavioral science (such as education, aging, child development, poverty), and even to some areas in the humanities, the federal government has sought information, created grant-giving agencies, and, in particular, created project grants for research with very specific and practical goals.

Government-sponsored research has significantly affected institutions, researchers, the relationship between individual researchers and institutions, and the nature of research; but more to the point it has significantly affected the way scientists and other researchers use library materials. By emphasizing problem-solving research, the government also has emphasized or demanded that research produce high-quality, timely, and useful results. If there is a problem to be solved, then clearly the need is for mission-oriented research, rather than basic research, to provide pertinent information very quickly.

Researchers under these conditions need information fast and often need the latest available information; the source of this kind of information has tended increasingly to be journal articles and prejournal publications such as technical reports and conference proceedings. The serial collection has, as librarians well know, become extremely important as well as extremely large and expensive. The journal and serial literature, the prejournal publications, and access-enhancing and synthesizing works have become preeminent in the sciences and most areas of the social sciences and have become a significant element in humanistic scholarship. Academic, research, and special libraries

24. Charles Osburn, *Academic Research and Library Resources: Changing Patterns in America* (Westport, Conn.: Greenwood, 1979).

must subscribe extensively to journals, newsletters, annual reviews, conference proceedings, technical reports, and other series, and they must subscribe to abstracting and indexing services, often quite specific ones.

Even in the humanities a shift has occurred from an emphasis on erudition and an understanding of the past toward "an emphasis on criticism as a creative activity; on formal, theoretical principles as a means to understanding man as a social animal or as a metaphysical being; and on the applications of methodology, skills, and knowledge of social sciences research—including quantitative approaches."[25] Even though monographic works retain their importance in the humanities, these are increasingly specialized, increasingly current. Osburn's description of changes in humanistic research is borne out by a recent study of the kinds of materials requested by scholars at the National Humanities Center: "These requests were for a larger proportion of journal articles, of a more recent body of literature, and for a higher concentration in the English language."[26] Yet the situation is not quite so clear and simple. There is evidence of a countermovement or a reassertion of the humanistic mode of research. Anthony Loveday, in challenging the Atkinson Report in Great Britain, asserts that "Today even the sciences are in company with the humanities in their more traditional pattern by constantly returning to a reexamination in a new context of apparently unrelated or outmoded concepts contained in older scholarly work."[27]

Humanistic research and study continuously examines and re-examines recorded human expression (creative, analytical, and synthesizing), both for its content and for the reasons it is what it is. As our present-day understanding develops and as new information about the past comes to light, humanistic interpretation and analysis enable us to see again with new eyes. The sciences, too, in their own ways reexamine the record of past scientists' work. Certainly the history and philosophy of science are healthy disciplines and the relations between science and other endeavors are a common subject of study.

---

25. Osburn, p. 121.
26. Robert N. Broadus, "Information Needs of Humanities Scholars: A Study of Requests Made at the National Humanities Center," *Library and Information Science Research* 9 (1987): 113–29.
27. Anthony J. Loveday, "An Appraisal of the Report of the University Grants Committee Working Party on Capital Provision for University Libraries (The Atkinson Report)," *Journal of Librarianship* 9 (1977): 17–28, and Richard J. C. Atkinson, *Capital Provision for University Libraries: Report of a Working Party* (London: HMSO, 1976).

The university proclaims and demonstrates its dedication both to preserving and making known all that was ever thought and to maintaining its deep involvement in the crucial knowledge-making, problem-solving work of society. Libraries' participation in the process and place in the system of scholarly and scientific communication, especially as science and scholarship now operate, lends new force to the assertion that the library is the heart of the university (and research institution).

Knowing we are at the heart does not provide us with easy answers about what kind of collection to build. Our understanding of the process and system of scholarly communication does, however, enable us to understand what kind of collection is needed. We recognize that library collections in general must serve current research and scholarly activities by keeping on hand or within ready access journals and recent monographs where current research and scholarship are published, but also by providing a collection of older journals and monographs where earlier research and scholarship have been published. In some collections there will be a need for documents from the informal domain, in others there will not be a need; in some collections extensive runs of older journals and the retention of older monographs will be important, in others they will not be so important. Institutions are different. One might expect cutting-edge research, another applied research, and a third the training of new researchers. The library collection in each will be different from that in the others; each specific collection will be governed by the kind of work being carried on with it. Understanding scholarly and scientific communication, thus, prepares us to identify our own community of users and to define our library's mission accordingly.

Mission

An organization's mission is the governing purpose from which all subsidiary purposes follow, but stated precisely enough to allow for realistic application. The standard statement of a library's mission— that it should provide reading matter and information services to its users and for its community—must be made more specific and concrete. A good collection is not merely an assemblage of materials but is a carefully selected whole, clearly appropriate for a specific community of users, within a specific community. Librarians must identify the user categories they can expect to deal with and then define the users' needs that the library can reasonably meet. The mission statement should show that these needs are understood fairly precisely. Librarians must define their user community, noting both individual users and predominant categories, and they must define accurately the larger community's demography and interests, or in the case of institutions or organizations, its operations and mission.

This and the previous chapters have dealt with the questions of what users need, what kinds of library materials exist, and how the various materials in collections might meet these needs. Librarians must understand needs, materials, and the ways materials are used by different kinds of users, in different situations, and with different subjects. Scientific and scholarly communication is a complex kind of use (or set of uses) and places a number of demands on a library and its collection, not least on those librarians responsible for understanding it as it is carried out in their particular libraries. Scholarly communication must be analyzed because of the insight it gives into the needs of many users in academic, research, and a number of special libraries, but also because of the emphasis it places on the individual librarian whose responsibility is to deal with scholarly and scientific users. Libraries are not inert, and librarians are not passive participants in the system and process. Of course this responsibility lies on all collection management librarians, but here is a particularly structured kind of use that needs and rewards our understanding. My definition of user categories tries to identify the typical needs of individuals in these categories.

These points are not new. Librarians have long dealt with their communities, and one result has been the development of distinct types of libraries. Whatever the immediate demand of the person at the door, we know that each type of library experiences a consistent type of use over the long term, and that if we prepare for that kind of use we can best meet the needs of the continuing, recurring users typical of the particular kinds of libraries. The needs of the typical reader, typical business executive, or typical high-school student using a public library are different from the needs of the typical sophomore, college senior, or senior faculty member using a university library and these latter needs are probably slightly different from those of similar users in a college library.

The major types of libraries—public, academic, school, government, special—can be further subdivided, and indeed *Library Literature* lists at least 50 different types of libraries (although within this number there is some overlap and some types are units within others). These libraries are initially defined, one might say, by their communities. An academic library is a library in a college or university, a special library is a library in an institution or organization, a public library is the library of a civic community. The community of users within each library type is distinct, although individual users move from community to community and category to category. Each of these types of libraries shares, as we know, features with the others. Yet we know that a public library does not, in most cases, serve a community of scholars, nor does the academic library serve a community of genre readers or juveniles. Individual researchers may use the public library and the person wanting romances or science fiction may use the academic library, but essentially each library serves different user communities and exists within different communities. Our initial definition of a library is based on its predominant community.

Each external community is different, however. A remarkable variety exists among the communities of the 8,800 or so public libraries listed in the *American Library Directory* and each has different users with different needs: urban, suburban, rural; industrial and agricultural; new city and old; prosperous and depressed; Grain Belt, Sunbelt, Bible Belt, Rust Belt; racially, ethnically, religiously, generationally, socioeconomically homogeneous or heterogeneous. Citizens in Las Vegas are likely to have different library interests and needs than those in Nashville, Boston, St. Petersburg, or East St. Louis.

Similar differences also exist among academic libraries. College librarians have worked hard to free themselves from the "university library syndrome," in Evan Farber's phrase, and to define their missions in terms of their own situations.[28] There are junior and community colleges, technical and liberal-arts colleges, universities with 2,000 students and with 50,000, some predominantly graduate or professional and others predominantly undergraduate. Some are rich, others are poor, and all have a simple mission: to survive. Some are generations old, others are new or newly constituted: the library in the former teacher's college turned comprehensive university has a different mission from the library in the long-established university. But it is not necessary to multiply examples.

A library's mission, then, if properly defined reveals its understanding of its external community and its user community, as well

28. Evan I. Farber, "College Librarians and the University-Library Syndrome," in *The Academic Library: Essays in Honor of Guy R. Lyle,* eds. Evan Ira Farber and Ruth Walling (Metuchen, N.J.: Scarecrow, 1974), pp. 12–23.

as of the unique process involving users, the materials in the collections, and the ways these materials are used. Where the library serves avid readers, circulation is important; where it serves scholars, use of primary materials is important; where it serves professionals, use of the most current information resources is important. The library must create and maintain a coherent collection suited to its users' needs, appropriate to their abilities and interests, as best as it can determine them.

The mission guides collection management operations. The library in setting its mission is also setting into operation its collection management program. The library's mission is to be well managed. The first step in management, once the mission is stated, is to evaluate the existing collection to determine how well it serves the library's mission, that is, to see how well it has been managed. Good management depends on the knowledge and understanding of individual librarians. The library must gather knowledgeable librarians who understand their community, its needs, and its library users' needs, but who also understand management principles and practices.

Chapter 5

Evaluation and Analysis

When evaluating we seek to determine our collections' intrinsic quality and extrinsic effectiveness. Evaluative judgments only can be made relative to stated standards or criteria and within the framework of the library's mission. The various evaluative projects and the methods used in them can be applied to the whole collection or to a smaller part of it, such as to map, chemistry journal, Spanish literature, or children's collections. Admittedly the prospect of evaluating a multi-million-volume collection is daunting, but if we attack smaller segments we can be fairly successful and, over time, can arrive at a cumulative evaluation. It is important, therefore, to think of many evaluations carried on continuously rather than of just one huge evaluation project.

A library of almost any size will have readily identifiable subcollections within it, each of which should be evaluated periodically. In a university library we could, for example, look at our list of journals serving the English literature collection, compare them with relevant standard lists, distinguish those suitable for undergraduates from those suitable for graduate students and faculty and judge whether we have the proper proportion of each, and measure the use they have been receiving. At the same time we could keep a file of new titles and requests received from students and faculty, consider adding duplicate copies and microform backups of heavily used titles, and work on a project to fill in any gaps in the periodical runs. This relatively small-scale evaluation is useful in itself; combining it with similar evaluations of the book collection would provide an accurate assessment of one segment of the whole collection, and combining it with similar assessments of other subcollections could in time provide an evaluation of the entire collection.

Concentrating on smaller evaluation projects also places the responsibility on individual collection management librarians to conduct evaluations and to see that appropriate action results. The individual librarian is best able to make the evaluation, understand its results, and take the necessary steps on the basis of it. Likewise, action at the smaller level may be more feasible than action at the level of the whole library. Evaluation is not an end in itself but must lead, if necessary, to action of some type, whether this action involves revised policies, altered procedures, changed staffing, new services, shifted allocations, increased cooperation with other libraries, or other changes.

Collection analysis is a key tool in evaluation. It provides data about a number of elements and activities. This data, such as circulation counts, average age of the books in different subjects, in-house use of journals, expenditures for different materials or subject areas, and the time needed to keep up with book reviews or new-book announcements, provides not only information we can use to evaluate our collections but also information we can use to manage them better. For example, lower circulation of books in one subject than in another could indicate that we are spending too much in the wrong area, that we should increase our library instruction activities in certain areas, that in-house use should be more carefully monitored, or, simply, that some subjects draw lower library use. Collection analysis provides data, but this data still must be interpreted and does not always, and certainly never automatically will, lead to evaluative judgments. The library profession is continually learning about the nature of collections, and as individual librarians we must discover and understand the individual character of these specific collections that we manage.

Our goals, then, are both understanding and action, and they are sought for our users and for ourselves. We evaluate and analyze, as F. W. Lancaster, one of the leading advocates of library evaluations, puts it, in order to judge the effectiveness of what we are doing, to judge the efficiency of our doing it, and to judge whether the results are worth the cost.[1] We want to determine whether our collection is of an appropriate quality and effectiveness for our particular users, and we want to determine whether the management process itself is effective and efficient. Evaluation and analysis are, therefore, key elements in a collection management program and should be established on a regular, ongoing basis.

---

1. F. Wilfrid Lancaster, *The Measurement and Evaluation of Library Services* (Washington, D.C.: Information Resources, 1977).

Evaluation

Evaluative methods must be used in combination, must be relevant to the purposes and scale of the evaluation project, must be relevant to the library's mission, and must be treated as experimental. To a still uncomfortable degree, each evaluative project must create its own methods and the procedures for implementing them. Allen Kent's major evaluation project at the University of Pittsburgh, now more than ten years old, had as one of its major goals simply the development of an evaluation methodology.[2] Partly as a result of work such as his, we now have a wide range of methods to choose from and some guidance in selecting the most effective. Blaine Hall's *Collection Assessment Manual* introduces us to a full range of evaluation goals and techniques and among its other virtues makes it seem possible to carry out a large-scale evaluation project.[3] Jutta Reed-Scott's *Manual for the North American Inventory of Research Library Collections* offers specific techniques and procedures; it also provides inspiration for adaptations.[4] Other examples of methods can be found through *Library Literature*'s indexing of reports of evaluation projects.

Intrinsic Quality. To judge the intrinsic quality of the collection—the absolute quality of the books, the periodical subscriptions, and the other items—we can compare holdings with lists of standard titles and ask experts for their opinions. The collection can be checked against compilations such as *Books for College Libraries* and against lists of core periodicals, best videocassettes, prize-winning books, films, or records.[5] This checking is, indeed, a standard procedure for selectors, and they and evaluators both, we must assume, use lists that are appropriate. We can ask experts to scan the shelves or shelf list and make judgments based on the mental list in their heads as well as on their understanding of how a collection serves, or fails, its users; they also can compile or recommend authoritative lists. In either approach we evaluate what is there by comparing it with what should be there, and we evaluate the collective quality of the holdings as well as the negative effect of the gaps.

---

2. Allen Kent and others, *The Use of Library Materials: The University of Pittsburgh Study* (New York: Marcel Dekker, 1979), p. vi.

3. Blaine H. Hall, *Collection Assessment Manual for College and University Libraries* (Phoenix: Oryx, 1985).

4. Jutta Reed-Scott, *Manual for the North American Inventory of Research Library Collections* (Washington: Association of Research Libraries, 1985).

5. *Books for College Libraries,* 3rd ed., 6 vols. (Chicago: American Library Association, 1988).

Unfortunately, there are many subjects and genres for which no authoritative lists exist, or in which experts are unavailable or they are reluctant to participate on practical grounds (too large an undertaking) or as a matter of principle (rankings like comparisons can be odious). In academic and research libraries where the rapidity of change in research interests and subjects renders any collection virtually instantly and continuously out-of-date, intrinsic quality is something to be reached for, and possibly achieved, but something that by the time we evaluate it may already have changed. Finally, there is an increasing suspicion that judgments of intrinsic quality, even coming from experts, reflect unfortunate biases of class, gender, method, or something else more than they indicate truths about the collection. We do, of course, care about intrinsic quality and take steps to achieve it, as best we can understand it, and there are areas in which lists or other measures of intrinsic quality do exist and should be used.

Standards. Standards, especially quantitative ones, provide another measure of intrinsic quality. It is a professional responsibility to promulgate standards, and library professional associations certainly have done so. Discussion of standards has been a staple of librarianship, and a basic overview of issues and a history of their development are given in two separate articles in the *Encyclopedia of Library and Information Science.*[6] The American Library Association provides standards for collections in college and university libraries, two-year learning resource centers, prison libraries, school media centers, and public libraries, as well as for units and services within these larger types, including rare books, manuscripts and archives, online searching and interlibrary lending, services to young and to older adults, and the training and education of librarians and assistants;[7] other library organizations also have set forth additional standards.[8] Nonlibrary accrediting bodies, such as for professional certification programs, often include relevant library standards.

Promulgation does not guarantee acceptance, however, and debate continues about both the usefulness of standards in general and the adequacy of any standard in particular. Some doubt exists that

---

6. Felix E. Hirsch, "Library Standards," *Encyclopedia of Library and Information Science* 16 (1975): pp. 43–62, and Naimuddin Qureshi, "Standards for Libraries," *Encyclopedia of Library and Information Science* 28 (1980): pp. 470–99.

7. "Standards and Guidelines," *ALA Handbook of Organization 1987/1988 and Membership Directory* (Chicago: American Library Association, 1987), pp. 251–53.

8. Reynold Kosek and Mary Anne Royle, "Library Standards: A Subject Bibliography with Emphasis on Law Libraries," *Public Administration Series: Bibliography* (Monticello, Ill.: Vance Bibliographies, 1983), p. 1316.

standards proposed by the profession will convince administrators of the institutions within which our libraries operate, either because our motives are suspect or because the administrators simply are unable to fund any significant improvements. Other librarians argue that standards are "based on a very limited research base, and it is difficult if not impossible to establish a relationship between achievement of the standard and the quality of the library services which will be produced."[9] On the other hand, supporters of standards in principle (whatever their feelings about any specific standard) see that attempts to define and justify them often have identified significant factors in collection management that should be monitored.

Quantitative standards usually have been applied to so-called input data, such as total size of the collection, volumes added per year, and expenditures for materials; they also could be applied to such output data as circulation statistics and counts of in-house use. Qualitative standards that have no quantitative measure are meaningless phrases. To say a college library should meet curricular needs is meaningless until there is some way to measure both the needs and the extent to which the collection meets them. On the other hand, it seems difficult if not impossible to prove that quantitative standards have a causal relationship with qualitative outcomes. Quantitative standards are most useful when applied to specific segments of the collection. Different subjects and users have different needs. A specific book-per-student ratio can make sense for one subject or library situation but not for all, or a library's overall adherence to a standard may not be borne out evenly throughout the collection. This specific application of standards also places, as it should, responsibility on the librarian closest to the collection.

Collection Levels. Intrinsic quality and standards are most practical when applied very specifically and when related directly to users' needs. Another way to apply them in evaluation projects, at least in academic libraries, is to use them to assess the ability of the collection to meet the needs of users at different levels, undergraduate through graduate. A number of university and research libraries, including members of the Research Libraries Group and other groups are working with a "conspectus" to profile their collections, subject by subject, systematically evaluating the level of study each part can support. Six levels are defined in the ALA's *Guidelines for Collection*

9. F. William Summers, "Standards for State Libraries," *Library Trends* 31 (Summer 1982): 77–83.

Development and in an article by Gwinn and Mosher about the RLG conspectus:[10]

> Level Zero. Out of scope: no holdings in collection and nothing bought.
> Level One. Minimal level: only a few items in the collection.
> Level Two. Basic information level: highly selective collection that introduces and defines the subject and indicates the varieties of information in it.
> Level Three. Instructional support level: collection supports undergraduate or graduate-level course work and sustained independent study. This level can be subdivided into initial and advanced study.
> Level Four. Research level: collection contains materials necessary for dissertations and independent research.
> Level Five. Comprehensive level: collection is exhaustive in a few, limited areas.

The concept of levels has several virtues. It is user-based, describing the collection in terms of what users can do with it rather than simply in terms of input or output. It tries to avoid mere quantitative criteria yet achieve a meaningful concreteness. It describes the local collection without comparing it to inappropriate external standards. It is very specifically detailed, so each of the hundreds (or even thousands) of subject units within the collection can be evaluated separately and appropriately. It permits communication and comparison among libraries based on a common definition of the levels. It applies to both the existing collection and the consequent collection development activity. It relates directly to the library's mission.

There is also one major criticism: it is a good evaluative device in libraries with research missions but it is not so useful in college, public, or other libraries. Indeed the RLG conspectus has been used by several ARL university libraries as part of the National Collection Inventory Project.[11] It is possible, however, to expand or subdivide Level Three to make it more applicable in college libraries, and it should be possible to adapt the levels to public libraries, possibly by using types-of-reader categories. A second criticism is that it is extremely demanding of time, professional expertise and attention, and procedural efficiency. The results can be excellent, but perhaps too costly. If, however, we think of evaluation by levels as inextricably

10. *Guidelines for Collection Development,* ed. David L. Perkins (Chicago: American Library Association, 1979), and Nancy E. Gwinn and Paul H. Mosher, "Coordinating Collection Development: The RLG Conspectus," *College & Research Libraries* 44 (1983): 128–40.

11. Reed-Scott, *Manual,* pp. 120–21.

linked with continued collection development and with developing national cooperation, then we can see the importance of this part of the collection management process.

Quantitative Profiles. Input and output data can be used to compile a quantitative profile of the library and, although susceptible to misinterpretation, can be used for internal management. Various library bodies, including ARL, ACRL, and state and federal governments, collect this type of data and much is reported in the *Bowker Annual.*[12] This data includes total volumes and titles, expenditures for materials, volumes or titles added per year (gross and net after losses and discards), titles and volumes specifically of books, periodicals, microforms, audiovisuals, and, recently, computer media. It is instructive within individual libraries to see these figures in a historical perspective as well as for specific years. Librarians need statistical data on size and growth to plan effectively for space, shelving, format alternatives, and appropriate staffing, and to spot potential problems in collecting.

Automated systems that can (or will be able to) record volumes, titles, and dollars, subdivide by subject areas, formats, acquisition accounting funds, and user group (such as a college academic department) and that can analyze the data with something like the Statistical Package for the Social Sciences will produce massive amounts of data. All this will have to be interpreted and applied: none of the data by itself is evaluative. Some can be quickly compared with quantitative standards, such as those found in the *Standards for College Libraries.*[13] Extrinsic methods also require information from outside the library, such as publication rates (described in chapter three), university budget and enrollment figures, and community demographic data.

A different approach, taken by Kendon Stubbs, is to perform a discriminant analysis on the ARL data to see which are most characteristic of a research library (presumably this could be performed with other types of libraries).[14] Discriminant analysis occupies a middle

---

12. "Library and Research Statistics," *Bowker Annual; Statistics of Ohio Libraries* (Columbus: State Library of Ohio, 1972–); *ARL Statistics* (Washington: Association of Research Libraries, 1971–); *ACRL University Library Statistics* (Chicago: American Library Association, 1978–); Lawrence J. La Moure, "Center for Education Statistics," *Bowker Annual,* 33rd ed., 1988, pp. 131–33.

13. "Standards for College Libraries," *College & Research Libraries News* 47 (1986): 189–200.

14. Kendon Stubbs, *Quantitative Criteria for Academic Research Libraries* (Chicago: American Library Association, 1984), and *1984 "100 Libraries" Statistical Survey* (Chicago: American Library Association, 1985).

ground between description and prescription. We cannot use this data to measure intrinsic quality nor use it as a standard, but we can use it to identify those elements that will make comparisons among libraries meaningful. Its data could be used to measure efficiency by comparing staff and processing costs with the quantity of materials held and added or to measure cost-effectiveness by comparing the quantity of materials added with the number of users served, as measured for example by turnstile counts, circulation, reference questions, degrees granted, and scholarly publication by users.[15]

Output data, mainly for circulation and other measures of use, provides equally important information and (its great merit) deemphasizes size and budget while pointing us more toward the service provided by the collection and, thus, more toward the extent to which the library fulfills its mission.[16] Nevertheless, even output data do not show what should be used nor the extent to which the collection is intrinsically good.[17]

Extrinsic Effectiveness. The preceding discussion of evaluation methods has moved from those measuring the purely intrinsic quality of the materials themselves, to those measuring ways the collection is or could be used, toward those considering extrinsic effectiveness. Input and output data are by themselves extrinsic measures, but when they are subjected to a discriminant analysis they can become measures of intrinsic quality. As we move further away from intrinsic measures, we begin to look even more closely at users, either their attitudes and opinions or their behavior. User satisfaction, and to some extent their success, can be measured by questionnaires, interviews, and the less certain evidence of suggestion-box receipts, complaints, and certain kinds of use data.

User Surveys. No matter how confident we are of evaluative methods applied to the collection, we also must evaluate users' work with the collection and their satisfaction. We can interview them directly, or we can devise a questionnaire for them that is similar to the ones listed in Blaine Hall's book. The interview almost always

---

15. Robert Hayes, Anne Pollock, and Shirley Nordhaus, "An Application of the Cobb-Douglas Model to the Association of Research Libraries," *Library & Information Science Research* 5 (1983): 204–8.

16. *Output Measures for Public Libraries: A Manual of Standardized Procedures,* 2nd ed., Nancy A. Van House, Mary Jo Lynch, Charles R. McClure, Douglas L. Zweizig, and Eleanor J. Rodger (Chicago: American Library Association, 1987).

17. Charles R. McClure, Douglas L. Zweizig, Nancy A. Van House, and Mary Jo Lynch, "Output Measures: Myths, Realities, and Prospects," *Public Libraries* 25 (Summer 1986): 49–52.

elicits positive remarks and is therefore suspect as a true measure of satisfaction. On the other hand, during an interview we can ask more complex questions about users' behavior and success than we can with a questionnaire. Even though the interview is time consuming to conduct and therefore can only be conducted with a sample of the user community, it demonstrates librarians' personal interest in user opinion, allows a positive interaction between librarian and user, and can elicit useful additional information. The questionnaire allows less guarded and more objective judgments from the users and can be given to virtually everyone who enters the library.

User satisfaction, however pleasant it might be to the librarian, is not the same thing as user success. To judge how well the collection serves the user, we must in some way measure the quality of users' performance that results from using the library. Do students get better grades, compile more sophisticated bibliographies, advance to richer collections? Do citizens vote more frequently or intelligently? These are not so much questions as research projects, however. On a more manageable scale we can ask specific questions about collection use and apply these answers, with caution, to evaluating users' success.

Analysis of Use

With use studies we can check our selection decisions, guide selection decisions into areas (subjects, materials, suitability for different categories of user) needing additional development, and organize management decisions about binding and mending, converting to microform, replacing and duplicating, storing, discarding, as well as shelf maintenance. We can devise or revise policies and services for users. We can predict patterns of future use of specific subjects or formats and plan appropriate steps. Use studies are exploratory and can raise more questions than they answer. Because we exist primarily to serve users, it is encumbent on us to see how they use our libraries. Automatic circulation systems can provide great quantities of data, but we must not think that circulation is the only use, nor even the only meaningful use a collection receives.

The important use studies conducted by Trueswell, Kent, Fussler and Simon, and Line and Sandison all tried to find ways to predict future use efficiently and accurately. They wanted to create a management tool to improve selection decisions and to guide maintenance, and especially to identify those items whose use had dropped so low that they could be sent to remote storage or discarded and

inconvenience the fewest users.[18] They all found that the single most
sure predictor of future use is past use. Other factors, such as language
of the materials, geographical origin or emphasis, age, format, their
location in the library, not to mention users' abilities, also affect use
and can be called on when the librarian does not have adequate
information about past use. Effective local management, however,
must have accurate and meaningful information about local use.

Analysis of use requires measurement. We can measure in readily
quantifiable terms such things as circulation, interlibrary loan requests,
turnstile traffic, cash intake at a photocopier, reference and information
questions, online searches, and sheets of paper coming out of the CD-
ROM printer. We can analyze this data to determine figures about
frequency of use within time periods, within specific parts of the
circulating collection, and by distinct segments of the user population. Not everything that can be measured precisely is worth
measuring, and vice versa. Much measurement is inevitably approxi-
mate and some is even highly impressionistic. We can collect massive
amounts of data, perform elaborate analyses, and still end up with
only the slimmest of usable results—although we may well understand
our collections better. Usable or not, all of our measurement data must
be interpreted.

Interpretation must consider factors that affect use, such as school
and college curriculum or a city's demography, the specific users,
materials, information, or services used, and, somehow, the value or
usefulness of the use. Data has no inherent meaning, comparisons
among libraries are suspect, and even comparisons within libraries
are difficult to make. We must, therefore, understand the elements
in use studies, that is, the nature of use itself, where it occurs, with
what materials, by whom, and, above all, its history in each specific
library.

Uses. Use must be recognized as *uses.* There are different kinds
of use, different intensities and frequencies, different ways of using
different kinds of materials, use of information or services as distinct
from use of materials, different uses by different kinds of users, not
to mention different amounts of use. We are forced by the limitations

---

18. Richard D. Trueswell, "Some Behavioral Patterns of Library Users: The 80/20
Rule," *Wilson Library Bulletin* 43 (1969): 458–61; Herman H. Fussler and Julian L. Si-
mon, *Patterns in the Use of Books in Large Research Libraries* (Chicago: University of
Chicago Press, 1969); Maurice B. Line and Alexander Sandison, " 'Obsolescence' and
Changes in the Use of Literature with Time," *Journal of Documentation* 30 (1974):
283–350.

on what we can measure to weigh quantity more than quality or kinds of use. Attempts to analyze the nature and extent of use in general and in particular libraries must recognize the complexity of what it is we call use and also the provisional nature of our analytical methods. Use studies must be considered exploratory in two senses: first, we are not sure yet that we can measure what we want to or what is worth measuring, and, second, we are performing these analyses to raise questions rather than, as yet, to answer them.

Location. Ultimately we must know what use occurs in our own libraries, but it helps to know what happens in other libraries. Richard Rubin's study of in-house use in a sampling of public libraries and citation analyses such as those reported in *SSCI Journal Citation Reports,* both cited in previous chapters, are obviously useful to librarians working in similar situations even though they do not apply locally. Both kinds of studies suggest what use could be occurring in our own libraries; both kinds provide us with insight into the nature of certain kinds of use of certain kinds of materials by certain kinds of readers. Citation studies are especially attractive because their data is precisely and sophisticatedly quantified. We can compare lists of journals ordered by citation frequency and sets of journals that have been cited by researchers working in specific subjects with our own subscription lists.

On the other hand, these studies cannot be used uncritically in local decision making, and certainly not for irrevocable decisions such as weeding. Maurice Line in particular has cautioned continually against inappropriate use of general data in specific situations.[19] One crucial element of local studies is that they occur in specific types of libraries, each with its own character and mission. As we measure and interpret the results of our measures, we must interpret in light of what we are. Useful and interesting as it is to read citation studies and other librarians' reports on use, we must conduct our own study with our own users and our own materials.

Circulation. It is easy to count what circulates; even without new automated circulation systems we can gather revealing data. Circulation records are precise and it is or will be possible to analyze them with sophisticated statistical programs. At the simplest level, we can count how many total items are checked out, and in most systems we also can measure circulation by subject (according to LC or Dewey classes), user types (resident or nonresident, faculty or

---

19. Line and Sandison, " 'Obsolescence.' "

undergraduate), time of the year, and certain special purposes (inter-library loan, reserve).

These figures become far more useful, however, when we can identify specific needs, compute percentages or ratios, and discover relationships. We want to be able to spot titles that need duplicate copies or subject areas that need additional materials. What percentage of the total circulation is accounted for by a specific subject? What percentage of the total holdings in a specific subject are in circulation? What percentage of the circulating items are checked out to faculty or graduate students or nonresidents? How does circulation data for a subject compare with population features, enrollments, institutional budgets? When do they peak, midway through a semester, during the summer vacation reading season, in times of community crises?

As these automated circulation systems become more sophisticated we can analyze circulation records by indexical features on the MARC record, such as publication date, language, country of origin, and format, and this can be performed in a variety of combinations. It should be possible to find out whether the faculty uses a distinctly different set of materals than undergraduate majors, whether nonresidents rely on the public library for different materials than residents do—different by date, subject, format, language, and so forth. A significant step in this direction has been taken by Paul Metz, who was able to relate circulation records to academic departments and thus gain insight into "supportiveness" and "dependency," as will be explained later.

All quantifiable data can seduce us into interpretive error, however. One can be tempted to make long-term decisions on the basis of short-term data, read blips as trends, assume that what is measured tells us about what is not measured, or simply convert decision making to formulae. It is also possible that data arrived at through elaborate analysis will only tell us what we already have discerned through experience: why count circulation when we daily watch shelves empty and refill? A good collection management program can answer this skepticism by responsible use of valuable data.

In-House and Noncirculating Materials. Of course circulation data applies only to those materials that can be checked out. Many materials do not circulate and many uses are confined to the library. If periodicals do not circulate, for example, then at least half the collection's use in an academic library will not be recorded in circulation data. In-house use may differ from use recorded by circulation: different subjects, different materials certainly, perhaps different purposes. The scholar who studies primary documents in the library might check out crime novels for bedtime reading, or might read glossy magazines in the library but check out serious poetry for quiet evenings at home. A researcher could slip in for a crucial financial figure or a citation, or could follow a trail of cross-references through volume after volume. What we hope to learn is how much in-house use there is, how it relates to circulation data, and what we should do with our collection management program in response to it.

In-house use seems greater than circulation use by four times or more, varying from library to library and from collection to collection or subject to subject and according to the method used to measure it. The ratio of in-house use to circulation use may, however, be consistent from subject to subject within libraries, even though it may also be unique to each library. The range of materials used in-house or that are noncirculating or that are not captured in circulation data vary from periodicals (noncirculating in many libraries), to reference books, indexes and abstracts, online information and bibliographic services, materials in special collections, maps, items sent to the bindery or to interlibrary loan, and a variety of restricted circulation items. We also must be alert to changes in users' needs: if they are in fact reading periodicals more than books, then we must put more effort into identifying and counting in-house use and perhaps relying less on circulation data.[20]

Kinds of Materials. Use varies with the kind of material being used. Use of books is different from use of periodicals, and both are different from use of microforms, newspapers, maps, CD-ROM indexes or data files, online search services, or our recordings of Beethoven quartets. A usable unit of measure for books is not applicable for journals or recordings. We must distinguish use of fiction from non-fiction books, collections from monographs, books with significant literary elements from those strictly informational, a directory from a handbook, and a book from a periodical. As for the periodical itself we must distinguish use of the article from the issue, the issue from the volume, the volume from the complete run, and, further, we must distinguish the magazine from the journal. If a book circulates, we count the book as having been used. If we pick up a journal from a study table, do we count the article, the issue, the volume, or the

---

20. Anthony Hinde and Michael K. Buckland, "In-Library Book Usage in Relation to Circulation," *Collection Management* 2 (1978): 265–77, and William E. McGrath, "Correlating the Subjects of Books Taken Out and of Books Used within an Open-Stack Library," *College & Research Libraries* 32 (1971): 280–85.

run? Even though we may not be able to compare among the variety of materials and media in our collection, data gathered over a number of years for each of the various materials can reveal patterns of use, trends to monitor, problems heretofore unrecognized.

Users. The various user categories should be a factor in our measurement of use, but although we have at times gathered data about who uses the collection we seem unable to measure the ways or the extent to which each of the categories uses our materials. In academic libraries we want to know what the faculty uses as distinct from what undergraduates use, what majors in a specific department use as distinct from those in another, what students in a particular class (or the set of a department's offerings) use as distinct from others, and what is used by nonfaculty or nonstudents. In a public library we want to know use by age, residency, and a variety of socioeconomic factors, as well as by the user categories. While we can find out how many of these various kinds of users come into a library and check items out, we do not know what exactly it is they use. Automated circulation systems have considerable potential to provide better understanding of our users' activity and thus help us better meet their needs.

Factors Affecting Use. Use does not necessarily show that patrons have found what they want or need. Several factors affect use, and chief among these are accessibility and availability. Materials that are not readily accessible, that are shelved in a storage unit, a branch library, or the rare books collection or only on microfilm, often will not be sought out unless they are crucial to the user. If an item is unavailable because it is already checked out, or it is at the bindery, or received but not yet cataloged and processed, or it is somewhere in the library in the process of being reshelved, the user is not likely to wait for it or recall it, unless it is crucial. Conversely, there are a number of ways that libraries can increase both use and use of the best materials. We can provide library use instruction, pathfinders and topical bibliographies, active catalog assistance services, consultation with instructors (in academic libraries), radio or television book talks, displays, and other forms of education and public relations. Use analysis can both alert us to problems and provide insights and suggest solutions.

The Nature of Collections

Use studies must be used with caution. When performed well they yield real insight into the nature of collections, and the practical management activities taken up in later chapters, such as selection, circulation policies, weeding and storage procedures, and preservation programs, heavily depend on this understanding of collections. Information scientists and bibliometricians have discovered much about the nature of collections, and collection management librarians have profited from their discussions of overlap and composite collections, core and obsolescence, and of the nature of collections in specific subject areas. Use studies have not yet, however, been able to provide us with data and information that can lead unequivocally to specific management decisions.

Overlap. Libraries that use the RLG conspectus to analyze and evaluate their collections rely in part on comparisons with similar collections in other libraries, chiefly in the form of overlap studies. Duplication of titles among library collections can be useful, as when it demonstrates the quality of the collections (any book held by all must be good) and also enables these collections to back up each other. At the University of Illinois, for example, a large share of outgoing interlibrary loan requests are for books owned but unavailable.[21] On the other hand, duplication of rarely used materials that could be readily shared would seem an unwise expenditure of the acquisition funds. Overlap is particularly important as we try to increase interlibrary cooperation. In a 1982 review of the literature on overlap William Potter summarized the issues.[22] Collection overlap is greater among similar than among dissimilar libraries, as measured by age, size, and type. Therefore, a cooperating group of libraries will have a wider range of materials to share if they are more different than similar. Among a group of cooperating libraries, each library's collection, regardless of size, will contain a significant proportion of unique titles, and thus every library will have something to offer the others. It may be that high overlap is more important among public, academic, and other libraries and that low overlap is better among research libraries with collection levels of four or five.

Composite Collection. Low overlap among libraries means there is a large and rich "composite collection," Paul Mosher points out, while a high degree of overlap indicates a common core collection among the libraries.[23] "Composite" is Mosher's term, but we could

---

21. Hugh Atkinson, "Atkinson on Networks," *American Libraries* 18 (6) (June 1987): 430–39.
22. William Gray Potter, "Studies of Collection Overlap: A Literature Review," *Library Research: An International Journal* 4 (1982): 3–21.
23. Paul H. Mosher, "The Nature and Uses of the RLG Verification Studies," *College & Research Libraries News* 46 (1985): 336–38.

just as well call it the collective, cumulative, or union collection.[24] The composite collection should contain as much of the world's library resources as will be needed. All cooperative agreements, from inter- library loans to the most elaborated and specific agreements, assume the existence of a composite collection. Union catalogs and biblio- graphic utilities make the contents accessible, but as we increase our efforts toward cooperation, we must also increase our efforts to develop the composite collection. It is not enough to assume that what is needed is being collected by someone else, we must ensure that it is. The RLG conspectus online is one such effort: it records the collecting level for every subject category in the conspectus by participating libraries. No one is coerced into buying what is not needed locally just to meet a national goal; each library can manage its own collections as it pleases, and yet we can be confident that a large, useful composite collection is being created. Whether we take a second step toward more explicit collecting responsibilities along the line of the Farmington Plan depends on our experience with the conspectus. At this time, overlap studies, the role of the Center for Research Libraries,[25] and specific cooperation agreements such as those described in *Coordinated Cooperative Collection Development*[26] suggest that we can cooperate effectively without such a formal and large-scale plan. On the other hand, if the publishing and price trends that are described in chapter three continue, it will become increas- ingly difficult to create and maintain an adequate composite collection.

Core.   Core is that part of the collection that is most pertinent to users; it is defined either by quality or by use. One view holds that there is a core of materials that should be provided by the library. An example of this kind of core collection was developed at Antioch College where it was deliberately chosen with the expectation that students should, and therefore would, use it: "One of [a library's] more important functions is to provide a kind of intellectual front or labora- tory where the initiation or testing of fresh ideas may take place or where their new expression may be found."[27] Reader advisory

---

24. Ross Atkinson, "Selection for Preservation: A Materialistic Approach," *Library Resources & Technical Services* 30 (1986): 341–50, and David H. Stam, "Collaborative Collec- tion Development: Progress, Problems, and Potential," *Collection Building* 7 (3) (1986): 3–9.
25. Center for Research Libraries, *Handbook* (Chicago: CRL, 1985).
26. *Coordinating Cooperative Collection Development: A National Perspective*, ed. Wilson Luquire (New York: Haworth, 1986).
27. Paul Bixler, " 'Core Collection' Is Dead—Long Live the Core Collection," in *The Academic Library: Essays in Honor of Guy R. Lyle*, eds. Evan Ira Farber and Ruth Walling (Metuchen, N.J.: Scarecrow, 1974), pp. 40–60.

services, exhibits and displays, or special shelving for items that we want to encourage use of, as well as weeding or sending out-of-date or out-of-fashion material to storage, are similar ways to identify or highlight a quality core of the collection.

The other way to define core is by use. High use is not necessarily high quality: it could simply be the most recently published materials, assigned reading in several classes, or materials dealing with some current social issue. Richard Trueswell's so-called 80/20 Rule is at work here.[28] Trueswell examined circulation records in a number of libraries and found that on average about 20 percent of the collection provided 80 percent of the circulation and called this general pattern a rule. Actually, however, his own evidence shows that each collection has its own size core: in one library 28 percent of the collection provided 80 percent of the circulation; in another little more than 15 percent provided that level of use; and other libraries provided different figures. The 80/20 Rule is far from a rule and, in fact, these exact figures seldom appeared. Furthermore, as we move above 80 percent user satisfaction (which is unsatisfactorily low), the percent of the collection that provides it goes up sharply, often to 60 percent and more. It is likely that it takes nearly two-thirds of the collection to provide a satisfactory level of circulation, and of course circulation use is only a part of the total use.

Nevertheless Trueswell's analysis of core is important and useful: a major share of the use is provided by a core of the materials. The librarian must know which items will be in the core, and Trueswell's analysis shows that previous use is the best predictor of future use. Trueswell has discovered not a law but a procedure that, if applied sensibly, will improve library management. Once we can identify the core of high-use materials, then we can operate our reshelving and maintenance operations more efficiently. We can reshelve items in this core more quickly, send them to mending or buy replacements and added copies, monitor the changes in the core as the user community changes, and in general focus our energies on the most-used or most-likely-to-be-used materials.

Obsolescence or Change in Use. Obsolescence is the tendency of materials over time to receive less use and, presumably, to become less valuable. Not all materials do become obsolete; materials in different subjects and different kinds of materials become obsolete at different rates, and obsolescence does on occasion reverse itself.

28. Trueswell, "Some Behavioral Patterns."

Received opinion is that periodicals become obsolete sooner than books and science materials faster than those in the social sciences and humanities. The matter is more complex than opinion allows, as suggested by the fact that half a dozen or more articles are published each year reporting studies of obsolescence or discussing aspects of the issue.[29] In fact, "decline in use" may be a misconception. Initial high use could merely result from the newness factor and could be unrelated to quality or usefulness, while later use rates, perhaps once per year, may in fact be appropriate and perfectly satisfactory. Use does not so much decline as it finds its own level.

Obsolescence itself is a value-laden term and discussion of it can be quite vigorous and practical applications quite political. *Obsolescence* implies a decline in the value, validity, and usefulness of an item and denotes as well a decline in the amount of use the item receives. Use and value are not necessarily related and several reasons can explain why a valuable item's use declines over a period of time. To avoid both the negative implications and the danger of simplistic thinking, I prefer to use *change in use* instead of *obsolescence*. Obsolescence implies age-related change and can lead to management decisions based on the assumption that the older the less-used items, the more readily should they be discarded or transferred to storage. The best criteria, however, is not age but use, precisely the point made by Fussler and Simon, Trueswell, and others. We must, therefore, conduct systematic studies of use in our own local libraries.

Supportiveness, Dependency, and Ethnicity. Subject collections are assumed to serve different groups of users: historians use history materials, geographers geography, chemists chemistry, philosophers philosophy. Where this assumption is true, a high degree of "ethnicity" exists. There are many disciplines, however, in which study depends on materials in other subjects, and, conversely, there are subjects whose materials support several disciplines. When academic library acquisitions budgets are based on the numbers of faculty and student users in different disciplines or departments, good collections are produced if there is a high degree of ethnicity but less good collections are produced when supportiveness or dependency is high.

Paul Metz, as reported in his *Landscape of Literatures,* investigated this issue through a study of circulation records in an automated system that recorded use of both books and periodicals and that allowed him

---

29. D. Kaye Gapen and Sigrid P. Milner, "Obsolescence," *Library Trends* 30 (Summer 1981): 107–24.

to identify the level (undergraduate, graduate student, faculty) and the discipline or department of the users.[30] He found that users in different subject departments varied in the extent to which they used materials from other subjects, that materials in different subjects were used in varying degrees by users from other fields, and that the three user levels varied in their use of subject materials. Students and faculty in technology seemed to depend on books and journals from the pure sciences; students and faculty in geography relied more on history materials than on geography materials; graduate students in all fields tended to be more ethnocentric in their borrowing than faculty or undergraduates.

Several conclusions seem to follow. Where there are large graduate programs there will exist a strong need for materials clearly within the subject fields; where there are applied science fields there will exist a strong need for pure science materials; materials in some subjects, particularly history, psychology, and mathematics, support an unusually wide range of users; the nature of academic programs locally will affect use. Growing interdisciplinarity in academic programs will definitely affect collection use and make it important for librarians to determine the degree of ethnicity, dependency, and supportiveness locally; branch libraries that increase subject isolation often are counterproductive. Metz's study is limited to one university so we must be cautious in drawing conclusions, yet his insights into use seem basically sound and deserve to be tested in other situations.

The Pittsburgh Study. Allen Kent's study of use at the University of Pittsburgh tried to determine how much of the library's collection was being used and would likely be used in the future, to evaluate the quality of acquisitions, and to select those materials that could be moved to storage.[31] Like Fussler and Simon at the University of Chicago, Kent and his associates were trying to solve a practical problem, not necessarily conduct an airtight analysis of use. The study has been criticized for both its methods and its conclusions, and it does illustrate some of the pitfalls that use studies cannot yet avoid. The project did show, however, that use studies are feasible, it gathered data that other researchers can analyze independently, and it argued for conclusions about use of materials in university libraries that have forced librarians to think very hard about their own collections.

---

30. Paul Metz, *Landscape of Literatures: Use of Subject Collections in a University Library* (Chicago: American Library Association, 1983).
31. Kent, *The Use of Library Materials.*

120   *Evaluation and Analysis*

What Kent and associates did was: (1) record the total circulation of all the library's books for a seven-year period; (2) record the circulation history over these seven years of 36,000 monographs acquired in 1969; (3) record journal use in six branch libraries; and (4) record in-house use and use in interlibrary loan and reserve. Their methodology is explained and the data is recorded; thus, the study itself is of continuing value, whether one finds its conclusions justified or relevant to one's own library. Their chief discovery was that recorded use seemed low. Circulation data showed that slightly less than half the collection and 40 percent of the new books did not circulate at all during this time, and this led Kent to conclude:[32]

> The hard facts are that research libraries invest very substantial funds to purchase books and journals that are rarely, or never, called for. . . .

Reaction to this conclusion was vehement, first on the grounds that Kent's interpretation of his data was inappropriate. A university research library, critics asserted, cannot be evaluated simply on use and especially not on use for only a seven-year span. The mission of a research collection is different from that of a college or a public library, and we should look at use only over many years and in terms of scholarly and scientific research produced by the users. Kent's reply to these criticisms seems more challenging than his first conclusion: should society pay for the acquisition, processing, and storage of books that are used once (or not at all) in five years? What is the quality and significance of use, and to what extent should the user be the judge of this? If a wanted book is not available locally, and it takes one day, one week, or one month to acquire it from elsewhere, what is the loss and who should judge? Given the increasing competition for funds, what is the trade-off between buying little-used books and, for example, slowing tuition increases for students?[33]

The other line of criticism was to attack his methods and assert that use was, in fact, far higher than he understood. In-house use in general seems to have been undercounted. Kent assumed a lower ratio of in-house to circulation use than is accepted now. With periodicals, use is so complex that simply to count what is picked up by reshelvers only shows what has been used, not the quantity of the

---

32. Kent, p. 2.
33. Allen Kent, Roger R. Flynn, Jacob Cohen, and K. Leon Montgomery, "A Commentary on 'Report on the Study of Library Use at Pitt by Professor Allen Kent et al.,' The Senate Library Committee, University of Pittsburgh, July 1969," *Library Acquisitions: Practice and Theory* 4 (1980): 87–89.

use. Robert Hayes later took Kent's data, reanalyzed it, and concluded that because "circulation data do not adequately represent the total use of a research collection" the actual use at Pitt was and would continue to be far greater than Kent believed.[34]

In a sense, Kent's study has been superseded by events—by a new age of austerity that has forced budget cuts on libraries no matter what their use level is, by OCLC and RLG that have improved the possibilities for resource sharing, and by other ways of evaluating collections that do not rely on use data, such as the RLG conspectus. Although Kent's study looked at the important elements and asked hard questions, it did not find a way to gather data that could be used to make decisions about storage and acquisitions allocations. The facts remain that we have not yet defined use adequately, we do not know what level of use is good or even typical, and we have not found a way to measure it accurately. We still seek understanding, and we now must turn from collections in general to two specific subject collections.

Subject Collections. Subject collections differ from each other and differ among themselves from library to library. Information scientists have produced many studies of scholarly communication and citation since Rolland Stevens' 1953 "Characteristics of Subject Literatures," but these have mostly failed to describe scholars' (as well as common readers') intellectual and information needs and the dynamics of their uses of collections.[35] Although much work must be performed before we fully understand the nature of collections in all the various subjects, we have basic knowledge in certain areas and can talk about the nature of certain subject collections. Here are two examples.

Psychology collections include reports of experiments carried in scholarly journals, conference proceedings, review articles in these same journals and in specialized handbooks, annual reviews, and collective volumes, scholarly monographs, popular books and periodicals, textbooks, a range of psychological tests and handbooks of testing and test evaluation, two important indexing and abstracting services (*Social Sciences Citation Index* and *Psychological Abstracts*, in print, online, and CD-ROM). They can make use of a variety of raw data, as well as data, theories, and clinical methods from sociology, social work, and education on one side and from physiology and medicine

---

34. Robert M. Hayes, "The Distribution of Use of Library Materials: Analysis of Data from the University of Pittsburgh," *Library Research: An International Journal* 3 (1981): 215–60.

35. Rolland E. Stevens, "Characteristics of Subject Literatures," ACRL Monographs, No. 6. (Chicago: American Library Association, 1953).

on the other. An academic collection serving researchers and professionals will have a different mix of these materials than will a public library serving a lay audience. Even in an academic institution a psychology collection in a branch or departmental library will be more narrowly defined than one in a central library serving users from several disciplines in addition to psychology. Furthermore, different institutions will emphasize different aspects of the field.

An English literature collection, in contrast, will contain original primary literature (books and periodicals with fiction, poetry, prose, drama, possibly manuscripts and archival materials), secondary critical literature, and scholarly or reference tools (concordances, dictionaries, bibliographies, indexes). The collection in a university research library will differ considerably in its selection of primary literature and in its mix of primary, secondary, and reference literature from that in a public library as well as from that in a college library. Furthermore, there can be noticeable differences among literature collections of the same level, depending on the library's history and situation and on the users' interests.

The psychology and English literature collections will differ from each other in their core, their rate of obsolescence or change in use, their dependency and supportiveness, and in the ways that they interrelate with similar collections in other libraries. They will also differ in maintenance requirements, costs of new materials, and pattern and quantity of allocations for serials, monographs, reference and indexing materials, special collections, computer media, and interlibrary loans. Yet the existence of these collection features reinforces my continuing assertion: each collection has a wholeness and identity unique to itself. From our understanding of the nature of collections in general we can move toward an understanding of our specific local collections.

Every collection has its unique character. We hope the character of our own collection has developed appropriately over its history to serve its primary users and fulfill our library's mission, and we want to continue to develop and maintain its quality and effectiveness. Evaluation and analysis become, then, integral parts of our collection management program through which we try to ensure that the quality of our work maintains the quality of our collection. Evaluation and analysis are processes that tell us good news, we hope, about our collections and also tell us about our management process. We refer back to our mission, try to meet our users' needs, and prepare ourselves for the ongoing work of selection and maintenance.

Chapter 6

Selection

"Selection" in this chapter refers almost entirely to new materials that are being added for the first time, whether individual books, periodical subscriptions, or information services. Selecting is certainly one of the most interesting of librarians' activities, for in selecting we are simultaneously involved with new intellectual currents as they flow through published materials and we are providing that essential service for our users, the materials and information they will need, read, and, we hope, profit from. Previous chapters dealt with what librarians must *know*—about materials, information, users, uses, existing collections, and the library's mission. This chapter, however, will explain what librarians must *do* in order to select well in their specific libraries. Focus will be on the process of selecting new materials, a process that depends on the knowledge of materials, users and uses, and the quality and character of the existing collection that have already been covered. This knowledge is as important for selecting new materials as it is for dealing with those already in the collection.

Selection is, ideally, the final step after the library has first drawn up a collection development policy, set up cooperative arrangements with other libraries, found alternatives to purchasing where possible, and won and allocated its budget. Selection takes place within allocation categories. Selection is almost always made by individuals, but the steps leading up to it are library-wide matters. Selection thus can be made easier and better with proper and prior decisions. In turn, however, these earlier decisions can be made only in light of the knowledge of specific decisions that selectors will have to make. Selectors work with collection development policies and within allocation categories, but they themselves should have contributed significantly to writing the policies and setting the allocations. Individual selectors also should set up plans for the short- and long-term development of their responsibilities within the collection. The

123

collection development policies and plans, cooperative arrangements, budget and allocations, and the actual selection process are all interwoven and interrelated. This complex is the heart of each library's collection management program.

Policies and Plans

The collection development policy is a crystalization of each library's understanding of how its collection can serve its mission. A written policy can guide selection of new materials and also can provide the framework for decisions about maintenance, renewal, preservation, and weeding. This policy serves as an assertion of the library's place in its institution or community, and as such can be used to justify budget requests and to evaluate the library's performance. It must be based on a clear statement of the library's mission, on an analysis of the community and users it serves and of these users' needs, and on an evaluation of the quality and character of the existing collection. The collection development policy is not a wish list or a generalized statement of librarians' ambitions, but it is a specific, realistic, and detailed profile of all the subjects in which the library will collect books, periodicals, and other materials or media. As defined in *Guidelines for Collection Development:*[1]

> A written collection development policy. . .(a) enables selectors to work with greater consistency toward defined goals, thus shaping stronger collections and using funds more wisely; (b) informs library staff, users, administrators, trustees, and others as to the scope and nature of existing collections and the plans for continuing development of resources; (c) provides information which will assist in the budgetary allocation process.

Every policy must be reviewed regularly and revised as needed. Academic programs change frequently, for example, when a college develops into a university, a once-popular subject is supplanted, or old faculty members retire and new members are hired. As a city's population ages or moves or changes its racial or ethnic makeup, as its economy shifts from heavy industry to high tech, as its recreational interests or social values change, its library's users and their interests

---

1. *Guidelines for Collection Development,* ed. David Perkins (Chicago: American Library Association, 1979), p. 2.

and needs also will change. Far from being cast in concrete and restricting a library's flexibility, a collection development policy with its provision for regular review actually becomes the mechanism for the library's regular review of its community, services, and collecting needs.

A selection plan, however, is the practical application of a collection development policy, usually drawn up and carried out by individual collection development librarians. The collection management librarian sets short- and long-term goals for that part of the collection for which he or she is responsible and translates collecting level designations into actual selection decisions in light of the library's participation in cooperative networks, new information and access technologies, and budget realities. The academic library trying to move a collection from Level 2 to Level 3 or the public library trying to strengthen its children's collection, or either of them simply trying to maintain an existing degree of quality while wrestling with price increases, changing users, straitened budgets, personnel turnover, or deteriorating materials must operate on more than a day-to-day basis. Libraries, like other organizations, can be long on policies but short on practical plans; we cannot have good plans without good policies, but good policies do not ensure good plans.

Public and Academic Libraries. In public libraries the collection development policy, not always so named, serves to explain and justify their role in the community and the role of the collection itself within it. Policies collected in Elizabeth Futas's *Library Acquisition Policies and Procedures* (1st and 2nd eds.) are often statements about much more than the collections.[2] Nevertheless, collections do receive explicit policy statements. These statements sometimes seem designed less to guide the librarians than to inform the governing and funding authority about its directions, to demonstrate that it has clear and carefully thought-out reasons for its collection (partly doing so as a defense against censorship attempts), and to demonstrate accountability. The constituencies of a public library are many and vocal. For its own collecting activities, as well as for the satisfaction of its users, public libraries must draw up collection development policies that deal in considerable detail with the different kinds of users and with the different services and materials it provides them.

To draw up a detailed and specific collecting policy, the public

---

2. Elizabeth Futas, *Library Acquisition Policies and Procedures,* 2nd ed. (Phoenix: Oryx, 1984).

library must analyze its community, and identify very specifically its actual and potential users. If the library serves the business community with up-to-date business information services or supports local drama and music groups with scripts and music, or if it plans to expand or shift its collecting emphasis, it must specify the groups it will serve. Equally important is to describe and define the procedures by which collecting decisions are made to ensure consistency over time and to assure the public that coherent collecting policy is matched by coherent collecting procedure. There should be a clear way for people to recommend additions to the collection, and there should be a clear procedure by which people can file complaints about what is in the collection. The collection development policy is a major safeguard against censorship, if it clearly outlines the procedures used in selecting, allowing access to, and maintaining controversial materials and subjects. This also ensures that librarians treat those citizens with complaints seriously and fairly.

In contrast to the public library that must think primarily in terms of users, the academic library must think primarily in terms of subjects. It must define both the subjects in which it is interested and the level of that interest. Much of the work during the 1980s was directed toward developing effective ways of defining subjects and levels, and this work was combined with that on the RLG Conspectus and the National Collection Inventory Project.[3] What individual librarians do to define collection development policies is closely related to what they do to evaluate the level of their existing collections. Financial straits, the increased volume and variety of materials, and the changes in higher education and academic research such as described by Charles Osburn together make a collection development policy an absolute necessity.[4] Without such a policy it is impossible to select new materials consistently, to resist undue pressure for inappropriate materials, or to guarantee that the collection being developed can in fact serve the educational and research mission of the school. A carefully written collection development policy is a subject-by-subject profile of the collection, broken down into as many subdivisions of

3. Nancy E. Gwinn and Paul H. Mosher, "Coordinating Collection Development: The RLG Conspectus," *College & Research Libraries* 44 (1983): 128–40, and Jutta Reed-Scott, *Manual for the North American Collection Inventory of Research Library Collections* (Washington: Association of Research Libraries, 1985), pp. 120–21.

4. Charles B. Osburn, *Academic Research and Library Resources: Changing Patterns in America* (Westport, Conn.: Greenwood, 1979).

each subject as is appropriate for the institution's program, and with each subject or subsection given a designated level of collecting intensity. The level of collecting intensity defines the users and determines the kinds of materials that are appropriate, such as audiovisual instructional aids for certain kinds of undergraduate programs or extensive microfilm collections of primary materials or access to data archives for research collections.

Libraries must cooperate in developing their collections. None can meet its users' needs without the cooperation of others. This mutual dependency must be recognized and then built upon. Academic libraries cooperate primarily to ensure the collection of and access to research materials; public libraries must ensure that all segments of the community are served. Academic librarians can follow several models of cooperation, from the Center for Research Libraries to specific subject-by-subject resource sharing among a few libraries. Public libraries could enter into county or regional projects in which one library would agree to maintain periodical runs, drawing volumes from the other network libraries; another would agree to develop a rich business information service and provide backup information and materials to the other network libraries; another would be designated as the center for literary classics, the library that has and to which others send important but less-called-for books of literature, philosophy, religion, and cultural history. Likewise, within specific systems a division of responsibility for different subjects and materials and for current and older materials could be developed for the branches and the central facility, and the relationship between specific branches and various neighborhoods and community segments could be defined. Multitype cooperation should increase, as it has been successful (although multitype collections also mean multitype governance, legal status, and financial situations, all of which make cooperation difficult).

Writing the Collection Development Policy. With mission defined, community described, user needs understood, and their own collections analyzed, librarians are ready to draw up the collection development policy. "Policies" might be a better word, for each segment of the collection must be covered by its own policy. The process of drawing up a collection development policy appears straightforward and conceptually simple. Librarians, as portrayed in Sheila Dowd's description of work accomplished at the University of California, Berkeley, first create a profile of subjects, usually as defined by Library of Congress classification and in as fine detail as is appropriate to the specific library.[5] Next, they assign a collecting level designation to each unit of subject classification, usually on a six-point scale, zero through five. Then they decide what languages to collect in by subject.

The six-point scale mentioned previously runs from zero to five.[6] Zero means nothing is bought in the subject, one means minimal level, two means basic level, three means initial and advanced study by undergraduates and Master's students, four means research level suitable for faculty and Ph.D. research, and five means comprehensive, that is, the intention to collect virtually everything published on the subject. The two extremes are the easiest to work with, but they are also rare. Few libraries can collect comprehensively in any subject at all, yet nearly all will have something on everything. The difficult levels are three and four, difficult both to define what constitutes graduate and research level materials and difficult to find and afford what is most pertinent to the specific library's collection. The selector's professional expertise, based on knowledge of materials, users' needs, and one's own library (its existing collection, the abilities and interests of its users, the budget), and the support of the profession through workshops, consulting, and publications (such as ARL "Spec Kits" and actual collection development policies in addition to those in Elizabeth Futas's books), must be brought to bear on this problem.[7]

The collection development policy is not a uniform, cut-and-dried document. Libraries are complex and dynamic; each is unique. A university with a graduate program in American literature, for example, might emphasize late nineteenth-century writers, omit any study of colonial writers, and seek to strengthen its program in post–World War II writers—with the result that a policy for American literature must be subdivided and each subdivision given a different level designation appropriate to the kind of study and research being conducted or anticipated in each. Furthermore, the nature of the program might emphasize work with primary texts over secondary, so that the library would be expected to contain an extensive collection of manuscripts, first editions, and literary periodicals, but possibly a thinner collec-

5. Sheila Dowd, "The Formulation of a Collection Development Policy," in *Collection Development in Libraries: A Treatise*, 2v., eds. Robert D. Stueart and George B. Miller (Greenwich, Conn.: JAI Press, 1980), pp. 67–87.

6. *Guidelines for Collection Development*, pp. 1–8.

7. "Collection Description and Assessment in ARL Libraries," Spec Kit 87 (Washington: Association of Research Libraries, 1982).

tion of current critical journals, so that its collection, though identical in level with that of other universities, would display a unique character. The policy must be written from the ground up in each library by the librarians most familiar with the collections and their users.

The emphasis on levels, while very useful, may cause a problem. Levels are perhaps more appropriate for research libraries than for college and smaller university libraries without comprehensive doctoral programs. More attention must be paid in these smaller libraries to such pedagogical concerns as providing multiple copies of books and periodicals for undergraduates, developing sound and up-to-date popular magazines and popular treatments of scholarly subjects, and providing for undergraduate independent study. We may want more focused collections that allow students to develop discipline, in the senses of a critical intellect, rich memory, and knowledge of the academic modes of research and analysis. The college collection development policy could, conceivably, emphasize topics or documents rather than levels. In the public library, where research uses may be minimal (although there are obvious exceptions, including local history, genealogy, and business information) but the range of users considerable, the level designations could be supplemented by user-categories. In all types of libraries, however, the policy must explicitly consider the ever-broadening range of materials and media and their role in the collection. Scholarly journals, information services, CD-ROM bibliographic files, audiovisuals, microforms, along with books, all contribute to the collection and should be recognized in the collection development policy.

Finally, the policy must be a written document, with provision for review and revision, and must be available to librarians, the public, and to librarians in other libraries. No matter how much effort has been expended in writing it, the real issue for the individual collection development librarian is how to translate this into a selection plan.

Selection Plans. A selection plan is the practical application of a collection development policy, as well as the management of collecting activities not covered in the policy. With the plan the individual selector interprets the language of the levels, addresses problems and opportunities with the specific collection (such as the necessity to update the popular science materials, cut periodicals, or spend a donor's major gift), makes short- and long-term plans for developing the collection, and coordinates his or her work with network or consortium libraries and with the acquisitions, processing, and catalog librarians.[8] Selection is not simply an item-by-item sequence of choices but is a process governed by a coherent and thought-out plan, and it is through the plan that the individual selector puts a personal stamp on the collection. Plans for implementing the collection development policy must be responsible, workable, and appropriate—responsible to fiscal reality, workable with the available time and personnel, and appropriate to actual users, needs, and programs in the community.

A responsible plan fits budget and allocations. Budget is an irrefragable constraint: one cannot, given most institutional encumbering and payout systems, overspend a budget. One purpose of a plan is to make sure one buys what is needed before funds run out. To stay within a budget the selector must set priorities among the various options for buying, distribute the buying throughout the fiscal year to establish a steady relationship with the acquisitions department and to maintain an overview of the materials to be bought as they are published throughout the year, and establish subunits within one's allocation. For example, the selector should make multiyear plans for filling gaps, developing specific areas within one's collection and responding gradually but systematically to new programs or new faculty, and then set aside a suitable amount for these each year. A sound plan demonstrates a purposeful expenditure of the allocated money, and even though it can be used to increase one's influence during the budget and allocation setting period, it primarily enables us to achieve significant collection management goals.

A workable plan depends on the selector's knowledge of the subject and its materials. One cannot plan to fill gaps in the existing collection if the materials with which to fill them are no longer available or are too expensive or if one does not have time or assistants to comb bibliographies and search the card catalog. Put more positively, the selector who is aware of gaps and of suitable and affordable materials that are available will be able to draw up a workable plan. Likewise, the selector who knows current publishing output and patterns will be able to identify suitable materials from a wide range of possibilities and will not, for example, try to build a level-four collection using only level-three tools. A plan that involves coordination with other libraries will work only if that coordination is personally established and maintained.

---

8. Ross Atkinson, "The Language of Levels: Reflections on the Communication of Collection Development Policy," *College & Research Libraries* 47 (1986): 140–49.

An appropriate collection at a given level, for instance three, will never be completely identical with any other level-three collection, just as the users of one library will never be identical with those of another. Certainly some important similarities will appear (one reason for verification studies is to find these), but as the individual character of each collection is developed or discovered, the selector will realize its uniqueness. This may be the most difficult part of the selection plan, the problem of building a collection uniquely useful to a particular library and its institution that is also consistent in quality and complementary in materials with collections of similar aspirations in similar libraries in similar institutions.

To set up a realistic, workable, and appropriate plan, the selector must be able to manage the various other elements affecting collections. Ensuring availability and access, conducting weeding projects and selecting materials for storage, discard, and preservation, assessing and evaluating the quality and appropriateness of the collection are all operations integrally related with selection. Selection builds on the past and looks to the future.

Budget and Allocations

A good budget must be adequate to support the library's goals; it must be stable and allow for long-term planning and development; it must reflect a specific and explicit institutional mission; and it must be created by the library administration. The library and parent institution or funding body meet to discuss the budget, with the library only one of a number of essential services and organizations within the community or institution. Public libraries compete for public funds with police and fire departments, schools, human services, and public works; academic libraries compete with laboratories and computer centers, travel and research leaves, and faculty salaries. The budget that is allocated is, therefore, a political achievement by the library administration, not simply a gift due us.

The library budget should be created from within the library itself. A major function of the library's administration is to demonstrate the connection between the library's budget and the library's role in the institution or community, not simply to plea for more but to show what more, or less or the same, can do for the quality of the programs and community. The budget request accounts for actual costs of materials and for managing the collection, and so it depends on sound data from collection management librarians.

The definition of adequacy is difficult and has to be made locally, in terms of actual local programs and needs. National standards or guidelines can prove helpful as a context but not as a formula. A stable budget is almost as important as an adequate one. Wild, unpredictable swings between plenty and poverty can create more damage than a consistently low budget. Effective collection management operates under the assumption that there is a long-term purpose for the library's collection activities. Libraries are not simply buying many new books each year, they are developing and managing, filling gaps, replacing worn-out and lost materials, developing new areas of coverage, and responding to and anticipating changes in the user community.

The final budget should reflect both the librarian's judgment of need and the community or institution's judgment of the library's value. The library plays a specific role. It must be able to define the cost of performing this role; it can expect the institution in return to recognize the costs of its programs and meet them or else scale back those activities that depend on the library's performance. The complexities of administration and of organizational and community politics may well make this task far less clear, far less direct, than it should be and may, therefore, demand considerable political or negotiating skills.

It is increasingly important for libraries to seek additional funding outside of regular budget channels, for both special needs or projects and continuing programs. Gifts and grants should be sought for special occasions and to build an endowment that can provide regular, continuing funds. Many private institutions depend entirely on endowments, and in other libraries endowments provide regular, continuing income. While never a substitute for institutional support, these extra-budget funds should be included in the collection development policies and selection plans.

Allocations. Budget money must be allocated at several levels. The administration can allocate for broad categories, such as books, continuations, and periodicals, but it is just as important for collection management librarians to allocate the funds they control. The collection development policy should guide the former, while selection plans guide the latter. At both levels, allocations should consider, with greater or less explicitness, the following:

> Subjects: the various Dewey or LC classes; broad divisions (fine and performing arts, humanities, sciences and technology, social and behavioral

sciences); academic departments or disciplines; subfields within subjects, such as medieval, Renaissance, Victorian and the other literary periods within English literature.

Users: the various user categories described in chapter four; undergraduates, graduate students (Master's, professional, Ph.D.), faculty; juvenile (children, preteens, and adolescents).

Formats: books, periodicals, audiovisuals, microforms, computer media, etc.; further distinctions within subjects and disciplines, such as journals, monographs, collections and proceedings, research reports, tests and measures in psychology.

Uses: current and retrospective; new and replacement; primary, secondary, and tertiary.

Acquisitions: discretionary, fixed, and subscription (books, blanket orders, and periodicals).

Management operations: network and membership fees; online searching and interlibrary loan; maintenance (mending, binding); preservation; storage; cooperative arrangements and resource sharing.

We must consider the costs of materials, including their preservation and maintenance, and the intensity of their use and need. It is desirable to have both fixed and flexible allocations: regular accounts for subject and other categories, and a desiderata fund for special needs. Fixed money pays for regular, ongoing buying while flexible money covers one-time expenses to redress problems (fill gaps noted in accreditation reviews, maintain science periodical subscriptions for a year), take advantage of opportunities (a publisher's or dealer's sale), buy major items (a new subject encyclopedia, a faculty request for microform set), or even simply to give, on a scheduled rotation, extra money to each of the subjects covered or units in the library's collection management operation. This combination of stable and flexible allocating enhances long-term planning.

Allocation Procedures. The idea is to justify the specific allocations. Most libraries work with some sort of quantitative data about the library, its institution and community, and the materials being selected, and yet most also try to avoid rigidity and do recognize the human effect of allocation decisions. A great deal of data is available: quantities, prices, and trends in publishing and media; circulation statistics and data on in-house use; community surveys and enrollment counts. We can try to understand the complex nature of library use and of user needs.

Formulas manipulate data to arrive at an allocation. Some might be called driving formulas and calculate such things as amount of use, costs of materials, and status of user—that is, circulation, average prices, number of faculty or course enrollments—to indicate a dollar amount to be spent. Others can be called governing formulas and use a variety of institutional data that describes institutional or community characteristics as a comparison or check on allocations. This latter formula assumes, for example, that if the institution spends three percent of its budget on fine arts, then the library should, too. Both formulas were described most recently in articles by David Genaway.[9] The latter approach seems fair, especially in austere times when everyone feels the pinch, but no one seems to receive more than anyone else. This approach, however, seems to ignore costs, quantities, and need, factors that the former formula responds to more assertively.

A successful allocation procedure cannot be a simple formula, but must consider both institutional and publishing data and must combine this with quantifiable data about need and use. Allocations must reflect costs and quantities, but also must reflect institutional priorities as revealed in institutional budgets, and must reflect actual use of materials as shown in circulation, interlibrary loan, photocopying, reference, and library instruction statistics.[10] They also must consider long-term goals as well as current activities and must provide for developing parts of the collection, for preservation and mending and replacement, for maintaining historical strengths in the collection, and for cooperative commitments.

Ultimately allocating is not so much a procedure as it is a policy decision. When making these decisions, librarians must demonstrate their steps and their rationale, but they also must recognize the point at which their own personal vision of the collection's character and direction come into play. Quantification and formula are important, but data, no less than policies and plans, must be interpreted by an informed and knowledgeable librarian.

9. David C. Genaway, "PBA: Percentage Based Allocation for Acquisitions," *Library Acquisitions: Practice & Theory* 10 (1986): 287–92, and "The Q Formula: The Flexible Formula for Library Acquisitions in Relation to the FTE Driven Formula," *Library Acquisitions: Practice & Theory* 10 (1986): 293–306.
10. William E. McGrath, "An Allocation Formula for Academic and Public Libraries with a Test for Its Effectiveness," *Library Resources & Technical Services* 19 (1975): 356–69.

Cooperation and Other
Alternatives to Ownership

Cooperation among libraries is an old tradition, now newly driven by practical need and commonality of interest. We are all interested in, and must occasionally make use of, others' collections. Problems of funding in our age of fiscal austerity and publishing plenty have made active, formalized cooperation a positive virtue and a standard operating procedure. Cooperation involves a number of aspects, of which these are most relevant:

1. Resource sharing, such as interlibrary loan and reciprocal borrowing privileges;
2. Coordinated collection development, such as that accomplished through the Farmington Plan and which is now being urged by many research and university libraries; and
3. Coordinated collection maintenance, such as cooperative preservation and storage projects.

Cooperation is not, however, the only alternative to purchase and ownership. Recent improvements and likely future developments in telecommunications and computerized information technologies may provide a number of alternatives to outright purchase and ownership of materials. With access to bibliographic, numeric, and text information in CD-ROMs and online databases and access to documents through telefacsimile a library can provide its users the information or documents they need quickly. "Alternatives to purchase" does not, unfortunately, mean alternatives to payment: purchase, alternatives, and cooperation all have dollar costs and also particular virtues and drawbacks.

One of the more effective voices arguing for access over ownership has been that of Richard De Gennaro who wrote several years ago about the need to use technology and resource sharing to maintain collections in an age of austerity. More recently he wrote that the "emphasis in libraries is shifting from collections to access" and that we must "continue to strengthen the library's book and journal collections, and, by using new technology, to enhance its ability to provide access to the resources of other libraries as well as to the growing universe of information in electronic form".[11] The key

---

11. Richard De Gennaro, "Austerity, Technology, and Resource Sharing," *Library Journal* 100 (1975): 917–23, and "Shifting Gears: Information Technology and the Academic Library," *Library Journal* 109 (1984): 1204–09, both reprinted in Richard De

concept offered here is "to provide access to the resources of other libraries." What is being emphasized now, in contrast to traditional informal, ad hoc resource sharing, is coordinated collection management.

Cost and quantity are the problems. No library can afford to collect all that it needs; no library could house all that it needs even if it could afford to acquire it. Libraries must rely on complementary collections, seeking through careful mutual cooperation to build and maintain large and useful composite collections. Coordinated cooperative collection management involves a formal agreement among libraries to develop and maintain their collections to their mutual benefit. Each library deliberately selects materials to add, bind, preserve, or discard knowing that its decisions are consistent with similar decisions in other libraries and knowing that each library can depend on each other library for developing a composite collection.

Three examples from among the many successful and varied programs are the Research Triangle Libraries in North Carolina (Duke, University of North Carolina, and North Carolina State University), the Shared Purchase Program of the University of California system, and the Center for Research Libraries. The central assumption in these programs is that each library must provide the materials its users need regularly in the course of most academic work but that only by cooperating can the libraries provide the materials needed by only a few scholars (and their advanced students). These particular coordinated cooperative agreements, then, involve research materials or materials that are neither widely held nor heavily used.

The Center for Research Libraries was established in 1949 by ten midwestern university libraries and today has more than 100 dues-paying members. CRL accepts the deposit of materials that member libraries wish to withdraw from their own collections but think should be kept available for use, provided these meet stated criteria. The CRL thus participates in collection management activities. The CRL also draws its own budget from member dues to purchase materials, and over the years has refined its collection development policy so that now it systematically acquires research materials from the Soviet Union and the Third World, European dissertations, serials (mainly

Gennaro, *Libraries, Technology, and the Information Marketplace: Selected Papers* (Boston: G. K. Hall, 1987), pp. 205–21 and 139–54.

newspapers and scientific journals), and commercially produced micro-form sets. Members may borrow free of charge, and CRL holdings are listed in OCLC and RLIN. A member-elected governing board over-sees operations and members are polled and reported to regularly on purchase decisions. Although the membership fee can be steep (a proportion of a library's acquisitions budget), members clearly find the CRL collection and services worth the cost.[12]

In the mid-1970s the University of California system, joined later by Stanford University, instituted a Shared Purchase Program by which a central committee administered a large fund drawn from an assess-ment of three percent of each university library's materials budget and purchased a variety of research materials, including serials and continuations, commercially produced microform sets, and manu-scripts and archives. Requests for purchase are initiated by collection development officers at any of the libraries and are evaluated by the system's central committee according to clear criteria, including the fact that the item must cost at least $1,500, that in the case of sets there is adequate bibliographic control, and that at least 85 percent of the materials purchased are accessible through interlibrary loan. The purchased sets are distributed among the several libraries, not necessarily going to the library that initiated the request, so that strong and coherent collections are developed and added to at one location. The program helps contain the system's expenditures for research materials, while ensuring that relevant materials are bought.[13]

The oldest of these three programs was started in the 1930s between Duke University and the University of North Carolina, with North Carolina State University joining later. Several kinds of cooper-ation occur. Because the schools provide different programs, each library can focus its purchasing, knowing what the others are buying in their areas of interest. The libraries also formally agree about the purchase, to cite three examples, of materials from specific countries, publications from state, national, and international governments, and about specific subjects, for example, the history of the French provinces. The program involves formal agreements and frequent

12. Center for Research Libraries, *Handbook* (Chicago: CRL, 1987).
13. Marion L. Buzzard, "Cooperative Acquisitions Within a System: The University of California Shared Purchase Program," in *Coordinating Cooperative Collection Develop-ment,* ed. Wilson Luquire (New York: Haworth, 1986), pp. 99–113.

consultation among collection development librarians and no doubt benefits from the close proximity of the three schools.[14]

All these programs involve research libraries and research materials. They avoid unnecessary duplication of expensive and less-used materials yet ensure adequate coverage of subjects or areas and try to create coherent, high-quality collections that are readily accessible. They are formally coordinated, with written agreements about objectives and procedures and with frequent consultation among collection development librarians. They originated in order to meet very specific needs but they also seem to position the libraries well for additional cooperative programs. They are both good models of successful cooperation and actual programs into which other libraries can tap or on which they can build.

Equal success was achieved in multitype cooperative systems involving more common materials. Several instances of school and public library cooperative collection development are described in *Collection Management for School Library Media Centers.*[15] In Illinois a statewide program of multitype cooperation is building on the already proved LCS multitype system, operating on the assumption that every library has something to offer others.[16] Indeed, in the LCS program the University of Illinois is a net borrower, not a net lender, and more than 50 percent of what it borrows are items it already owns but are temporarily unavailable.[17] The Illinois LCS program and statewide, multitype program building on it are both examples of what might be called laissez-faire cooperation, cooperation based not on formal agreements about collecting responsibilities but on the individual collecting practices in each library that have led to a rich composite collection in the state. Overlap studies have shown that most libraries contain many unique items. In addition successful laissez-faire cooperation depends on good bibliographic control, inexpensive communications technology, fast document delivery

14. Joe A. Hewitt, "Cooperative Collection Development Programs of the Triangle Research Libraries Network," in *Coordinating Cooperative Collection Development,* ed. Wilson Luquire (New York: Haworth, 1986), pp. 139–50.

15. *Collection Management for School Library Media Centers,* ed. Brenda H. White (New York: Haworth, 1986).

16. Karen Kruger, "A System Level Coordinated Cooperative Collection Development Model for Illinois," in *Coordinating Cooperative Collection Development,* ed. Wilson Luquire (New York: Haworth, 1986), pp. 49–63.

17. Hugh Atkinson, "Atkinson on Networks," *American Libraries* 18 (6) (June 1987): 430–39.

systems, and a willingness to borrow and to lend, rather than on formal agreements.

Criticism of cooperation focuses on costs. Costs are high: interlibrary loan operations, the Center for Research Libraries, network, and consortia membership fees, and telecommunication charges all run into thousands of dollars, and the time and energy librarians must spend devising, monitoring, and evaluating cooperation may be incalculable. Thomas Ballard has argued strongly that in public and nonresearch libraries money spent on interlibrary loans and cooperation should be better spent acquiring additional books and periodicals.[18] Several libraries have had to withdraw from cooperative agreements because use and need could not justify membership fees. The Farmington Plan was terminated because participants no longer found it cost effective, although the plan was valuable in part for having shown by their absence that several key features are necessary for successful cooperation, namely central authority, ongoing evaluation of principles and procedures and of specific results, precise bibliographic control, and clearly drawn purposes.[19]

The success of a cooperative venture depends on clear understanding and agreement about the goals of the program, about the procedures for meeting these goals, about a method and timetable for evaluation, and about the involvement of the people most intimately responsible for the program's operation. Effectiveness and efficiency as well as cost benefits must be measurable and must, when measured, meet expectations. Individual libraries must be able to retain their independence. These cooperative agreements should be integrated into each library's collection development policy and, especially, into each librarian's selection plan. By doing this we ensure cooperation at both the administrative and operations levels and, thus, better focus our own collecting efforts on our immediate needs and derive more benefit from our relationship with other libraries.

The clearest summary of the purposes, problems, possible models, and policy and procedural requirements of a cooperative collection management program, as well as suggestions to nonadministrative librarians about how to initiate programs, can be found in Mosher and Pankake's "Guide to Coordinated and Cooperative Collection

18. Thomas H. Ballard, *The Failure of Resource Sharing in Public Libraries and Alternative Strategies for Service* (Chicago: American Library Association, 1986).

19. Hendrik Edelman, "The Death of the Farmington Plan," *Library Journal* 98 (1973): 1251–53, and Edwin E. Williams, "Farmington Plan," *Encyclopedia of Library and Information Science* 8 (1972): pp. 361–68.

Development." Even though it assumes that the primary audience is research libraries, almost everything it says is applicable to any other size or type of library, and even its vision of a grand, national composite collection has meaning and value for school, public, and special libraries:[20]

> Ultimately, cooperative collection development should provide a national network of dependencies and distributed responsibilities. Through the online database capacities of the various utilities, and through faster and more efficient borrowing and lending systems, large libraries will be able to provide a national research resource collection, available to any library, of any size or type, with a terminal capable of accessing the data.

The Selection Process

Selection is the quintessential professional act, requiring, in Jesse Shera's words, knowledge of men and of books. It is both art and science—or more exactly, personal judgment and systematic procedure. Experience and knowledge, sympathetic understanding of the library's mission and its users' needs and capabilities, and an ability to work within an organization mark the effective selector. One must determine the needs and demands of users and the quality of the potential materials. One must balance these sometimes incompatible criteria within the very specific context of one's own library, a balancing made easier if a good collection development policy is in place.

Selection is more than a series of individual decisions about what to buy. There is direction. The librarian may inherit a collection development policy but can implement it through his or her own selection plan. There are constraints. The budget and allocations are set by the library administration; the money must be spent within the fiscal year; the materials are not always available. There are, however, opportunities to win grants or gifts, set long-term plans that focus acquisitions money efficiently, and improve vendor profiles. Selection is a process in which the selector manages a number of elements, coordinates his or her work with other librarians, and develops the collection toward appropriate short- and long-term goals.

This selection process involves three steps. (Of course actual work is not so rigidly schematic; we often perform two or even all three

20. Paul H. Mosher and Marcia Pankake, "A Guide to Coordinated and Cooperative Collection Development," *Library Resources & Technical Services* 27 (1983): 421–22.

steps at one time.) First, we identify those items that could belong in our collection. Next, we select from these those that are particularly relevant or pertinent to our users in our situation. Third, we decide which of these pertinent items we must buy now. The three steps of identifying the relevant, selecting the pertinent, and deciding on purchases apply equally to books, periodical subscriptions, audiovisual materials, CD-ROM services, etc., including, as will be discussed in later chapters, selecting for mending, weeding, and conservation. In these three steps we constantly try to link users and materials, based on our understanding of how our users would be able to meet their needs with the materials we have selected.

Identifying Relevant Materials. Potentially we are interested in all materials dealing with the subjects we collect that are appropriate to the users we serve. The collection development policy guides us here by identifying subjects, users, and levels. A good policy should define the range of our search for relevant materials, and the more explicit the policy the better. If the policy uses levels as defined in *Guidelines for Collection Development* and calls, for example, for graduate-level collecting in agriculture, English language materials only, then we should know where to look to find those materials (books, periodicals, audiovisuals, CD-ROM indexes, etc.) that are relevant.

The actual work of identifying materials can be complex. Standard bibliographic tools list books, periodicals, and so on: we can scan the relevant sections of the *Weekly Record*, the *British National Bibliography, Choice* cards, or vendor slips; we can consult the subject sections of *Ulrich's* or *Magazines for Libraries;* we can read through the titles in *CD-ROMs in Print.* For some subjects or for some types of users we may have to look beyond the standard sources to find pamphlets, society publications, reports, alternative press materials; we may have to write publishers for information and lists. Current, new materials are one thing, materials for retrospective development are another, so we may also want to deal with *Microforms in Print,* sale catalogs, and out-of-print booksellers. Helpful at this point are the standard textbooks of selection by Broadus, Curley and Broderick, Evans, Gardner, and Katz, as well as the more specialized *Selection of Library Materials in the Humanities, Social Sciences, and Sciences* or *English and American Literature.*[21]

21. Robert N. Broadus, *Selecting Materials for Libraries,* 2nd ed. (New York; Wilson, 1981); Arthur Curley and Dorothy Broderick, *Building Library Collections,* 6th ed. (Metuchen: Scarecrow, 1985); G. Edward Evans, *Developing Library and Information Center Collections,* 2nd ed. (Littleton, Colo.: Libraries Unlimited, 1987); Richard K. Gardner,

The key element at this point is the selector's knowledge of bibliographic resources and the ability and occasion to use them effectively. One's knowledge of publishing patterns, the nature of the literature in the field, users' broad interests, and special needs not likely to be met by typical materials or publishers or gathered from common sources of supply, is important in making the large sweep. Our responsibility at this stage is to seek widely.

Selecting the Pertinent. Selecting the pertinent requires knowledge of subjects and understanding of users. On the one side, we will judge the quality of the materials and whether they are of a form and at a level suitable for our collection; on the other, we judge the actual needs and abilities of our users. We must have a selection plan. The selection plan specifies such matters as short- and long-term goals and the balance between current and retrospective development, new and replacement items, primary and secondary literature, and faculty and undergraduate, generalist and specialist needs. To select the pertinent requires attention to the specific item.

Unfortunately, we usually do not select with the item in hand or with the user at hand. We rely on reviews, bibliographic citations, descriptive annotations and advertisements, and certain triggering factors such as prizes, best-seller lists, and citation reports. We look at curriculum and enrollments, use studies, news of issues in local papers, and information from user surveys. We consult our cooperative arrangements and alternatives to purchasing and on occasion ask individuals or groups for advice about purchases. For example, in school or public libraries the selector might want to consult a committee before selecting controversial books, and in a university library the selector might want to consult an academic department's library committee for advice about desiderata or periodical subscriptions.

It is increasingly difficult to rely on reviews because books go out of print so quickly and users often hear of (and want) materials before they are reviewed, although they are still helpful perhaps as a part of the process of selecting belles lettres, added copies, replace-

Library Collections: Their Origin, Selection, and Development (New York: McGraw-Hill, 1981); William A. Katz, *Collection Development: The Selection of Materials for Libraries* (New York: Holt, Rinehart and Winston, 1980); *Selection of Library Materials in the Humanities, Social Sciences, and Sciences,* ed. Patricia A. McClung (Chicago: American Library Association, 1985); and *English and American Literature: Sources and Strategies for Collection Development,* ed. William McPheron and others (Chicago: American Library Association, 1987).

ments, and expensive desiderata such as microform or reprint sets. In academic libraries selectors must instead rely on their own knowledge of a field's subject needs, supported by such books as *English and American Literature,* while in public libraries they must have an understanding such as conveyed in Helen Haines' *Living with Books.*[22] Bibliographic citations provide much crucial information about level, authority, and likely applicability, as Ross Atkinson has shown in his "The Citation As Intertext."[23] Selectors must anticipate demand before it speaks, must judge quality on some basis other than reviews, and must (in academic and research libraries) be aware of the library's place in the process of scholarly and scientific communication.

Knowledge of subject gives one expectations for materials. One subject might require lengthy up-to-date treatment of the sort most likely to come from a university press, while another subject might require pamphlets or ephemeral material issued by a special interest group. One decides that the item is likely to be of good quality, suitable to one's users, in a format appropriate to the subject and user and consistent with the collection, and likely to be used and to prove useful. For a college library's literary criticism collection one would first identify books and periodicals of literary criticism, but then one would have to cull those that cover the literature studied in the curriculum, are suitable for undergraduates, and are not already extensively represented in the collection, and then finally select those that are needed immediately, are clearly going to be used in courses, and are within budget.

Purchase Decisions. The actual decision to purchase an item is the third step and often depends largely on very practical criteria, chiefly price, immediacy of need, and status of the user. Because an item is pertinent does not mean it will be ordered automatically. Price is a factor: some things simply cost too much, or the allocation is spent for the year, or we can buy several other items for the price of this one. Immediacy is a factor: some things are needed sooner than others, for example the high demand for multiple copies of a best-seller, reserve reading for a course already under way, or a researcher anxiously awaiting a rival's just published study. When an item can be identified for a particular user category, such as undergraduate or

22. Helen E. Haines, *Living with Books: The Art of Book Selection,* 2nd ed. (New York: Columbia University Press, 1950).

23. Ross Atkinson, "The Citation As Intertext: Toward a Theory of the Selection Process," *Library Resources & Technical Services* 28 (1984): 109–19.

concerned citizen, then the status of that user category, as defined in the collection development policy or mission, can be a deciding factor. An academic library that serves the undergraduate needs first, or conversely that serves research faculty needs first, has a clearly defined user status. None of this is a matter of either subjective or mechanical judgment; the selector is working in an actual situation, one that changes from day to day and one that only he or she knows in all its details. It is at this point, too, that the selector's relations with the Acquisitions Department and awareness (or coordination) of the several elements in the acquisitions system come into play.

The Acquisitions System. Materials come into the library in several ways, which is to say, there is an acquisitions system. The acquisitions system includes discretionary orders, subscriptions for periodicals and standing orders or continuations, buying plans (blanket orders and approval plans), depository agreements (as for federal documents or a company's archives), gifts and grants, and cooperative arrangements and alternatives to purchase. The three-step process just described applies to discretionary orders and to selection of individual subscriptions, but it takes place within the larger system.

Ideally discretionary, single-order decisions are coordinated with other elements, particularly with buying plans. There are a number of advantages to the various kinds of buying plans, among them timely receipt of materials (usually sent on publication and often before reviews or announcements appear), receipt of materials before they go out of print, savings in order-processing costs, often savings through discounts for subscriptions, and a rationalizing of the work of selection.[24] These can be written to fit most library's situations, from all-inclusive blanket-order plans to profile-driven approval plans. If, for example, the selector knows that university press books will come automatically through approval plans or blanket orders, then he or she can devote more time to identifying relevant publications from other kinds of publishers or even to reviewing the collection for gaps or maintenance needs.

The main disadvantage of these plans is that they do tie up a significant share of the budget and that share usually is allocated for current materials. In times of severe austerity, selectors may want more choice, or the nature of their collection may dictate that more money

24. Robert D. Stueart, "Mass Buying Plans in the Development Process," in *Collection Development: A Treatise,* 2 vols., eds. Robert D. Stueart and George P. Miller, Jr. (Greenwich, Conn.: JAI, 1980), pp. 203–17.

be spent for retrospective materials than for current, or the collection might need materials not readily brought in through such plans. Furthermore, usually certain segments of the collection are served better than others by them: an American approval plan can bring in American publications, but that means that some other effective and equitable way must be found to bring in foreign publications and foreign-language materials.

The various elements in the system should be complementary, and usually the Acquisitions Department is responsible for coordinating them. Acquisitions Departments have three broad areas in which to assist selectors. First, they manage relations with vendors and publishers. They submit orders and make payments, take out subscriptions, claim delayed orders and missing issues, evaluate vendor performance, and regularly review approval-plan profiles. Second, they initiate in-library processing of all materials received. Third, they manage finances of purchasing, monitor expenditures, and provide data about receipts, expenditures, and publishing. Because they know that the selectors need information about prices, that they often are working with the public on orders and therefore must be able to report back on the status of these orders, and that vendor relations do matter to selectors, Acquisitions Departments should provide a variety of information and should provide a clear procedure through which selectors can receive the information they do need. (For more complete discussion of acquisitions work, see Magrill and Corbin, as well as both Tuttle and Osborn on serials management.[25])

Selectors can in turn assist and cooperate with their Acquisitions colleagues. Selectors have certain obligations, such as prompt response to requests for profile revisions, accurate identification of items to be ordered, some preorder searching (if staffing allows), and regular and systematic submission of orders throughout the fiscal year. They also must understand that the Acquisitions Department is the bearer not the author of unpleasant messages about price increases and out-of-stock and out-of-print reports. The Acquisitions Department also can perform marvels with bad citations, recalcitrant vendors, and obscure publishers, and often are the library's main source of information about the publishing world from which we derive our resources.

---

25. Rose Mary Magrill and John Corbin, *Acquisitions Management and Collection Development in Libraries,* 2nd ed. (Chicago: American Library Association, 1989); Andrew D. Osborn, *Serial Publications: Their Place and Treatment in Libraries,* 3rd ed. (Chicago: American Library Association, 1980); and Marcia Tuttle with Luke Swindler and Nancy I. White, *Introduction to Serials Management* (Greenwich, Conn.: JAI, 1983).

Conclusion

The selection process, then, is a web of relationships rather than a simple flow chart. Decisions depend on a number of factors and can be revised or canceled; selection and acquisition librarians are hemmed in by a variety of factors. Selection requires bibliographic knowledge, sympathetic understanding of users' needs, and an ability to work within a complex organization. There is nothing merely mechanical about it, nor is it an art practiced with splendid and independent panache: selection is a complex, professional performance.

Chapter 7

Access and Availability

Our collections are intractably physical. A book, a map, a cassette, even a machine-readable file must be put someplace that is accessible and kept track of while it lives out its useful life. Not only must it be accessible, but it also must be available in usable condition when needed. To achieve access and maintain availablity we have devised rigorous cataloging and indexing principles and have tried to design buildings that accommodate users and protect materials. The physical materials change, however: with time and use individual items deteriorate, are lost or moved, and must be replaced by new editions or different formats; thus the collection as a whole grows and ages. The problems of access and availability become more complex and quickly transcend single buildings and single libraries. Access and availability ultimately depend on storage systems and interlibrary cooperation.

Previous chapters dealt with the nature of library materials, the character of individual collections, and the principles and processes of selection, all directed toward serving our users' needs, as we understand them. The emphasis now shifts to access and availability; that is, to helping our users identify what it is they need and what we have and then getting this material, or the contents of this material, into their hands. For collection managers these concerns in the past have been at best secondary, usually left to someone else, whether other librarians or users themselves. Within libraries, however, these have long been principal concerns and indeed much of library history is the history of these two services, broadly understood.

Access requires bibliographic control, and we speak of bibliographic access when discussing cataloging, classification, indexing and abstracting, bibliographies, and our reference and information services

147

that deal with the information in and the contents of our collection's materials. Access also requires physical control of the things in this collection, mainly the ways we arrange the physical materials on shelves, in buildings, in storage systems, and in networks of libraries. Both bibliographic and physical access serve similar purposes; there is a continuum of purposes that each must be designed to meet and that we as collection managers must be sure our library achieves. These purposes are to:

1. Record the library's holdings.
2. Describe the items in the collection to distinguish among them and highlight features of each that are important to users.
3. Help users identify those items that are relevant to their needs.
4. Extend use as widely as possible through the collection.
5. Indicate the locations of items in the collection.
6. Make it possible to get to and retrieve items on the shelf, in the library, in the library system, in the library network.

Availability is the degree to which things are usable when needed. Availability is affected by circulation policies and procedures, by shelving locations and reshelving procedures, by the maintenance of materials in usable physical condition, by the number of copies of particular items, by replacement of lost, stolen, or worn-out items, and, to introduce a different issue, by the extent to which a collection's size obstructs or inhibits effective use. In addition to making sure that things are bibliographically and physically accessible, we must make sure they are physically available. Not only must they be accessible, but they must be on the shelf when they're needed; not only must they be on the shelf, but they must be usable and not falling apart, mutilated, or defaced. Effective interlibrary loan service, prompt retrieval of materials stored at a distance, and even a variety of document delivery services increase availability. Availability is an important measure of a library's performance and quality: it can be measured, and it can be improved.

Bibliographic Access

Bibliographic access allows users to identify items they need and to determine whether the library has them in the collection. Libraries provide bibliographic access in the process of meeting the access needs mentioned previously, and do so with a range of tools and services, some produced locally (such as cataloging), others purchased (such as indexes and bibliographies). At the same time librarians provide access to collections outside their own libraries. From our realization that no library can be self-sufficient, to the more active idea that a library is a window through which we can look out into other volumes in other rooms, to the very active, technologically sophisticated interactive links among libraries, we have thought of bibliographic access as a central aspect of our own services and of our cooperative relationships.

Catalog. Every library must catalog all its holdings, if only for its own benefit as inventory control. We cannot manage a collection if we do not know what is in it. No matter what the form of the catalog—cards, book, microfiche, computerized online or on CD-ROM—it must list the single items in the collection. The public catalog, however, is a crucial user service that now is an integral feature of every library. In deciding what to consider as single items—a book, but also chapters, bibliographies, charts; a serial, but also individual issues or articles or bibliographies in articles—and then in deciding how to list these so that users can find them, we turn the catalog into an access tool. As such it can be remarkably rich. The current versions of automated catalogs may be a significant advance over the card catalog in the number of access points and the combinations of access points that they offer, but their accomplishment is technological more than intellectual: they make access points of cataloging details, but the details themselves long ago were identified by catalogers. Different details are of different utility to different users; what is helpful for the advanced graduate student is not necessarily helpful to the common reader, the high-school sophomore, or the business analyst. Just as the collection should be suited to the user community identified in one's mission, so should cataloging. The collection manager should have a role in helping each library decide what degree and level of cataloging are appropriate for its collection and its users.

Classification. Although machine-readable cataloging has increased the number of access points, these are almost entirely bibliographic details rather than subject details. Classification is another form of bibliographic access, which takes us beyond recording our ownership of an item and describing of its bibliographic details and into attempting to place it in an intellectual or subject context. Classification allows users to comprehend the item as part of a larger intellectual or subject context, and it can be used to place an item in useful proximity to others on the same subject. The extent to which the catalog also gives location information depends on the library. We are accustomed to call numbers, but certainly in small libraries where simple shelf arrangement lets users find what they need, a call number is not absolutely necessary. We also are accustomed to open stack libraries and to call numbers not only directing us to the right place but also indicating something of the item's subject classification.

Indexing, Analytics, and Subject Bibliographies. We do not provide so comprehensive and convenient a system of indexing as we do of cataloging. Indexing of periodicals is selective; not all titles are indexed, nor are all the indexed titles indexed thoroughly. What indexing we do provide is almost entirely commercially produced outside the library, but this indexing is not consistent: terms, formats, and quality vary from index to index. Furthermore, this indexing is not keyed to our catalog nor does it provide holdings information, so that users must both find the most appropriate index and also make a separate effort to find out what is available among the indexed items. The one area where libraries have performed indexing in the past, that is, the provision of analytics for collective volumes, is far less common now than formerly. In addition, we have erected an obstacle—price—between users and the latest form of indexing, the online bibliographic database. There are reasons for all this, of course, but neverthless we cannot blandly absolve ourselves.

Bibliographies are as essential an aspect of library access as catalogs and indexes. In their classification, comprehensiveness of coverage, authority of selection, and fullness of description the best of them extend the local catalog and current indexing. Herein lies their value as access tools, but also their inconvenience: they lead out of the local collection to the broader one. In some libraries, such extension is welcome, even expected, but in others it frustrates more than it assists.

Collection managers must examine issues of appropriateness, coverage, and cost. What level of indexing should we adopt, that which is suitable for scholars and specialists or that which is suitable for undergraduates and the general public? How much of the costs of commercial products do we pass on to users and what provision do we make for the needs of users who cannot afford our prices? How do we index locally owned materials not indexed commercially, and, conversely, what problems of access are created when indexes cover materials not owned locally? Cataloging work is performed in a separate department by a group of professionals with their own training, traditions, and expertise. Indexing usually is performed by similarly specialized professionals, and outside the library to boot.

Collection managers must become reasonably familiar with these practices, not to license meddling but to make possible regular consultation and coordination between them and catalogers.

Extending Use. Access tools allow users to find what we have if they know how to use the tools effectively, but in reality users find relatively little of all that our libraries hold. By extending use to more of our materials we hope to serve users by helping them find what they need and to serve our collection by distributing use and thus reducing wear and tear and justifying the costs of acquiring it. Access tools and access points by themselves are not enough, so we have long offered reference, information, and reader advisory service and, more recently, emphasized user education (especially in academic libraries). Displays and book lists, accessions lists, posting dust jackets, and other publicizing activities also inform users of what we have that they probably were not aware of. Rather than thinking of these services as separate from collection management, we should recognize that they are integral with it. We should be as anxious to make our collection known as we are willing to buy what users request.

Access to Other Collections. A quick review of library history shows several ways in which access to other collections in other libraries has become possible. First, union catalogs, which came to first fruition in the late nineteenth century and were conscientiously maintained until recently, brought libraries into significant contact. Their purposes, reviewed by Eugene R. Hanson in an *ELIS* article, were to facilitate interlibrary lending, to standardize bibliographic description and cataloging practice, and to enlarge the bibliographic list of known publications.[1] In the United States there were county and multicounty, state, regional, and national union catalogs, many involving multitype libraries. These varied in what they included, some focused on a subject (such as medicine or regional history), while others focused on a format (particularly serials); still others were comprehensive in subject and format. Those maintained as a card catalog were useful to their members but not so much so to libraries outside the network. The publication, however, of the *National Union Catalog* and the *Union List of Serials* were remarkable bibliographic triumphs, surely among our profession's finest moments.

A number of library catalogs have been published, and these, along

---

1. Eugene R. Hanson, "Union Catalogs," *Encyclopedia of Library and Information Science* 31 (1981): pp. 391–445.

with such works as Robert B. Downs' *American Library Resources* and Lee Ash's *Subject Collections,* have provided an in-depth picture of American libraries and have made bibliographic access possible at a broader level than that of individual titles. Whole collections have been identified for the scholar, the student, and the ambitious amateur. Users gain through these catalogs not just the location of specific items but the description of coherent and authoritative collections. With union catalogs, published catalogs, and subject guides, interlibrary loan became not just a blind but hopeful reaching out to other libraries, but a very purposeful and informed means for bringing user and material together.

What the national bibliographic utilities—OCLC, RLIN, WLN— have brought in addition to technological advance is sheer size: more books and periodicals, in more libraries, more access points, more interlibrary loan capacity, more potential for additional technological innovations. They contain items not listed in the *National Union Catalog* or *Books in Print,* include invaluable subfiles such as the *Eighteenth Century Short Title Catalog* on RLIN, list virtually all locations of items, and with their own interlibrary loan subsystems have made interlibrary borrowing fast and sure. Starting perhaps as tools of cataloging cooperation, they have become central to bibliographic access.

More focused versions of these utilities can provide an even closer access link between libraries. The LCS system in Illinois is surely a prototype for the future, besides being tremendously effective at the moment. It offers direct access to the online catalogs of other libraries combined with access to circulation services, and also provides related document delivery and telefacsimile transmission systems operated by users in any library in the system (and with the "system" expanding to include virtually all libraries in the state). And, as mentioned previously, these systems are not only for scholars and do not lead only to the esoteric and rare, but provide ordinary users with their ordinary and everyday needs: the University of Illinois specifically benefits from LCS for it can retrieve from other libraries copies of books and periodicals that it already owns but are checked out, at the bindery, lost, or somehow unavailable.[2] These direct links among libraries can only increase in sophistication and efficiency. They also may dramatically affect governance and administration, for a statewide university system

---

2. Hugh Atkinson, "Atkinson on Networks," *American Libraries* 18 (6) (June 1987): 430–39.

now can have a statewide university library system with considerable coordination among them all, resulting in enhanced autonomy (individual libraries can define themselves more specifically) and enhanced collections and access services. Public libraries can break out of the constraints of political jurisdictions into increased cooperation with neighboring and multitype systems.

The composite collection, although far from a reality, is a realistic goal, but with it must come accessibility. Cooperative relationships among libraries can provide the composite collection; we must be careful also to provide the access. This composite is not just a backup for our own collections to which we refer when all else fails; this larger whole is the collection, of which each of ours is but a small part. In practical terms of bibliographic access what this means is that we must participate in bibliographic databases, must put retrospective conversion high on our list of priorities, must work toward mutually exchangeable library cards and privileges, and must work cooperatively with other libraries. If accessibility is a major justification for a library's existence as well as one of its major goals, as it must be, we as librarians must look, ultimately, outward.

Physical Access

A library building's first function is to house the collection, but it must provide housing that allows users and librarians access to the collection. The typical library building is a compromise between these two not entirely compatible functions, so perfection in buildings is not to be expected and has not been achieved. Furthermore, each library building exists in a unique situation so that what is true of one can never be true of another. There is, however, the accumulated wisdom of people who have designed, built, moved into, and lived with libraries, as well as a good deal of common sense and informed judgment to guide us in thinking about library buildings and the ways they enhance physical access. The amount of building space given to the collection, how the collection is arranged within this space, the collection's rate of growth, the building's approach to capacity, and the ways capacity can be increased all affect physical access. Good collection management requires good facilities management.

Broadly speaking there are four kinds of library buildings: those designed primarily for users and not for storage of materials (such as a separate reading room), open-access facilities housing materials but allowing users free access to them as well as space to sit and read, closed-access facilities likewise accommodating readers, and secondary storage facilities exclusively devoted to storing materials. The second type is the most common library today, although the third was once so and may regain popularity; the fourth kind, secondary storage, also is increasingly common as an adjunct to the second. The first kind is of no consequence here; the others will all be covered to some extent in this chapter on access. They all are designed with consideration given to their use of space for storing materials, for providing amenities (heat, light, convenient maintenance of building and collection) and services to the reader (seating space, reference service), and for accommodating certain collection related services (reshelving, user access). Different types of libraries may well require different types of buildings, but the general outlines we will cover should apply in all. Discussion will focus on the most common type of building today, the open-access library providing space for the collection, users, and librarians, staff, and their work.

Access to the collection first of all depends on the amount of space that the collection takes up in the building and the arrangement and shelving of the collection within this space. In an open-access library, arrangement and shelving are primarily by subject, but we also arrange materials by format where different formats cannot efficiently be interfiled. Books are not normally interfiled with audiovisuals, unbound periodicals, newspapers, maps, or microforms, nor are nonbook materials typically arranged by subject. That is, all unbound periodicals could be kept in a separate room but shelved there according to Library of Congress classification, by broad subject (as determined by the library), or by title. A closed-access facility could arrange and shelve materials by size, order of accession, or format.

When deciding how to arrange and shelve their collections, librarians must determine both the most cost-effective and the most accessible use of space, but these are incompatible requirements: a library building must be a compromise between accessibility and cost-effective storage. Cost-effectiveness can be calculated and projected readily, although the factors that affect it will vary in degree from library to library. The ratio of books to nonbooks and among subjects, the growth rate of each of the collection's various subjects and formats, and requirements of different categories of users all can be quantified and their effects on arrangement and shelving calculated. For example, a research library that devotes at least half its collection budget to periodicals, that acquires large microfilm collections of research materials, and that serves a large body of graduate students and faculty must provide for arrangement of its collection differently than a small undergraduate college or a public library would.

Metcalf, Leighton, and Weber's book about academic and research library buildings, *Planning Academic and Research Library Buildings,* notes the following factors affecting arrangement and shelf space:[3]

1. Growth rate varies by format: periodicals can take up progressivley more space just as they take up progressively more of the acquisition budget; in some libraries audiovisuals will grow faster than books.

2. Growth rate varies by subject: fiction might grow faster than nonfiction in a public library, education faster than religion in a state college, and in all libraries the growth of subjects will be affected by publishing patterns and, especially, the collection development policy.

3. Growth rate varies by category of user: an undergraduate library might grow by one to two percent per year, a research library by four percent, and within a large library the collections for different users will grow at different rates depending on the collection development policy.

4. Book size differs for different subjects: art has a higher proportion of folio-sized books than do other subjects; law books are twice as thick as fiction.

5. Within different subjects, there are different numbers of sub-classifications and different rates of growth: twentieth-century American literature collections grow faster than eighteenth-century collections.

6. Some subjects include a higher proportion of reference books than others, thus taking up more shelf space in different locations.

Noting growth rates leads to thinking about a building's capacity. Given the multiplicity of uses in the typical library building and the multiplicity of subjects and formats, each with different space needs and growth rates, it is no easy matter to determine when a building is full, let alone to project when one might become so. Each library can, of course, calculate its own rate of growth over preceding years

---

3. Keyes D. Metcalf, *Planning Academic and Research Library Buildings,* 2nd ed. by Philip D. Leighton and David C. Weber (Chicago: American Library Association, 1986), chapter 1.

and can make reasonable projections about future rates, and can try to include such unpredictables as changes in academic program or character of the student body, urban demographic and economic changes, and even the character of the library. Growth continues and must be accommodated. Metcalf argues that shelf space that is 90 percent full is unusable, and that 86 percent is the maximum working capacity.[4] Furthermore, when shelf capacity has reached 75 percent, the library must start developing additional space, particularly if that means a new building, which can take up to ten years to design, fund, and build. Building capacity is harder to judge because of multiple uses; there are ways to increase capacity, but they all affect either the space for other uses or the ease of access to the collection.

Each library has its own growth rate. Nationally, libraries have grown steadily throughout the century. Academic libraries—particularly university libraries—seemed to grow at a rate that doubled every 16 years, or so Fremont Rider observed.[5] Today, however, a majority of the nation's academic and public libraries possibly have reached maturity, a stage in which growth continues but at a fairly low rate. According to Keyes Metcalf, whose concept "maturity" is, university libraries will grow at about two to three percent per year, while college libraries will grow slightly less.[6] A decade or more ago the concept of zero growth was commonly accepted, but even in the face of inflation and recession, publication increased and most libraries continued to grow, as previously noted in chapter three. Knowledge increases faster than it becomes obsolete; publications increase faster than they wear out. No matter what our intentions, a "healthy" library (argues Metcalf) will grow and grow faster than we expect.[7] If it were possible to achieve zero growth, it would be so only within a single building; within a library system zero growth is impossible. A mature collection in a mature community or institution may not see a growth in users, but its collection will nevertheless continue to grow and will require additional space and additional staff to care for it.

As a collection nears its capacity, more maintenance problems arise. Because of uneven growth rates, a full collection begins to require frequent shifting to accommodate growth in one part by moving into space taken less densely by another. Shifting takes people and time,

---

4. Metcalf, pp. 153–55.
5. Fremont Rider, *The Scholar and the Future of the Research Library: A Problem and Its Solution* (New York: Hadham, 1944).
6. Metcalf, p. xiii.
7. Metcalf, p. 158.

takes people away from other activities, adds to personnel costs, and almost always leaves a residue of misshelved and damaged books, no matter how skillfully and conscientiously shifting is carried out. Shifting is limited by, or else must cause revisions in, the arrangement of materials and services. Periodicals must be shifted into book space, books into reader's space, microform cabinets into corners, staff into hallways. The collection, like a living system, chokes on its own growth.[8]

Access decreases as the building nears capacity. Reshelving slows down because shelvers must spend more time shifting books on the shelves and more time shelf reading; fuller shelves means more damaged books and more time and money spent finding and repairing these books. Additional space can be won in a variety of ways, but most of them are stopgap and most make access more difficult. We can increase capacity by narrowing and eliminating aisles, adding shelves at tops or bottoms of sections, extending ranges, setting two rows of books per shelf, or adding ranges in poorly lit corridors and corners. Narrow aisles, however, inevitably mean dark, uninviting aisles; additional shelves means shelves out of reach; long ranges without cross-aisles slow users' travel. With all this comes the increased likelihood of misshelved or damaged books. Nor are we considering the space users need to sit and read or write, use microfilm readers, spread maps out on light tables, and so forth. Clearly, if a major library goal is to provide users with convenient access to collections, we cannot let our buildings become overfilled.

No-Growth Collections. To the skeptic, the most sensible solution to space problems is to limit growth. If it is true that large collections are less accessible than small ones, then it is absurd, if not culpable, to let libraries balloon out of control. Rather than construct new buildings or wings, hire additional librarians who will have the time to select more precisely and to weed unneeded material. Such was the argument of essays collected several years ago by Daniel Gore in *Farewell to Alexandria*.[9] The counterargument was that we do not know what the ideal maximum collection size is, nor is there proof that size does obstruct users, and, above all, information, knowledge, and publications are expanding faster than our population. It is irresponsible to ignore this growth. A collection must stay ahead of

---

8. Richard A. Stayner and Valerie R. Richardson, *The Cost-Effectiveness of Alternative Storage Programs* (Clayton, Victoria, Australia: Graduate School of Librarianship, Monash University, 1983).

9. Daniel Gore, ed., *Farewell to Alexandria: Solutions to Space, Growth, and Performance Problems* (Westport, Conn.: Greenwood, 1976).

its users: libraries bring not only what users know and want but also what there is that can be known and wanted.

On the other hand, there are increasing numbers of slow-growth libraries and of libraries that have capped growth in their main facilities. Metcalf noted that mature libraries grow at a lower rate than new libraries, and nationwide libraries are maturing. Libraries also continue to live in austere circumstances and will increasingly forgo ownership for access. So although no growth is not an explicit goal, decreasing growth is a reality. Even limited growth, however, adds a huge quantity of material that must be shelved accessibly. Many library buildings have reached capacity, and growth can be accommodated only by moving materials out of the main library into storage facilities. This sort of nongrowth has occurred in several university libraries[10] and recently has been implemented at Westminster College (Pennsylvania).[11] There the goal is a 300,000 volume collection in the main library that allows growth by weeding, storage, conversion to microform, and, it is hoped, use of telefacsimile access. Additional librarians will be employed to handle the time-consuming work of weeding and selecting for storage. Growth cannot be stopped, but it can be managed.

Browsing and Shelf Arrangement. Physical access enhances bibliographic access. The location of shelving, the kind of shelving used and the ways materials are arranged on the shelves, open or closed stacks, the use of storage facilities, and the value of branch libraries all are major considerations, as well as the matter of the relationship between location and classification. Underlying our thinking about physical access seems to be a firm belief in the value of browsing, a Missourian's "show-me" atttitude that belies our intense involvement in the variety of bibliographic access tools and services. Also influential is a belief in a core collection of materials that most users will need ready access to.

Browsing is a complex activity, imperfect and inefficient yet useful and powerful. We know from our own experience that often a book on the shelf grabs our attention more than an entry in a catalog. Libraries make use of this phenomenon. Periodical display areas for the latest issues, separate shelving for new books, posting dust jackets,

---

10. Jay K. Lucker, Kate S. Herzog, and Sydney J. Owens, "Weeding Collections in an Academic Library System: Massachusetts Institute of Technology," *Science & Technology Libraries* 6 (1986): 11–23.
11. F. E. Smith, "The Static-Capacity Library at Westminster College," *Technicalities* 5 (4) (1985): 10–12.

and face-out shelving are some ways to call attention to certain materials. In some cases we do this to increase or extend use; in others, we do it because we realize that users come to the library partly to inform themselves of what is newly published, not necessarily to read it.

Browsing is also an integral part of more purposeful library use. Dewey and Library of Congress classifications are both in large part location systems; that is, they classify materials according to the predominant subject of their contents but they do so in such a way that similar materials are brought together on the shelf. They emphasize exclusive, coherent subject groupings more than interrelatedness or recency or format or type of treatment. Browsing is more effective in some subjects than others. Literature collections with the works of an author all in one place, along with critical, scholarly, and biographical works, seem particularly suited to browsing, at least for a certain sort of user interest. Similarly, fiction collections with books arranged by author or genre (crime novels, romances, foreign novels in translation) can lay out for readers a wide range of the library's holdings. Public and school libraries make very effective use of shelf arrangement, and even academic libraries benefit from the virtual self-classification of literature, although they do make less frequent use of genre arrangement. For research and for recreational reading, therefore, the shelf arrangement of literature can be very effective. This also is true for other core subjects and disciplines such as history and mathematics. But what if the subject were environmental pollution? It is impossible to provide a browsable collection of materials in this case, except in a small special library devoted exclusively to the subject.

Other ways of arranging have been tried, several of which are described by Richard Hyman in *Shelf Access in Libraries*.[12] Ribbon shelving, where the most interesting books (in librarians' eyes) are shelved at chest level along a whole range of sections, with related reference books, related studies, and odd-sized books on shelves above or below, seems to appeal perennially to librarians trying to focus user's search, and may work in children's collections or in certain kinds of branches of public libraries or dormitory collections in universities. Setting up a core collection, either a highly distilled one for the entire library or several larger cores in divisional arrangement has worked,

---

12. Richard J. Hyman, *Shelf Access in Libraries* (Chicago: American Library Association, 1982).

too. A number of years ago the Detroit Public Library developed a Reader Interest Classification scheme that sought to arrange books according to users' interests (as understood by librarians) rather than by traditional subject analysis and classification; although since abandoned, it remains an intriguing concept. In fact the history of librarianship is replete with attempts by librarians to lay out their collections in ways they hoped would catch readers' attention and improve their access to the materials.

Yet browsing is notoriously imperfect. The best books are already checked out, the periodicals are being bound, important general treatments and collections of essays are shelved elsewhere, the subject itself is so complex that materials on it are found all over the library, not to mention not even in the particular library, and often the user cannot judge the book as well as a good review can, or cannot find essential details of publication that good cataloging regularly ferrets out (such as actual date of publication, the fact that the book in hand is a reprint, or a pseudonymous author's real name). The problem of how to extend use into more of the collection has not been solved by physical arrangement. To organize a collection in hopes of increasing browsing may at once frustrate users and deny them best access to the material they most need and really want.

Branch Libraries. A logical extension, if not indeed a historical outgrowth of browsing and shelf arrangement, is the branch library, that building separate from the main library with a selection of the same materials in it. Branches exist to make collections more accessible. Academic branch libraries have won tremendous user approval for the very reasons that librarians who believe in the efficacy of physical arrangement have long championed: they seem to enhance bibliographic access. A subject's materials along with specialized librarians are housed separately on the assumption that academic specialists will benefit from the coherence of the collection (and appreciate its proximity to office and classrooms and the cachet of special treatment). Advocates of core collections and browsing often advocate branch libraries, too. Other librarians resist branch libraries on the principle that knowledge is whole not part, and branches simply ignore intellectual reality and foster a sterile overspecialization, that great flaw in the academic mind, or decry their cost in manpower, heat and light, duplication of staff and materials, and the problems of bibliographic control.

To some extent the problems of bibliographic control and access are solved by computer technology. The online catalog is easy to

maintain and unaffected by the existence of one or 100 branch collections; the online circulation system lets users know the circulation
status (and by implication the on-the-shelf status) of books in branches,
and even can be tied into a delivery system, thus reducing the problem
of access. These solutions reduce the pressure for duplicate copies
of books and subscriptions or additional staff, but probably in large
library systems that include a number of branch libraries there is
already a need for more copies and staff. Dispersion, while itself a
problem, is not necessarily the cause of other problems. The question
of intellectual integrity is more complex, as is shown in Paul Metz's
study of ethnicity, supportiveness, and dependency, *Landscape of
Literatures*.[13]

If there are trends under way in academic branch libraries, they
are toward broad subject areas rather than single subject collections.[14]
Simple fiscal reality limits our ability to set up many new libraries
because space, personnel, and duplication are too costly. Security,
too, prevents us from letting users into unsupervised branches. The
idea of a branch as a small, exclusive offshoot of the main collection
seems to have given way to the idea of divisional collections—such
as a science and technology or a fine-arts library. These complement
the main library, with similar hours and circulation policies but with
minimal duplication of materials and exceptions to use policies.

For branches in public library systems the question is not whether
they should exist, but in what form: should their collections be
miniature versions of the collection in the main library or should each
branch provide a unique emphasis and, consequently, a collection
with its own unique character? Technological developments do not
answer the question, nor do national standards or trends, because
each urban community and each neighborhood served by a branch
library is unique. The question can be answered by analyzing the needs
the branch collection must meet. In some cases, a branch stocked
with materials selected by a centralized body and that essentially
duplicate main library emphases and collections is exactly what is
needed; in other cases, the branch must have nearly complete
autonomy to select what its community needs; in still others, the
branch can be treated as a separate resource center with a collection

13. Paul Metz, *Landscape of Literatures: Use of Subject Collections in a University Library* (Chicago: American Library Association, 1984).
14. Robert A. Seal, "Academic Branch Libraries," *Advances in Librarianship* 14 (1986): 175–209.

that serves its immediate users and also serves other branches and even the main library from its collection.

All branch libraries exist to provide better access for users. In expanding urban communities with poor public transportation it is more effective to take the library to the people rather than to let them find their way to the library. In public or in academic libraries, branches have been treated as simply another part of the main building or as a single, self-sufficient building. Useful or wasteful, cost-effective or expensive luxuries, they have not yet been used to help solve access problems caused by growth and aging.

Access in Storage Systems

It has become impossible to deal with large collections, to solve the problems of growth, aging, changing use patterns, of warehousing and access, in terms of single buildings. There are very practical problems: we cannot build buildings large enough to hold the millions of volumes we own and provide the necessary services and user amenities, and even if we could construct the building, we cannot find space for it or space is too expensive. There are political problems: we cannot convince central administrations to fund another new huge library building. Even the basic problem of access to a large collection cannot be solved with a new building. We have been forced to think of alternatives to new primary buildings, and in doing so we have stumbled onto an opportunity. Problems of access and availability are better dealt with in a storage system rather than a single building. They can be managed more economically, more efficiently, and more clearly for the users' benefit. When seeking storage alternatives to the traditional library building we must develop storage systems.

Leighton and Weber in their updating of Metcalf on academic libraries conclude that "the future of campus auxiliary facilities seems assured. . . It would not be surprising if. . . the larger university libraries may have 50 percent of their collections in a secondary-access facility within a decade or so into the next century."[15] Public libraries face similar problems. John Boll argues that any library with more than a million volumes should be moving parts of that collection into storage so that by the time the collection has reached one and a half million volumes at least 33 percent of it is stored.[16] Metcalf approaches

---

15. Metcalf, pp. 34–35.
16. John J. Boll, *Shelf Browsing, Open Access and Storage Capacity in Research Libraries* (Urbana: University of Illinois Graduate School of Library and Information Science, 1985), p. 29.

the issue from consideration of obstacles presented by overfull stacks, while Boll considers that browsing, or the presumed virtues of open access to the entire collection, becomes less effective as the collection grows.

All libraries face the problem of accommodating a growing collection. There are six alternatives to simply building a new, expensive library building:

1. We can make more exhaustive use of the existing building, which is, of course, what all libraries have done by squeezing out reader space, staff office and work space, and public space. Obviously, this alternative cannot work forever.

2. We can weed the collection and convert paper materials to microforms and new electronic formats. Weeding does not cause dramatic reductions, however, and conversion works only for a time and then it, too, takes space: microforms need storage cabinets and reading equipment, not to mention as strict environment controls as paper. Electronic publishing will affect reference services and document delivery but significant effects in regular collections will not occur for a generation or more.

3. Stack reformation, chiefly the addition of higher shelves, narrower aisles, and rearranged stack areas, such as more exhaustive building use, has an obvious upper limit for storage, and, equally obvious, will make library use less pleasant, perhaps less possible, for users.

4. Compact storage on movable shelving will offer modestly accessible but quite close storage, and can maintain the browsability of collections.

5. Use of local shared facilities, such as classroom space on a campus or municiple building space in a community. This alternative, too, seems to have an upper limit, in addition to putting the storage solution into a politically complex relationship.

6. Construct an alternative storage facility designed primarily for a collection: this makes more efficient use of storage space, provides climate controls suitable for the collection, is located perhaps at some distance from the main library where land and construction costs are lower, and might serve more than one library or institution.

There are three models of storage systems: local, shared but distant, and membership in something such as CRL. In considering these, however, we must keep in mind the nature of collections and use, the library's mission, and the problem of compromise between cost and convenience. In particular we must try to maintain the integrity of collection units. Not all subjects are browsable, yet most do reward those who visit them in person. It is not desirable to break up coherent subject collections.

The most immediate storage is the traditional central library. I use the word "central" because almost any library of any size does in fact use more than one building but also maintains one of its multiple buildings as the one with either most of the collection and services or with the administration located in it. Public libraries and university libraries generally follow this model, as do most school libraries and many college libraries that have branch or departmental facilities. Many special libraries serving large corporations have several facilities dispersed in several cities. Certain kinds of networks also have a central library, or possibly a series of central libraries that can treat each of the others as a kind of branch or remote facility.

A local—that is, on-campus or in-town—facility could be used, whether refitting an existing building or constructing a new one. The purpose of the building is to store books not people, so its amenities can be spared. What it needs are space, shelving that enables the most material to be held (many storage facilities shelve by size, not classification), proper environment, and limited provision for staff and, possibly, for a limited number of users. Square footage of floor space is a primary consideration and in cramped quarters can well be gained by building down; books do not need windows, so sublevel construction is suitable. Floor space can be devoted almost entirely to shelving because there is little need for users to visit the facility. Shelving must be efficient: shelving by size, shelving by accession number so that no space need be left on shelves for expansion, using mechanical compact shelving, adapting the latest warehouse technology that places books in labeled boxes, set and retrieved by mechanical arm, tracked by computer.[17]

The library can join an organization such as the Center for Research Libraries, to which it can send discarded materials and from which it can borrow materials purchased with accumulated membership fees. Although this is not alternative storage of one's own materials, by being an alternative to purchase and local ownership it can be included here.

---

17. Norman Tanis and Cindy Ventuleth, "Making Space: Automated Storage and Retrieval," *Wilson Library Bulletin* 61 (10) (June 1987): 25–27.

Similar alternatives could be developed regionally and statewide. The University of California Shared Purchase System is an example. A central administration takes an allocation from funds that are distributed to the system's libraries and makes purchases from these, in accordance with written policy and procedures, and then assigns the purchased materials to one of the system's libraries. We solve a storage problem by converting it to a matter of cooperation and access.

At the same time we also must think about what it is that is being stored: the higher the amount of use, the more the retrieval costs and, possibly, the less dense the storage, for some provision has to be made for retrieval staff or for user access. The more use that is expected of the materials put into storage, the more the facility has to allow for browsing and ready retrievability. Different uses and different users require different storage facilities. The more daring the library administration, the more technologically sophisticated the storage can be; the more technologically sophisticated, usually the more costly. Costs can be calculated. Richard Stayner and Valerie Richardson analyzed the costs of storage and the costs of retrieval, including factoring in the users' needs and degree of demand.[18] Storage in the central library is more expensive than in a special storage facility, but delivery costs from the farther building are more than from the central facility. We must consider both demand and the likely kind of use. It might make sense to move entire blocks of materials, rather than single items, to the distant, special storage and allow user access, browsing, and on-site use, in limited or rather Spartan reading areas.

These all belong together on a continuum of uses. They are not alternatives in the sense that we will choose to use one rather than another. The longer a library is in operation, the wider the range of storage alternatives it must adopt. Their distinguishing features are not technological but are the procedures for access and retrieval. We should think of a sequence of facilities, from immediate access and retrieval by users to delayed access and delivery from a distant facility, with each facility in between being farther from the center, more densely stocked, and causing greater retrieval costs. Figure 1 shows these storage systems graphically.

The guiding principle, however, is not to do only what is possible but to try to do what is needed, and to allow a considerable degree of flexibility, adaptation, and change in the future. We can look ahead to a storage system that involves a central library, specialized branches,

18. Stayner and Richardson, "Appendix."

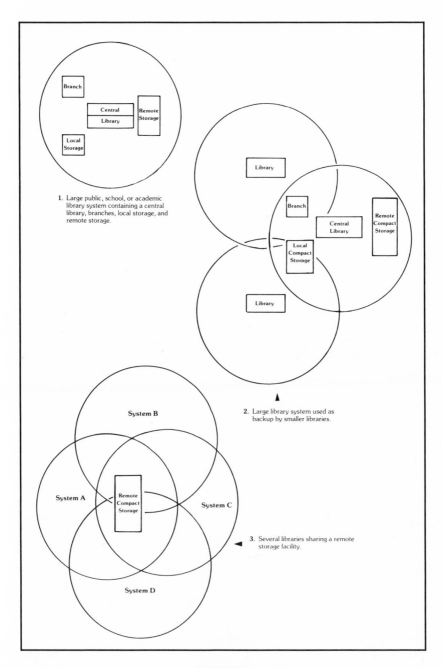

1. Large public, school, or academic library system containing a central library, branches, local storage, and remote storage.

2. Large library system used as backup by smaller libraries.

3. Several libraries sharing a remote storage facility.

FIGURE 9.
Storage Systems

nearby storage facility accessible to users, a remote facility shared with other libraries and containing the castoffs of our collections, and an even more remote facility supported by several libraries and responsible for purchasing, storing, and lending valuable but seldom-used materials. To this system should be added those other libraries in one's network from which regular interlibrary borrowing and lending is encouraged and readily accomplished. A composite collection, as described in chapter five, depends on such a system. A mature library and, even more, a nation of mature libraries, can survive only if such a system of collection storage is in place, intact.

Availability

It is not enough to develop a system of access; libraries also must guarantee that their materials are available. Availability is in the eye of the user and the only meaningful definition of availability, the only meaningful measure of it, must come from the user. Output measures, discussed previously in chapter five, turn attention from size and rate of acquisition to use, usually as measured by circulation, and as librarians have analyzed use more thoroughly they have come to see that it is affected by availability. Users will not use what they cannot find and their failure to find what they want in one visit will make them less inclined to try again on another visit. It certainly makes little sense to spend millions of dollars for books and periodicals and still have users who are unable to get what they need: a library with a low rate of availability is neither cost effective nor useful.

Availability is as hard to define and measure as use. It refers to users' ability actually to get what they want in the library. If they know exactly what they want when they come in, then it should be easy enough for us to tell whether they succeed. If they know what they want but are willing to make do with something else, then the situation is more complex: there may be frustration but not failure. The intensity of their desire has to be considered, as well as their willingness to wait. Someone coming in expecting the latest best-seller knows from experience that there will be a wait. Likewise, the user who expects a popular weekly to be in every Tuesday will know that occasionally it does not arrive until Wednesday. On the other hand the student whose paper is due in a week cannot wait for a book to be recalled, an interlibrary loan to be processed, a periodical to be returned from the bindery, or our regular search procedures to turn up a misshelved item. When the user is not seeking a known item but instead wants materials on some topic, then availability is much harder to judge. A large library surely will have some relevant materials on nearly any subject its regular users would want, but just as surely may not have something, or enough of something, that is directly pertinent. Furthermore, users may want one thing but actually need something else. The question of availability, then, depends in part on users and in part on the library.

Several efforts have been made to analyze precisely the factors that decrease availability, and they all came to roughly the same conclusion. Saracevic, Kantor, and Shaw's 1978 study is perhaps the classic analysis; Paul Kantor subsequently refined their analytical method; and John Mansbridge surveyed these and a number of other studies.[19] According to Mansbridge's analysis, libraries have an average availability rate of 61 percent; that is, to put it less positively, four out of every ten people who try to find a specific book in their library fail. In only ten percent of these failures is the cause the library's failure to have the book, so the problem of availability is not a problem in selection or collection development. The main causes of users' frustration are circulation, user mistakes, and library mistakes.

One of the most useful aspects of the work of Saracevic, Kantor, and White and then of Kantor's further refinement is their ability to pinpoint why books were unavailable when wanted. According to Kantor's book, *Objective Performance Measures for Academic and Research Libraries,* specifically chapter 1, the following seems typical. (His figures are not universally true; his is not a widespread survey of the causes of failure but rather an attempt to show how to discover it in each library.[20])

Causes of Nonavailability	*Percentage of Failure*
Nonacquisition of book	11%
User problem at catalog	5%
Book needed is checked out	14%
Book not checked out but not on shelf either:	
lost, missing, misshelved, in process somewhere	21%
User mistake at the shelf	16%

19. T. Saracevic, W. H. Shaw, Jr., and Paul B. Kantor, "Causes and Dynamics of User Frustration in an Academic Library," *College & Research Libraries* 38 (1977): 7–18, and J. Mansbridge, "Availability Studies in Libraries," *Library & Information Science Research* 8 (1986): 299–314.

20. Paul Kantor, *Objective Performance Measures for Academic and Research Libraries* (Washington, D.C.: Association of Research Libraries, 1984).

What Kantor has shown is that if a user were looking for 20 books on a list, he or she would find only nine. Of the 20, the library would own 18 and would list them in the card catalog. Of these 18, the user would make a mistake and find catalog cards for only 17. Of these 17, two at least would be checked out, and of the remaining 15, three or four would be missing (lost, misshelved, or somewhere in the process of returning from circulation to shelf or being mended), and two would in fact be on the shelf but overlooked by the user: a total of nine books found from the original 20 wanted. Of course, if the user asked for assistance, then the book missed in the catalog and the two missed on the shelf certainly would be found, as quite possibly would the three or four missing ones. Still, the unaided user is in for a long day of frustration.

We can look at this brief history and take some comfort. The books we did not buy that the user wanted are perhaps out of scope or from a time when we were not buying in that subject or at that level; or perhaps they are readily available through interlibrary loan; or perhaps they have just been published and are in fact on order or even received and being cataloged. Given these possibilities, our selection or collection development record is satisfactory. That books are circulating is, of course, the whole point for buying them. The user's problem at the card catalog could have been because of a library error, but more likely is the result of the inevitable complexity in the catalog of a collection of any size: multiple authors, title main entries, corporate authors, complex filing rules—any one of these could have stumped our user. Likewise, once at the shelf the user understandably could be confused by the call number (particularly if the library is a large one with several possible locations for any given number) or by the arrangement of shelving. Not all the user's problems are our fault. Some are, however, and even those that are not are problems only we can solve. The library has a responsibility to ensure availability, especially because typically our users can find barely half of what they need that we do, in fact, own.

There are other instances of library "failure" than are mentioned in Kantor's study, which deals exclusively with books. Periodicals present their own set of problems—latest complete volumes being at the bindery, single issues missing (perhaps being claimed, perhaps not), single issues of weeklies being lost somewhere in the library, a high likelihood of current issues of popular periodicals being in use at any given moment. An increasingly significant cause of user frustration, however, is the deteriorating physical condition of library materials. The brittle condition of acidic book paper in a large share of the collection, the heavy use a core of the collection receives, theft and mutilation, and the more or less petty depredations suffered by books at the hands of highlighters, sticky fingers, and our own book drops either make books virtually unusable or cause us to set them aside into safe but inaccessible storage. The subject of preservation, maintenance, weeding, and renewal will be covered in chapter 8.

There are user failures, too, which are no surprise to librarians. They misread catalogs, miscopy call numbers, overlook (or fail to understand) location designations such as "folio" or "reference," or misunderstand our signs and directions. Librarians have been known to make the same kinds of mistakes and even in their own libraries. Libraries are complex places; catalogs and periodical indexes are complex tools. We should not be surprised that users have problems and make mistakes but should take active steps to help users before they have stumbled. Library use instruction programs are as important to collection management as to reference and information services.

These problems affect different users in various ways. Undergraduates are most affected when material in the core collection is checked out, mutilated, defaced, or worn out. Public library patrons likewise will have problems with very popular materials or materials on popular subjects. Scholars and advanced graduate students on the other hand will be more affected by the deterioration of research materials. Different libraries, then, will have different problems, or the same problems but in different degrees, and will want to take different measures to deal with them.

We have an obligation to maintain the availability of our collections, to assign personnel to this work, and to budget for it. Libraries do not yet have a clear idea of what the costs of a maintenance-and-preservation-for-availability program might be. They are likely to be steep. But as in any other situation, preventive maintenance of collections is cheaper than fixing up after the roof has caved in. Several steps can be taken. Circulation and reshelving policies and procedures can be improved, that is, brought into line with what is appropriate for the particular library. To deal with binding tie-ups, libraries could contract for faster work (perhaps at a greater cost to the library, but a justifiable cost) or set up their own binderies. Inventories are common in small libraries, uncommon or nonexistent in large ones: large ones should rethink their policy here. Shelf reading, no one's favorite activity, is very important and in busy libraries must be thorough and continuous. Procedures for replacing mutilated and lost items must be implemented: hand-wringing does not help. Every library, not just the large research libraries or those with special collections, needs a repair and preservation program. Collections must be reviewed and programs for regular repair and replacement set up; particularly important for core collections—collections of perennially popular or constantly used materials—is to set up a collection renewal program.

Circulation. We pride ourselves on our healthy collections, our open-access shelving, and our liberal circulation policies. Justifiably so. The book is to be used, and to be used best it must often be taken home. Once out of the library, however, and in someone's home or office it can no longer be used by anyone else. One person's satisfaction is another's frustration. We try to compromise between the two needs by shortening loan periods, recalling loaned books when needed by someone else, fining people who keep loans too long, and establishing reserve and reference limited-circulation collections. Once the borrowed book comes back the problems are not over; it still has to be returned to the shelf in good time and maintained in good, usable condition.

This whole operation includes the obvious function of recording loans, but also the reserve collection, duplicating copies when needed, spotting books needing repair as they return from borrowers, reshelving, interlibrary loan, document delivery, and managing the storage system. Sometimes known as access services, these ought to be thought of as availability services. In many libraries they are fragmented and separate from decisions about which books go into reference, into restricted circulation, or receive maintenance and preservation work. Management is not the concern at this point in the discussion, however; the point is that we recognize that there is a whole complex of related functions. Who is to manage them, how they are to be coordinated, the degree of centralization and automation are really local decisions to be based on the size, personnel, and history of each library.

Regulation of Borrowing. The main function of circulation is to check out books, or so we commonly think. Michael Buckland in *Book Availability and the Library User* suggests instead that we should think of it as regulation of borrowing.[21] His view has considerable merit, particularly as more and more libraries install automated

---

21. Michael K. Buckland, *Book Availability and the Library User* (New York: Pergamon, 1975).

circulation systems that seem to allow more flexibility and variety of regulation than traditional manual systems. There always have been options in circulation practices, but they were limited by the nature of the system. They did serve a regulatory purpose, however, and so went beyond simply recording who had what. The purpose has been to manage availability for both those who have the materials checked out and for those who might want them soon. Borrowers must be allowed adequate time with the material they have borrowed, while others must be able to reasonably expect to receive the materials without undue delay; we should not have to harass borrowers with recall notices nor frustrate potential borrowers with vague promises.

How can a circulation system regulate borrowing so that we can serve both sets of users? Buckland discussed the results of his research into the regulatory possibilities of circulation systems, chiefly the shortening of the loan period (see especially chapter seven). If we shorten the loan period, do we frustrate the borrowers, do we increase renewals, do we really increase the use of books? Buckland found encouraging results—no, no, and yes. Borrowers, he found, return books at the last minute before they are due, no matter how long or short the loan period. Shortening the loan from a semester to three or even two weeks did not inconvenience borrowers, not did it cause them to renew books more frequently than when they had a semester-long loan. On the other hand, the shorter loan period did in fact increase the rate of availability: more books were available on the shelf when users asked for them when the shorter loan period was in effect. Buckland's research has seemingly provided important proof and has been verified in other studies, such as that of Saracevic, White, and Kantor.

Along with adjusting the loan period, what else can we do to regulate borrowing effectively and purposefully? Automated circulation systems seem on the one hand to allow us to make very precise adjustments in loan periods and on the other to gather data that we can use to make effective management decisions. The check-out aspect of circulation can be adjusted in a variety of ways. Loan periods can easily be varied according to the status of the user (undergraduate or faculty member, adult reader or school student, taxpayer or non-resident), by the subject matter or format of the material (fiction might have a shorter loan period than philosophy, sheet music shorter than books, current materials shorter than older materials), or by special circumstances. In academic libraries we might make loan periods shorter after the halfway point of the semester than before; in public libraries we might reduce the loan period on tax materials from February through April or extend the period for fiction during the summer vacation season. Whatever our decisions, we now have choices, and the choice enables us to regulate circulation to enhance availability and, increasingly, to take individual cases into account.

Many variables mean many decisions and much oversight. Complex technology has created a complex situation that in turn requires making complex decisions after considerable thought and consultation. Perhaps the subtly complex system leaves users hopelessly confused and our gain in control is offset by a loss of goodwill. A whole new area of library operation has opened up that needs more concentrated attention than it has yet received. Loan policies and procedures, flexible yet firm restrictions and enforcements, discrimination among materials, subjects, types of users and uses, wants and needs, all must be thought through, cleared with proper authorities and sounding boards, and then publicized and implemented sensibly. The fact that so-called lockout provisions have not been used to their fullest potential yet indicates that our management has not kept up with our technology: we have not yet decided what to do, whom to do it to or for, when to do it, or even why to do it.[22]

Duplicate Copies and Strengthened Collections. Other obvious ways to increase availability of popular items are to buy additional copies and to build up heavily used collections. In his analysis of availability, Michael Buckland included the effects of duplicate copies (see his chapter 8). It is standard practice to buy additional copies of bestsellers, scholarly and popular classics, and curriculum perennials. We do not always, however, learn of the need for duplicates soon enough. An automated system should be able to identify books for which there are several hold or recall requests or that have been loaned frequently within a short time span and could then trigger an automatic suggestion to order duplicates. Circulation data also could be used to discover areas of the collection receiving high use, and knowing this we then could consider adding to allocations for those subjects. Allocations must be based on publication patterns and quantities, users' needs as we understand them, and actual use of the collection. Promptness in replacing lost or deteriorated copies, adding duplicates, and strengthening high-use subject areas will increase availability and user satisfaction and can be achieved with an effective system. Materials budgets

---

22. Henry J. DuBois, "From Leniency to Lockout," *College & Research Libraries News* 47 (1986): 698–702.

must, however, include allocations for duplicates and replacements.

Reserve Collections. Reserve collections in academic libraries provide ready access to, and assure availability of, items on course reading lists. In most cases they allow only short-term loan, typically two hours, and are revised every term. By including a permanent reserve collection of constantly needed titles they also function as a limited core collection. Reserve operations do require separate personnel and space and thus can be quite costly. They also present several minor problems, such as teachers bringing in their lists at the last minute or producing lists based more on hope and delusion than on realistic assessment of their students' needs and interests. If librarians can freely add material to reserve lists in response to demand at reference desks, then they have better control over the efficacy of the reserve operation. A budget for additional copies and close cooperation between reserve and reference, as well as effective communication between reserve and faculty, will assure that the right materials are kept available.

Reshelving and Shelf Maintenance. Although it may be, as William J. Hubbard says in *Stack Management,* that most libraries consider stack management a part of circulation, many others do not.[23] Where it is in the administrative chart is not so important as what it is and whether it gets done. Without it, materials in the collection simply will not be available. Stack management consists of four broad activities: paging or retrieval, shelving and reshelving, shelf reading and stack maintenance, and monitoring.

While open-stack libraries have made paging much less common than formerly, on the other hand the increase in storage systems will require efficient retrieval operations. Regular, quick, accurate retrieval from and return to storage of materials will be required, especially as storage systems increasingly include materials that continue to receive predictably regular use. Storage, as explained previously, will no longer be solely for unused materials but will be for materials that it is more cost effective to store remotely and retrieve on demand than to store in the main (and more expensive) facility.

New materials must be placed and already held materials reshelved as they are returned. Because collections are very dynamic—always growing, always growing irregularly—stack management must deal with them as constantly changing things. Where relative classification

---

23. William J. Hubbard, *Stack Management: A Practical Guide to Shelving and Maintaining Library Collections* (Chicago: American Library Association, 1981), p. viii.

is used and new materials must be interfiled with old, shifting becomes a constant problem, particularly because different parts of the collection grow at different rates. At least parts of a growing collection must be moved fairly frequently: new wings, different configurations of shelving within existing buildings, new storage facilities all mean major moves.

Reshelving itself is an operation that requires efficiency. The time it takes for a returned book to move through circulation, to the appropriate staging area, and then to the shelf must be as fast as possible; furthermore, books must be accessible during this process. Materials used in-house, likewise, must be picked up regularly and frequently, quickly staged and sorted, and quickly reshelved. That the reshelving also must be accurate goes without saying, although librarians must recognize the inherent managerial problem of combining speed with accuracy. We must be sure to provide our shelving staff with thorough training, ensure constant oversight, and reward them for their important work.

We know that open-access shelving means a higher incidence of misshelved materials because users replace things themselves and disarrange them as they retrieve what they need. The increasing need in mature collections for shifts and moves causes considerable disarray and disorder on the shelves, no matter how carefully the shifts are managed. We must care for the materials while on the shelf, straighten fallen books, replace bookends, shift books so that tall ones are well supported (while maintaining proper order), dust, and clean away litter.

This matter of shelf reading and shelf maintenance probably receives inadequate attention in most libraries; it is costly in time and personnel, it does not meet an immediate need (unlike shelving), it is not interesting work, and it usually is a low priority, left for less busy times. Where it is carried on, the workers usually are part-time and temporary, undertrained, high-school or college students. Effective personnel management is important. The work is far from exciting or challenging but it is vitally important. Highly centralized, bureaucratic management is probably not so effective as more personalized, decentralized management. Giving individuals fairly broad responsibility for specific parts of the collection might produce high-quality shelf reading and maintenance.

To plan for shifts and moves, to accommodate growth, and to catch problems of maintenance before they reach insolvable levels, we must monitor the stacks. Regular surveys of materials on the shelves, measurement of the number of new volumes arriving, and recording use data for the various parts of the collection should help to keep us abreast of the collection's growth and change. Spread sheets, such as those described by Lawrence Auld in *Electronic Spreadsheets for Libraries,* are an effective way both to both record and arrange the information so that it becomes usable in stack management.[24]

The larger and older the collection, the more complex its maintenance will be. Accessibility and availability must be the primary goals in stack management, yet growth and change, use in-house and out, physical deterioration, and more elaborate storage systems all combine and multiply to make collections less accessible and less available. Collection management cannot ignore these problems.

Selection for Storage.   Assuming that the library has developed a storage system, it next must develop procedures for assigning materials to storage and retrieving them when needed. Who will select and according to what criteria? What provisions are established for access, and what procedures for prompt retrieval? The main criteria are use (present and likely future), the kind of use, the cost of storage and retrieval versus the cost of retaining an item in the central library, and the nature of the collection. Some of these criteria are quantitative and can be readily identified. In fact, to the extent that assignment to storage is based on use measured by circulation and to the extent that retrieval is managed by the Circulation Department, then management of the storage system should be a function of this department.

Other criteria are qualitative, however, and here it is more appropriate that collection management librarians make storage decisions. The kind of use materials receive is a crucial factor: some materials must be consulted in person by users before their utility can be decided. Some materials must be browsed and their true usefulness cannot be determined from the catalog. Some collections are valuable precisely because they are coherent collections, not merely a shelf of discrete items. In each of these cases the decision takes into account the materials, the specific storage facility, and the provisions for users' access.

Interlibrary Loan.   Systematic use of interlibrary loans is a crucial part of collection management. Borrowing is not a shameful admission of one's collection's inadequacy or of personal failure in selection decisions, but is a simple fact of life. No one has everything; everyone has to borrow. We borrow what we do not have; we even borrow

---

24. Lawrence Auld, *Electronic Spreadsheets for Libraries* (Phoenix: Oryx, 1986), chapter 10.

what we do have but cannot get our hands on. We borrow materials in scope as well as out of it, at our self-defined level or at a higher or lower level, in print or out of print. We borrow for all users, even, increasingly, for undergraduates. Most libraries cannot buy everything their users need, whether they are undergraduates or the common reader, scholars or specialists. With books going out of print faster than ever, and with periodicals being so prolific, so specialized, and so expensive, it is unrealistic to resist providing interlibrary loans for any of our users. And if we borrow, we must lend, within the limits of practicality and fiscal responsibility.[25]

The issues probably are not controversial. What may give pause is the problem of making interlibrary loans a planned part of collection management. For this to happen, we must be able to assert that a specific title will be attained only through interlibrary loan, not through purchase, and to make this assertion we need both a firm grasp of our collection development policy and a precise, clear understanding of how each title in question does or does not fit it. After this we must know how long we can expect to wait for a borrowed item and how long it is reasonable to expect the user to wait. On the other side, we need a complex, varied interlibrary loan operation that can draw on various sources, as is appropriate and as needed. Our cooperative arrangements and our network and consortia memberships are crucial at this point.

If interlibrary loan is to be a regular part of our work, then we must recognize the requirements and costs of performing it well. Each library needs an adequately staffed operation, both to send out requests and to retrieve and send out loans. Increased traffic places burdens on everyone, and if the system is not to collapse under its own weight, requirements for accurate citations, care in handling, and rigorous attention to due dates are crucial. Reference librarians must help users find the accurate citation (or get it for them), staff must learn proper book-care techniques, and users must honor our regulations. Above all we must recognize the real and large costs for personnel, photocopying, postage, facsimile transmission, and fees. These are not considered permanent purchases but are placed in the same class as memberships and fees for networks, consortia, and utilities.

25. Geraldine King and Herbert F. Johnson, "Interlibrary Loan (ILL)," *Encyclopedia of Library and Information Science* 12 (1974): pp. 196–211, and Thomas J. Waldhart, "The Growth of Interlibrary Loan Among ARL University Libraries," *Journal of Academic Librarianship* 10 (1984): 204–08.

Document Delivery. Document delivery services take items to patrons outside the library. They also are costly and few libraries have instituted them on a wide scale. Technology has brought as yet only tantalizing possibilities, not reliable and financially bearable mechanisms. The collection manager, however, must acknowledge that delivery provides the ultimate in availability. Even if we do not yet think in terms of specific delivery services, we must increasingly consider document delivery as an alternative to document ownership. That is, we must think of ourselves serving as the channel or switching center through which documents pass on the way from their location to the user.

Special libraries, especially those in corporate or industrial settings, are more likely than other types to provide document delivery. Public libraries' bookmobiles and delivery to shut-ins are more an outreach service than a part of collection management, although the phone-reference services might be considered a kind of information-delivery service, if not quite a document delivery. Academic libraries have tried document delivery.[26] Perhaps academic librarians could compute costs for delivery the same way they do for retrieval from storage and set up either a regular service or guidelines for an ad hoc service. Logically, document delivery should be a regular feature in most libraries, but practically the costs seem excessive, especially when most users can simply visit the library where we have already done much to make materials readily accessible and available.

26. George D'Elia and Charla Hutkins, "Faculty Use of Document Delivery Services: The Results of a Survey," *Journal of Academic Librarianship* 12 (1986): 69–72.

Chapter 8

Preservation, Weeding, and Renewal

No collection is available if the materials in it are in such terrible physical condition that they cannot be used. Indeed it is an article of faith among librarians that access and availability are improved, and use thereby increased, when materials are in good physical condition and the shelves not cluttered with unnecessary volumes. Conclusive proof for this belief may be lacking, but we nevertheless continue to cite improved availability and increased use as the major justification for preservation and weeding activities. These are not our only justifications, of course, for the problem of deteriorating collections has, we now recognize, reached catastrophic proportion. The thought of weeding probably occurs to everyone who finds a shelf full of multiple copies of one-time best-sellers, especially when librarians are asking for more space to house their growing collections, but librarians (especially public librarians) have been weeding for years. What is new is the degree of awareness of both issues and the extent to which we are making preservation, maintenance, and weeding an integral part of our collection management programs. Important as selection is, we know that to ensure access and availability we must set up a process of continuous collection review.

Preservation and Maintenance

The only thing new about our present concerns with preservation is the size of the problem. Brittle paper, cracked bindings, mutilated periodicals, pages smudged and marked to illegibility; scratched records and microfilm, stretched tapes, faded prints; and, not sufficiently infrequently, fires, water leaks, dust, air pollution, heating and ventilating systems run amok—these are the signs along the road of

179

deteriorating collections. The materials we buy, the hard use they receive, and the way we keep them all contribute, and it is a hard truth that the best and most useful suffer more than the unwanted and unused. Deterioration is the most disheartening form of our collections' dynamic nature.

Bad as the brittle-books problem is, for a number of libraries it is less serious than other problems, such as defacement, mutilation, or simple wear and tear. Not that libraries were unaware before, but they did not always sense a crisis. Possibly, too, we downplayed maintenance work because it seemed too closely allied with the negative aspects of our profession's public image, that of the antiquarian, hoarding, parsimonious caretaker shrinking further into dingy corners with repair tape and glue, rather than with the image of the modern librarian out on the cutting edge of scholarly communication with researchers and computers, at the vital center of a web of information exchange, and reaching out into previously unserved communities with our latest paperbacks and films. What we recently have done is turn that dingy corner into a well-lit center of high-tech artisanship, staffed with Conservators and Preservation Officers, operating with funds from our newly budgeted Preservation Program. Good.

To slow, reverse, and rectify deterioration we must institute preservation programs, rationalize maintenance routines, and systematically renew the most heavily and regularly used part of our collections. These steps are expensive, lack the glamour of new-book selection, and do not contribute to our growth statistics. Nor do they catch the eye of institutional administrators. We must ourselves make the case for them, perhaps add to our annual statistics about volumes added and periodical subscriptions held the statistics for the number of volumes repaired, restored, duplicated, converted to microfilm, and identified in neighboring libraries, and acknowledge the important status of those librarians who do the work. The problem is worse than we think, and the cost more than we can pay; yet to fail will further decrease the availability of our collections.

The Problem: Physical Condition. About 150 years ago technology provided us with paper in abundance, all made with a highly acidic sizing and wood chips, that decayed gradually by itself and more quickly in reaction with ink, heat, high humidity, varying temperatures, sunlight, dust, and chemical air pollution. The decay takes the form of brittleness, so that turning pages causes them to break off, but even if left unused on the shelf book paper will crumble. The bindings also deteriorate. Their glue and paper dry up, turn brittle, crack, and pull away from the book block. When books were held together by over-sewing and magazines by staples, further damage was done; pages broke more easily and the metal increased deterioration.

Technology also provided new formats: edition binding, so-called cheap editions, paperbacks, the pamphlets of polemics and popular culture, newspapers, and magazines thrived on what we now know was bad paper and bad binding. Popular reading, schoolbooks, Bibles and documents of religious persuasion, political and social publication, scientific and technical writings, commercial prospectuses and advertising not only marked European and North American culture, they made it possible. In this country homesteaders were drawn west by pamphlets and prospectuses, while established cities developed with technology brought in on paper plans and were nourished on printed versions of European culture. Ironically, the efflorescence of print culture in the nineteenth century has turned out to be tragically impermanent.

To that flawed medium we have added problems of our own: overheated and high-humidity buildings designed for people not paper; inadequate air-conditioning systems that create radical swings in temperature and humidity and so alternately expand and contract paper and bindings; air polluted with dust, ashes, and chemicals that react with the acid in paper to increase deterioration; and a seemingly mad urge to get more and more people to use our collections more and more frequently. Probably the single most serious cause of book and periodical deterioration is handling, that is, use by patrons in the library and at home (not to mention environmental hazards between library and home), reshelving and shifting that knock books around in a variety of ways, book returns that drop book on top of book, crowded shelves where more and more books are jammed into less and less space, straitened budgets that do not allow for sufficient copies of high-demand titles nor an adequate binding schedule for periodicals. Bad environmental conditions and mishandling are multiplying factors in the formula for deterioration.

Nonpaper materials are no less vulnerable. Film scratches, tears, feeds mold, and fades. In addition microfilm, motion pictures, slides, filmstrips, and overhead transparencies also endure a great deal of use because of their educational value. Models and realia, however durable their materials, receive rough use and often haphazard storage. Sound records warp and scratch, and their grooves clog with dirt; tapes stretch and can be ruined by magnetism. Computer disks and tapes are equally vulnerable. Nothing lasts, and as with paper, the more use the more damage. Some specifics on the nature, most common problems, and storage requirements of the main library materials, as set out by Carolyn Clark Morrow in her *Preservation Challenge,* include:[1]

Paper
Should be alkaline at pH 7.5 or better; higher pH allows paper to compensate for pollution from acidic air and particles (ANSI standard).

Studies at Yale and the University of California, Berkeley, found that fully 86 percent of the book paper is highly acidic paper.

Paper can be deacidified. Individual leaves can be treated with homemade chemicals and large quantities of books can be treated with the Wei T'o Process, but truly large-scale deacidification technology, such as that being developed by the Library of Congress, will not be available until the early 1990s, and then only if current problems are solved.[2]

Acidic paper often turns brown with age and in interaction with other chemicals and sunlight; it also turns brittle.

Brittleness is measured by the "fold test." If a corner of a page breaks off after two double folds, the paper is brittle beyond repair. Brittle leaves will break away from bindings or simply crumble. Brittleness is not directly related to discoloration or other outward signs of deterioration. Brittle paper cannot be restored, but leaves or single sheets can be encapsulated or laminated; books cannot be restored.

At Yale, Stanford, and the University of California from 26 to 46 percent of the collection has brittle paper.

Film
Of the three kinds of film—silver halide, diazo, and vesicular— the first is most permanent, although easily scratched, and most expensive.

---

1. Carolyn Clark Morrow, *The Preservation Challenge: A Guide to Conserving Library Materials* (White Plains, N.Y.: Knowledge Industry, 1983); see also *Permanence of Paper for Printed Library Materials* (New York: American National Standards Institute, 1985).

2. Richard D. Smith, "Mass Deacidification: The Wei T'o Way," *College & Research Libraries News* 45 (1984): 588–93, and "Report on the Library of Congress DEZ Project," in *Association of Research Libraries. Minutes of the 109th Meeting, October 22–23, 1986, Washington, D.C.* (Washington, D.C.: Association of Research Libraries, 1987), pp. 81–88.

Permanency is of the film itself and of the image. Film can turn dry and crack, can be torn, scratched, burned, and melted; images fade, discolor, blur; color images lose their brilliancy and integrity.

Storage is best in cool, dry, dark boxes, cans, and drawers, with further protection from scratches and tension stress.

Digital tape and disk

Magnetic processes can be altered by magnetic fields, optical processes by handling, heat, chemicals; tapes can stretch and tear, disks break and scratch.

Careful handling by staff and users is essential; protective storage is necessary.

To this deterioration add deliberate mutilation and theft and ignorant misuse. We are plagued by highlighters, by scholars and others leaving a trail of marginalia, underlinings, and a variety of smudges from coffee stains, cigarette burns, ink-blots, and food crumbs, among the more speakable debris, by carelessness in rain and snow, with pets, with hot surfaces and humid corners. Worse, though, is deliberate mutilation, a supremely selfish and antisocial act; not only does it rob other users of an article or illustration, but it always takes the best and most asked for. Sometimes mutilated pages can be replaced, at a considerable cost in photocopying and skilled, labor-intensive work, but mutilation often breaks bindings and thus initiates a worse deterioration. Incidence varies from library to library. One study found that 15 percent of education periodical issues had suffered mutilation, but it did not examine books and did not study periodicals in other known high-damage subjects, such as sociology, business, and literary criticism. The inconvenience to users is considerable, for another study found that more than 70 percent had encountered ripped-out articles.[3] How to prevent mutilation and what to do to rectify it are perennial and important issues.

Opinion varies on prevention. Assuming that we want to maintain open access, then we must rely on users' goodwill and can do little more than inform them of the problem through exhibits, newspaper

---

3. Mary Noel Gouke and Marjorie Murfin, "Periodical Mutilation: The Insidious Disease," *Library Journal* 105 (September 15, 1980): 1795–97, and Carroll Varner, "Journal Mutilation in Academic Libraries," *Library & Archival Security* 5 (4) (Winter 1983): 19–29.

stories, and signs in the stacks, and provide inexpensive photocopiers as close to the stacks as possible (with change machines and some provision for small emergency loans). These steps work to an extent. More restrictive steps include converting bound volumes to microfilm and setting up a serviced, closed stack periodical operation, but the cost of these might be higher than that of the problem, both in actual dollars and in diminished access. We must, however, make every effort to replace and repair the damaged books and periodicals. If it is our best material that suffers, we must make our best effort to keep it accessible and available.

Theft is a more rational problem. Thieves steal for money; libraries contain valuable books and pictures; therefore they steal from us. Conventional security measures can go a long way toward preventing theft, although these often seem incompatible with traditional attitudes and practices favoring open access and a minimum of supervision. Some people do steal simply to avoid checking materials out and this is a problem, too. Modern magnetic security systems and sealed-window buildings may have reduced this kind of petty theft. Still, there seems to be a remarkable number of items missing from our shelves, although this, like mutilation, is something that seems to vary from library to library.[4]

The Preservation Program. At the moment we know the problem and its causes, but we have not yet been able to do much to arrest it. The difficult thing is to move from consciousness raising to effective action. Our buildings are built, our use statistics are up, our budgets are down, and the manufacturers and publishers are insufficiently concerned (their job is to produce and sell, ours to buy and preserve). Old libraries with a central core of bookstacks were book ovens that baked and baked; modern modular libraries are humid arenas intermingling book and reader; the library of the future may well have an air-conditioned stack area separated from users, as well as adjunct storage facilities that are heavily air-conditioned and inhospitable to people. Paper manufacturers are producing more non-acidic book paper; sewing, gluing, and casing technology has been reformed; we may well manufacture different formats according to different standards of physical quality and distinguish between use and preservation formats. Digitalization seems a promising technology for preservation and even for certain kinds of use, while there is

---

4. Marvine Brand, ed., *Security for Libraries: People, Buildings, Collections,* (Chicago: American Library Association, 1984).

renewed confidence in microfilm.[5] All this is the future, though, and does not help us to get from here to there nor to help us reclaim the past.

Libraries must develop preservation programs—all libraries. Large research libraries and large public libraries may suffer from this problem most acutely, having both a large deteriorating collection and a large body of users still hoping to find the collections available, but every library—school, college, corporate, rural—has and will continue to acquire materials that are more likely to deteriorate than not. A preservation program, however, is not simply a conservation operation; the latter may be included but most likely only in the best-funded libraries. We can do much that does not require expensive, sophisticated personnel and materials. During the past decade large university and research libraries have been drawing up preservation programs, so that we now have a fairly clear picture of what should be done.[6] Other libraries can use these examples to make up their own programs to fit their specific needs and budgets. True, the costs of a full-scale, highly aggressive program probably are enormous and far beyond the means of most libraries. The more the emphasis in these programs is on prevention rather than restoration, however, the more likely will the costs be bearable and the results truly beneficial.

Before setting up the program we must ascertain the extent of the problem in our library, draw up realistic goals that take into account what we can afford to do and what is appropriate for our library, prioritize these goals so that we can tackle the most important first, and devise fairly specific plans for individual parts of the collection, for different parts have different needs. Above all, we must relate the preservation program to the collection development policy.

We know the problem is large, but we do not really know the exent of the problem in each individual library. Virtually all paper in a library of any age at all will be highly acidic paper, but the degree of incapacitating brittleness varies because of the unique history of environmental conditions, extent of use, and the care of the staff. The extent of the preservation problem is part of the character of each collection and each subsection within collections. We want to know the kinds of preservation problems we face, the extent of each in quantitative terms, that is, both numbers of items and degree of

---

5. Alan Calmes, "New Confidence in Microfilm," *Library Journal* 111 (September 15, 1986): 38–42.

6. Jan Merrill-Oldham and Merrily Smith, eds., *The Library Preservation Program: Models, Priorities, Possibilities* (Chicago: American Library Association, 1985).

damage done, and we want to know how this all sorts by various parts. Are periodicals generally in better shape than books, books better than films, travel better than fiction, scholarly studies better than primary texts, etc.? Several libraries have surveyed their collections for preservation needs, and the results are summarized in Carolyn Clark Morrow's *Preservation Challenge.*[7] The methodology and broad outline of these collection reviews are as important to us as the specific details.

Each library must set its own goals, and these must be realistic. Neither despair nor overarching ambition is appropriate. Regardless of its size, a library can take reasonable, cost-effective steps to prevent or slow down deterioration, and probably will already be doing repair and maintenance. The goals must be realistic, but just as important they must be appropriate. Reference at this point to the collection development policy is extremely important, as well as reference to the library's mission, current use statistics, and likely future emphases. It makes no sense to set aside time and personnel to deal with materials in a subject that is no longer studied or is long since out of favor with the public. Although a preservation program will draw on the expertise of conservators (whether directly as staff members or indirectly through workshops and handbooks), its scope and goals are developed by the collection management librarians.

Knowing the magnitude of the local problem and setting realistic goals that are consistent with the collection development policy, the library is ready to start up its preservation program. The program contains four major segments, each with its own elements:

Prevention
1. Improved climate control in buildings
2. Disaster plan
3. Staff and user education

Cooperation
1. Active participation in cooperative preservation arrangements with other libraries
2. Quick and precise bibliographic control of items that are being converted or conserved

---

7. Morrow, pp. 178–80.

Repair and Conservation
1. Active and purposeful maintenance program
2. Regular commercial binding
3. A variety of conservation operations, including format conversion such as microfilming
4. Trained and conscientious staff adequately supported with salary, supplies, equipment, and continuing education

Administration
1. Clear, firm place in the library's administration, with authority and responsibility
2. Personnel committed to it
3. Ongoing segments and special project segments
4. Cost analysis and realistic budget

Prevention. Most problems are more easily prevented than corrected, usually more cheaply, too. While prevention does not undo the damage, it will prevent more. Knowing what causes deterioration, we should be able to take several steps to prevent it. We should select materials that will last in the environment and with the use that occurs in libraries. Knowing how heat, humidity, light, and rough handling magnify inherent tendencies toward deterioration, we must manage, modify, or build suitable buildings and educate ourselves and library users in proper handling. Prevention is first of all an attitudinal matter, and once attitudes are changed then most of the rest will follow.

Climate control in buildings is one very effective way to preserve our materials. Inadequate controls can directly cause problems such as foxing and mildew, and they accelerate the deterioration of badly made materials. In too many buildings, climate control is either run by remote control, run by people not directly connected with the library, or run by hope and patience, hope that the weather will cool off and patient bearing up until it does. We know what the ideal temperature and humidity are for paper and for film, and in most buildings we know what to do to achieve these conditions (or at least a reasonable compromise between human and paper needs): what we do not always have is the money to convert an inadequate climate system to one that works or the personnel to give it the constant attention it needs. Existing construction can be converted, but the high cost of doing so might not be justified by the return in preserved collections. Compromise and make-do might be the only steps we can take toward effective climate control. The minimum to strive for is stability.

The prospect of new buildings or wings or major reconstruction, however, gives us the opportunity to include proper climate controls in the design; considering the dollar value of collections there is no reason an effective case cannot be made for including this feature in all new construction. Unfortunately, what librarians know is not always what institutional administrators and architects know, so our needs, which will add to construction costs but reduce collection maintenance costs, must be stated clearly and effectively in terms they can understand. Metcalf on *Planning Academic and Research Library Buildings* includes current information and standards for temperature (65 degrees), humidity (50 percent), light (maximum ideal ultraviolet radiation), and air filtering, as well as giving valuable advice about how library buildings differ from other kinds of buildings.[8]

A disaster plan is easy enough to set up, if one follows the sound advice available in John Morris's *The Library Disaster Preparedness Handbook*.[9] No library is immune to the kind of disaster that can seriously damage large parts of collections. True, not many libraries exist in imminent danger of earthquakes and mudslides, and most are built well enough to withstand huricanes and tornadoes, so that "disaster" involving serious loss of life and damage to structures may be unlikely. Nevertheless, a host of more limited disasters occur regularly everywhere. Broken water pipes, leaking roofs, flooded basements, electrical fires accompanied by smoke, water, and chemical damage, collapsed walls, roofs, and floors are the stuff of everyday life in all buildings. People can get out of the way; books cannot. Disaster plans have less to do with evacuation procedures, although these should be included, than with names of emergency personnel to call, steps to take to protect books on the shelves and the materials with which to do so, some experience in these steps and with these materials (that is, training sessions), and, less easy to develop for many libraries, places to take damaged material for fast emergency treatment. Easy as it is to set up a disaster plan, it is not necessarily so easy to carry out such a plan when disaster strikes. Practical advice from those who have

---

8. Keyes D. Metcalf, *Planning Academic and Research Library Buildings,* 2nd ed., by Philip D. Leighton and David C. Weber (Chicago: American Library Association, 1986), *Preservation Planning Manual* (Washington, D.C.: Association of Research Libraries, 1982), and *RLG Preservation Manual* (Stanford: Research Libraries Group, 1983).

9. John Morris, *The Library Disaster Preparedness Handbook* (Chicago: American Library Association, 1986).

suffered is invaluable, and the Cunhas' book and bibliography, *Library and Archives Conservation,* is helpful.[10]

User and staff education can have immediate positive effects in slowing deterioration. Assuming that most improper handling is inadvertent, then telling people how to handle materials becomes one of our major responsibilities. User education must be continual because people forget (and in school and academic libraries students are constantly changing). Education also must occur as close to the site of use as possible, and it must be pedagogically sensible. Bookmarks, signs, informational handouts, or even oral reminders from circulation personnel; training sessions for shelvers; technical processing; and professional staff followed by proper supervision. A degree of strict enforcement also may be necessary, in the form of keeping food and drink out of stacks and reading areas, fining patrons returning damaged books, and prosecuting thieves and vandals (if we can catch them). One hard fact, however, is that we must work hard to replace and repair mutilated, defaced, and stolen materials: angry as these make us, we cannot hide behind a sense of righteous indignation and neglect to undo the damage. For one thing, there is evidence that mutilation breeds more mutilation; for another, our job is not to blame and complain but to make materials available. User education, then, must be effectively managed.

Maintenance, Repair, and Conservation. If use causes the most damage to library materials, then a regular and systematic maintenance program is a key feature in an overall preservation program. We must repair the damage and take what steps we can to minimize further damage. This is actually one area in which libraries have long been effective, and most libraries do have repair facilities, personnel, and work routines. To these should be added the use of proper materials and techniques. This whole maintenance operation can be divided into the following functions: shelf maintenance, reshelving, on-site repair, in-house repair, binding and rebinding (in-house and con-tracted), format conversion, and conservation.

Each library must have a knowledgeable staff, that staff must select the appropriate treatment for items, and the treatment must be per-formed according to the latest standards for permanent materials and techniques. Selection for preservation is as important as original selec-tion for purchase, and the former like the latter must adhere to a collection development policy and must be based on an understanding

10. George M. Cunha and Dorothy Grant Cunha, *Library and Archives Conserva-tion: 1980 and Beyond,* 2v. (Metuchen: Scarecrow, 1983).

of different kinds of materials and categories of users and uses as well as on the character of the local library. Three basic decisions must be made. First, we must decide whether to keep an item at all and invest time and money in it. Second, we must decide whether to keep this item in its original format or convert it into some other media, such as microfilm. Third, we must decide which treatment is appropriate, whether converting or conserving. To make these decisions, we must have good information about costs and an understanding of our library's needs. In academic libraries, this understanding should include:[11]

> academic activity, the strength of historical collections, the cost and cost-effectiveness of specific preservation activities, knowledge of alternatives to in-house preservation, and an understanding of disciplinary patterns of information use.

School and special libraries are more likely to need only current materials and to have little need for preservation. They will need mending and binding, of course, but they should be able to rely on academic and some public libraries for historical materials. Public libraries have more complex circumstances to deal with. Certainly local history materials, whatever archives the library is responsible for, and a limited number of rare treasures require true preservation; beyond that, however, the extent to which extensive preservation is to be undertaken depends on exactly the points listed previously, translated from academic programs to public users and their concerns. Policy, and the accompanying program whatever its extent, must govern.

Shelf maintenance should be a part of regular shelf reading duty, during which damaged books are pulled, and potential damaging situations cleaned up (missing bookends replaced, too-tight books given room, dusting). Climate conditions in various parts of the library could be monitored by reshelving staff. It is important to stop damage before it gets worse: one of the most common problems with books is covers that pull away from endpapers. Regluing is inexpensive and quick. Torn headbands and spines are other easily mended problems. Large libraries could decentralize this simple repair, setting up small work centers on-site in branch libraries and various departments. On

---

11. Dan C. Hazen, "Collection Development, Collection Management, and Preservation," *Library Resources & Technical Services* 26 (1982): 3–11.

the other hand, mending is sometimes as easily undone as done and it may pay to send heavily used books to be completely rebound. Costs here can be calculated, and the costs of duplicate or replacement copies can be factored in as well. A good time to spot damaged books is during the reshelving process, both in circulation departments and in staging areas where materials used in-house are gathered. As suggested earlier, management that places more responsibility in the hands of the people actually doing stack management work, that is, the shelvers, might improve both their morale and the condition of the collection. Hubbard's *Stack Management* offers valuable guidance on this aspect of a maintenance program.[12]

Treatment requires a local mending operation, and that operation, a staple of every library, must use materials, procedures, and techniques that meet the latest standards for preservation. Much that we used to do we now know is damaging, and some of the techniques we know are costly, although we can hope for prices to decrease as the market for proper materials increases. More and more handbooks and manuals with up-to-date information are becoming available. Jane Greenfield's *Books: Their Care and Repair* is one of several recommended books included in Lynn Westbrook's article, "Developing an In-House Preservation Program: A Survey of Experts."[13] The scope of the local mending operations varies from library to library. In some it consists of first aid to regluing endpapers, headbands, and spines; in others, major repair up to actual rebinding; and in still others actual conservation work in which books are disbound, paper cleaned, deacidified, or encapsulated, and bindings reconstructed. In almost all, however, the local operation relies on both commerical binderies and conservation centers. The local mending operation is, thus, probably the place where decisions about preservation treatments should be made (in consultation with subject specialists when appropriate).

Preservation concerns enter into regular maintenance and binding. Materials and procedures must be acid-free, permanent, nondamaging, and safe for workers. There should be someone knowledgeable about binding technology on the library staff to recommend certain binding practices and to contract knowledgeably. Library binders have traditionally bound for strength rather than for permanence, but

---

12. William J. Hubbard, *Stack Management: A Practical Guide to Shelving and Maintaining Library Collections* (Chicago: American Library Association, 1981).
13. Jane Greenfield, *Books: Their Care and Repair* (New York: Wilson, 1983), and Lynn Westbrook, "Developing an In-House Preservation Program: A Survey of Experts," *Library & Archival Security* 7 (3–4) (Fall/Winter 1985): 1–21.

increasingly they are able to provide suitable strength as well as realistic permanence. The classic problem of binding periodicals so that they can be easily and safely photocopied must be addressed.

Binding operations are crucial for virtually all libraries, even for those that rely on microfilm for back volumes of periodicals. There are always materials that have to be bound and kept in paper— periodical indexes, for example, as well as certain very high-use periodicals, some paperback books, and books to be rebound. Michael Buckland's study of access availability, cited in chapter seven, calculated the payoff in availability of taking out more expensive contracts for faster binding turnaround and for setting up in-house binding operations.[14] Each library has its own situation to deal with, so each library must make its own calculations. Cheapest is not always best, either for the binding work itself or for our users. Tiered binding operations or contracts might be considered that would get some materials such as abstracting and indexing periodicals back sooner than others, whether this rush work was performed by a modest in-house binding operation or through a more expensive contract with a commercial binder.

The cost in availability must be acknowledged. Books sent for mending or binding obviously cannot be used, but neither can books too fragile or defaced. Efficiency, speed, and accurate records ensure the least time off the shelf and precise information about where an item is in the mending process. Regular and systematic shelf maintenance recognizes that problems soonest identified are soonest mended, as well as cheapest. First-aid maintenance can be scheduled to put materials back on the shelf within 24 hours. Binding contracts can emphasize, and pay the price of, fast turnaround. Repair or replacement of mutilated materials, purchase of added copies and microfilm backups, and rebinding instead of repair all add to our costs. We must recognize this cost and build it into our budgets.

When we decide to convert deteriorating paper into some other media—format conversion—we have several options, chief of which at the moment is microfilming. While we have not yet convinced users (nor ourselves) that microfilm or microfiche is a pleasure to use and have not made it a true alternative to printed paper for ordinary use, librarians must acknowledge its utility as a preservation format.

---

14. Michael K. Buckland, *Book Availability and the Library User* (New York: Pergamon, 1975).

Properly produced, used, and stored, film is a major defense against deterioration. Other options are preservation photocopying and reprints on long-life paper and the potential of digitalization technologies. A strong case was made for digitalization and much hope held out for it, but at this time we do not have the assurance that it is indeed permanent, neither the digitalized image nor the equipment to retrieve it.[15] Paper can be very durable, not to mention usable, and the National Archives and Records Administration has reaffirmed its archival value.[16] Film, digitalization, and paper combine to give us an array of preservation formats from which we can choose according to user needs as well as a format's physical characteristics.

Preservation microfilming must be carried out according to production as well as storage and use standards, and it requires wide cooperation to ensure that we film what deserves filming, do so as economically as possible, and provide adequate bibliographic access. Cooperation is especially important, and several cooperative projects now under way, as described by Nancy Gwinn in *Preservation Microfilming*, are models of effective work.[17] Not only are microfilming projects costly in time and materials, but the difficult decisions about exactly what to film require expert judgment, best achieved through cooperation among professionals in several libraries and in conjunction with relevant learned societies. The Research Libraries Group, the American Philological Society, and the American Theological Library Association are all working on cooperative projects through which there are mutual plans about what to copy, assurance that copies will be purchased (or costs shared in some other way), and good bibliographic control. Improvements in the *Library of Congress Catalog of Microfilm Masters* will in time also serve the whole library community.

For most materials in most libraries intellectual content is the most important consideration, so conversion of deteriorated material to any suitable alternative media makes perfect sense.[18] Even basic mending alters formats somewhat and is, therefore, preservation of the contents not the format. Preservation of the format, the object itself, is called

15. Clifford A. Lynch and Edwin B. Brownrigg, "Conservation, Preservation, and Digitalization," *College & Research Libraries* 47 (1986): 379–82.

16. Calmes, "New Confidence in Microfilm."

17. Nancy E. Gwinn, ed., *Preservation Microfilming: A Guide for Librarians and Archivists* (Chicago: American Library Association, 1987).

18. Gay Walker, "Preserving the Intellectual Content of Deteriorated Library Materials," in Morrow, *The Preservation Challenge*, pp. 93–113.

for when that item is of particular value in and of itself. Rare book treasures, association copies, and materials of great local interest are obvious candidates for preservation. We should not, however, over-look the growing scholarly interest in the formats through which information, knowledge, and creative literature have passed. We cannot study, understand, or honor intellectual achievements of the past without due consideration of the complex contexts in which they took shape and were presented to readers or auditors, and this context included the format itself, the ways it was presented to the public. For example, science-fiction novels in expensive permanent-paper reprints do not recapture the often lurid, certainly nontraditional appearance and special appeal of the paperback originals, bought in out-of-the-way stores, read in privacy, and shared only with a select few sympathetic friends. If academic libraries serve scholars who are interested in this context, it is public libraries that have built the original collections: both academic and public libraries, then, have an obliga-tion to deal with the physical form as well as the intellectual content of their collections. We must not ignore the things themselves, which is to say that the choice between format and contents is not a simple one and we should not slip into simplistic thinking about it.

If the format is not to be altered, then conservation itself must be undertaken, either locally or commercially. An ambitious conser-vation laboratory is not for every library, although every library should be aware of where the nearest (or most suitable) one is located. Many libraries should look toward either setting up a conservation lab or providing the regular mending department with staff, materials, and expertise to do some local work. There is much that can be done effectively and knowledgeably. It is likely, in fact, that basic mending operations will develop into conservation labs simply because we now know the crucial role that proper mending plays in preservation programs. Timely mending can prevent serious, costly damage and deterioration and is far less time-consuming than conservation work or even commercial rebinding. With more and more conservators being trained there will be more and more basic practical advice and help more widely available. There are several centers that do such work and several programs that train conservators.[19]

Administration.   No program can be successful without adminis-trative commitment to it, and this is especially true of a preservation program that should combine, or draw on, several operations in the

19. Cunha and Cunha, vol. 1, "Appendix."

library, some traditional, others new. Preservation is not a frill, not devoted only to rare treasures or special collections, but applies to the entire collection and subsumes traditional maintenance, binding and mending, and subject specialist work. An administrative commitment must include a realistic budget (although at this time we know so little about costs that it is difficult to define "realistic"), adequate personnel properly trained and definitely committed to preservation, clear authority within the various administrative lines, and responsibility for success. The exact configuration of personnel will depend on the scope of the program and its specializations, but in any program the personnel should develop projects and plans. Projects have beginnings and ends, clear objectives, and clear accountability measures; plans provide long-term direction for projects and operations within the program. A preservation officer (manager, administrator, coordinator, head) will be responsible for winning the budget, coordinating the various personnel and their projects, maintaining smooth working of the ongoing operations, and dealing with other administrators in the library.

More difficult than assessing damage is determining costs realistically and then finding the means to pay them. Several libraries have undertaken ambitious preservation programs and as a result we have some idea of what the costs will be. Testifying before a Congressional subcommittee in the spring of 1987, David C. Weber, representing the American Library Association and the Association of Research Libraries, pointed out that libraries now are devoting about five percent of their budgets to preservation.[20] Prevention costs are not overwhelming, especially because they include the costs of the traditional activities of mending and binding. If, however, we seek to rectify a century and a half of deterioration, no library can afford to work alone. Cooperative action with some sort of assistance from foundations and the federal government is necessary.

What still must be done, however, is to calculate accurate local figures so that we can estimate what a given sum—for instance, $10,000—will produce in preservation or cost in further damage if not spent. Such costs also must be factored into the deliberations about setting up storage systems and cooperative collection management arrangements among libraries. We still do not have a good analysis of

---

20. David C. Weber, "Brittle Books in Our Nation's Libraries," *College & Research Libraries News* 48 (1987): 238–44, and "Preservation Programs: The Fiscal Support at Stanford and Other North American Libraries," in *Library Preservation Program*, pp. 88–92.

actual per-item preservation costs, nor of the cost of not doing anything, although Patricia McClung gathered accurate figures on the costs
in one preservation program, which was a real step toward accurate
understanding.[21]

National Cooperation. No matter how good the local program,
true preservation success needs national cooperation and national
planning. No library can afford to go it alone; every library that seeks
special funding will have to call on others to help justify its special
claims; all libraries will rely on collective professional information and
knowledge. Cooperative microfilming projects, cooperative storage
systems, conservation centers, and conservation of individual items
in individual libraries are examples in which this collective wisdom
is utilized. Yet we have not developed a true national program, one
that meets goals such as these set forth by Pamela Darling. Cooperation on preservation is not simply two or more libraries getting
together, it is the entire profession working to:[22]

1. Strengthen local programs of basic maintenance protective care.
2. Continue to refine and use safe, simple techniques for minor
   repair and protective wrapping of fragile materials.
3. Strengthen and increase the number of regional centers with
   their expertise and educational work, as well as actual conservation work.
4. Lobby for improved materials and for national manufacturing
   standards for paper and film.
5. Divide preservation responsibilities among libraries, publishers,
   and large-scale projects according to subject, imprint, format,
   and date.
6. Develop a national bibliographic system through which to
   communicate about holdings and preservation activities.
7. Increase the number of people who understand preservation
   in libraries.
8. Cultivate widespread awareness outside libraries.

Of these eight goals, we may be well under way with all but
numbers (5) and (6). I have just described local programs and in the

---

21. Patricia A. McClung, "Costs Associated with Preservation Microfilming: Results
of the Research Libraries Group Study," *Library Resources & Technical Services* 30 (1986):
363–74.
22. Pamela Darling, "Planning for the Future," in *Library Preservation Program*,
pp. 103–10.

process shown how these must involve cooperation with others and make use of cooperative and commercial conservation centers. Awareness is growing. There is a National Commission on Preservation and Access and an increasing number of trained and knowledgeable librarians.[23] The various cooperative projects described do divide up preservation responsibilities, but they are a tiny step in a massive undertaking. Ross Atkinson has suggested that most libraries will handle their own most important materials on their own, but that a whole enormous class of less valuable materials will be lost unless we collectively, cooperatively preserve them.[24] This is a dramatic plea, too recent to have elicited widespread agreement. When thinking about preserving collections, as when thinking about building them, we must recognize the concept of a composite collection. While each of us has local goals and objectives, in an activity so costly and time-consuming as preservation we must see where we fit into the national or international composite collection. On the one hand we all have our individual treasures, unique materials, and integral collections that we will try to preserve on our own, and on the other there are the classics and essential books and periodicals that are widely collected and on which we can cooperate, and have been cooperating, to identify and preserve. Atkinson's proposal assumes this composite collection concept.

Preservation, finally, has two claims. We preserve in our own individual libraries in order to continue to make available the materials we already own and to maintain the integrity of carefully developed, coherent collections. These local efforts can be successful only if we cooperate with other libraries and remain aware of what the whole profession is doing. Local availability, however, could be an excessively narrow or shortsighted rationale; if we seek only to make available what our local users want, we could be lead to individually and collectively jettison much of our past and to abandon the most basic of our profession's ideals, that of collecting and preserving the accumulated voice of the past. We are, after all, both arena and warehouse, and we are so for the same reason: libraries provide the materials with which we can improve our understanding of ourselves,

---

23. Patricia M. Battin, "Preserving America's National Heritage: The Response of the Commission on Preservation and Access," in *Bowker Annual,* 33rd ed. (New York: Bowker, 1988) pp. 88–91.
   24. Ross W. Atkinson, "Selection for Preservation: A Materialistic Approach," *Library Resources & Technical Services* 30 (1986): 341–53.

our times, our past and our future. "The purpose of large-scale coordinated preservation," asserts Ross Atkinson,[25]

> is not merely to help the future understand the past, but also to provide the future with the ability to understand itself—to supply a ground of knowledge upon which the future can build and against which the future can contrast and thus identify and define itself.

Collection Renewal

Selection builds the collection, preservation preserves what we have, and weeding removes what is not used. A good portion of our collections, however, must be replaced and replaced continuously. This includes the core of frequently used books, periodicals, and other materials that are in constant demand because of college courses or popular reading tastes as well as a core of essential books and periodicals even if they receive little use. The topic may be eternal but the materials in it are temporary and temporal. *Collections* must be renewed, just as individual items must be replaced and repaired. Many of our users are better served by a renewed than by a merely new collection.

The materials in this core wear out from overuse, and over the years the core grows thin in quality but larded with inappropriate gifts and books long since outdated. We need multiple copies and microfilm is not adequate for high use items. Publishers let their backlists dwindle and print the classics only in paperback. We accept gifts sight unseen, and buy books on sale simply because they are a bargain. Every library has a dozen copies of *Huckleberry Finn,* but only four of those are in fit condition and of these only two are of intellectually respectable editions. Users and user interests change; the juvenile collection full of unread cowboy stories shows this. To the casual eye the collection looks rich, but it has actually atrophied and needs renewing.

Not only do books in the core wear out, but they are themselves the object of constant scholarly study, popular interest, and additional publication. It is not enough to replace our worn-out copies of *Hamlet,* we also must keep adding the latest, newest editions, studies, and scholarly tools, the latest popular editions and student guides, and the latest recordings and videotapes of significant productions. If this is true with the humanities, it is just as much so with the social and

---

25. Atkinson, p. 347.

technological sciences. As the arguments about the death penalty or abortion or euthanasia surge and permute and draw on new or different evidence, new and different attitudes, new and different thinking, we must both repair and replace older books and periodicals and also keep up with the new publications. No sooner does new science replace old science, driving it into the outer darkness of ignorance and error, than does the historian of science step in to gather up all the old stuff and study the nature of error and the development of new understanding.

Renewal costs time and money. It is similar to retrospective collection development because the librarian must spend considerable time looking through standard bibliographies rather than sorting vendor slips or scanning new reviews, but instead of filling gaps the librarian is preventing gaps from opening up. On the one hand it requires good information about what is being used, while on the other it also requires that we judge what is likely to be used or is needed. The modern poetry collection in an academic library must have the texts, must have some biography, and must have criticism, but the criticism must be leavened with explication. Latest critical theories and approaches, often highly sophisticated, are fine for faculty and graduate students but seldom so for undergraduates who need much more practical help; the local business executives need *Value Line,* while the first-time investors need the latest sound beginner's guide to stocks and bonds. We must accurately judge our users.

Renewal, then, is partly restocking our inventories as they are depleted but also continually reexamining and rethinking the character of our collections, watching not only the physical condition of the materials but also the intellectual quality of their contents. The former is relatively easier, but both are equally important. Intellectual quality— or relevance—changes as rapidly as physical condition, and keeping abreast of these changes can be as exciting as keeping up with the latest publications. There is no reason collection renewal cannot be as rewarding as selection of new materials; it is, however, more difficult, requires actual legwork, and is difficult to systematize.

Weeding and Storage

Collection renewal requires not only replacement but also removal of materials. Weeding for discard or for storage is the systematic review of the collection in search of materials that can be withdrawn and discarded or moved to alternate storage. Weeding for discard obviously takes things out of the collection and so requires careful selection, appropriate checks, and effective public relations. Weeding for storage is not so final but can certainly cause users and librarians inconvenience or worse. Weeding is not an end in itself—there is no moral imperative to weed, despite our current age's fondness for lean cuisine, light drinks, and trim bodies—but it is a means to the important end of making our collections more accessible, and the items in them more available. Weeding is not a simple, mechanical process but requires a deep understanding of the nature of collections and, specifically, of one's own collection.

Weeding for Discard. Weeding is time-consuming. No matter how efficiently organized, a weeding project requires individual attention by professional librarians to a large number of individual items. It certainly takes as much time and attention as selection of new materials. Occasionally—never ideally—we weed in an emergency: we suddenly become aware of having run out of space or our budget request for additional shelving or a building wing was denied and so we have no choice but to reduce the size of our collection. Considering the amount of high-quality labor that must go into it, any weeding project must be carefully thought out or, better, the library should have developed its own guidelines and procedures for regular weeding; that is, libraries should have in place a weeding program. This program should include a clear description of the purposes, criteria, procedures, personnel, and disposal alternatives.

The first step in weeding is to define the purposes of the project. There are degrees of thoroughness and different reasons for weeding. We weed to gain space, to make remaining material more accessible, to identify a core collection, or to fill out a storage system. We must decide how much time and personnel to devote to the project. Purposes must be in line with our collection development policy, as well as with individual librarians' plans for their collections. Purposes should control how we weight the various criteria that apply in selecting and what procedures we use. Purposes apply to the library's overall weeding program, possibly setting some sort of timetable for weeding projects and providing broad guidelines for the individual librarians, and purposes apply in the work of individual librarians. We don't start until we have decided where to stop.

The criteria that are applied in the hundreds or thousands of decisions are: use, quality or value of contents, relevance, and physical condition. The weight given to each will vary by the program's or project's purposes, the type of library, the character of the individual collections, the particular items being examined, and the special conditions occurring at the time of weeding. As with purposes, these criteria must be in line with the library's collection development policy and the librarian's plans. Usually we thin out collections; occasionally we will lop off large chunks, as when an academic program is eliminated or a community undergoes major change and makes a large set of materials irrelevant to the library's mission. Ideally, these criteria can be applied coolly, but emergency situations force us to weed in desperation and throw out things we might much rather have kept, and might in fact have been able to keep had we had a long-running weeding program.

Of these criteria it is tempting to give most weight to use, which is the argument of Stanley J. Slote in his *Weeding Library Collections— II*.[26] Citing the Pittsburgh Study and other analyses of use (or lack of use), he accepts that circulation is an adequate record of use and that time since the last circulation is the best measure of the likelihood of future use. Weeding, then, is a simple matter of examining circulation records to see when a book last circulated. There are, he asserts, two classes of materials, core and noncore, that is, those that are and those that are not used. The library must decide what level of demand it wants to meet and define its core accordingly. If it wants to be able to provide a collection that meets 95 percent of demand, then it will define its core as those materials whose likelihood of use, based on past circulation records, will meet the demand. This could mean that one weeds every book that has not circulated in 25 years or ten years or even less. Slote does, of course, allow librarians to make a number of exceptions and is no doubt less draconian in practice than in theory.

Most librarians will be more cautious than Slote, however. Use, for reasons discussed previously in chapter 5, is too complex a matter to be left simply to circulation records or even to in-house tagging procedures. An item's quality or value does not depend on the amount of use it receives, and conversely use does not mean that an item is worth keeping. People often come to the library looking for information about subjects and will use whatever the library has, good or bad, up-to-date or out-of-date. In many cases, we should replace a much-used book with a newer one or even abandon books in favor of periodicals or other formats. We know, too, that use can rise and fall and that certain materials though infrequently used are nonetheless

26. Stanley J. Slote, *Weeding Library Collections—II*, 2nd ed. (Littleton, Colo.: Libraries Unlimited, 1982).

valuable. Academic libraries experience cycles of use according to the courses offered, the faculty on the staff, and the long-term shifts in student interests; public libraries experience similar if less-predictable patterns; special libraries all experience sudden wide shifts in corporate or research emphases. No librarian will ignore the fact that an item seems to go unused, but neither will any librarian fail to look beyond circulation records for evidence of use and try to determine why a book is not used, provided there is time to do so.

Physical condition is sometimes more compelling than nonuse, and usually is a direct result of use. A book that is falling apart is a book to be weeded, if it cannot be repaired or replaced. Given the nature of book publishing today, the worn book frequently cannot be replaced, leaving librarians with little choice but to weed heavily used books, which certainly is an ironic situation. This problem stresses that weeding, storage, and preservation must be considered together. When attempting to make collections more accessible and materials more available, then selection for discard, for repair, or for alternative storage can be one single operation.

These criteria will vary by type of library, category of user, subjects, and kind of materials. Physical condition is probably more of a hindrance to use in a school than in a university library, where materials are increasingly found boxed, tied, or enveloped simply because they must continue to be available even though in terrible condition. Public libraries are midway between school and academic libraries in the importance of physical condition. Clean, sound books probably do get more use than dirty, broken ones, but some users will not be deterred by evidence of heavy use. The browser and the genre reader might be put off by bad condition more than the commmon reader or scholar. Academic librarians might concern themselves more with books for undergraduates than the books for graduate students and faculty; public librarians might be concerned more with popular reading collections than with local history materials. Above all, librarians must understand the use in their own libraries and the character of their collections.

Weeding criteria differ in complex ways for books and periodicals. Certain periodicals carry strictly current news and are almost instantly out-of-date; other periodicals contain articles that never diminish in value, despite changes in intellectual fashions. Contents of other periodicals long out-of-date may regain current value. Interest, for example, in women's history sends use back to nineteenth-century magazines for evidence of nineteenth-century attitudes of and about women. The same can be said of books, and sometimes the most topical become, later, the most valuable. Weeding for discard, preservation, or storage must take into account these kinds of differences.

Jay Lucker and others in an article describing a periodical weeding program at MIT libraries explain clearly a situation that is actually very complex. His advice is sensible, as, for example, suggesting that when weeding periodicals we remove long unused runs of a few titles rather than simply weeding everything over a certain age. Weeding is not a simple matter and we should not let ourselves undertake it without thinking very hard and thoroughly about what we are to do.[27]

Procedures for weeding will vary according to a number of factors. The procedures must fit the circumstances; they should also include a schedule to give the project impetus at one end and closure at the other. Slote's book does give good advice and the literature is full of reports on a variety of weeding projects. Should we weed the whole collection or just part of it, and if just part, which part? If weeding the whole collection, should we proceed straight through from A to Z or should we select certain parts as having more pressing needs? When undertaking a project, some time frame or schedule is important; if, on the other hand, a weeding program is in effect, then the scheduling already has been established. We might, for instance, weed regularly two hours per week or every first day of the month or every June.

The personnel involved are integral with the procedures. It might be desirable for student workers to sort through the collection item by item, looking for books that have not circulated in ten years, for duplicate copies, and for obvious evidence of wear; the books they find can be set aside and then examined by librarians for a final decision on whether to discard, store, or repair. Exactly how use will be determined will vary from library to library, depending on whether it is a circulation record, evidence in the books, or some sort of tagging applied to books. On the other hand, it might be better for librarians to perform the whole project, for example, when weeding a reference or special collection. Procedures and personnel will be affected by how the weeding criteria are weighted: if use is the prime criterion, then student workers can check for it; if quality is the prime criterion, however, then really only professionals can judge and there is

27. Jay K. Lucker, Kate S. Herzog, and Sydney J. Owens, "Weeding Collections in an Academic Library System: Massachusetts Institute of Technology," *Science & Technology Libraries* 6 (Spring 1986): 11–23.

little point to preliminary culling. When it is condition that is most important, then the final decision must be made by conservators or similarly trained people. Often we will apply a combination of criteria, perhaps sending student workers to scan for use; asking librarians or faculty to judge the quality of the items, the coherency of the collection, and the nature of likely use; and then asking librarians again to determine the physical condition and choose among the alternatives.

Once weeding selection is made, then others must be called in to review the items. These could be other librarians, as when a reference collection is being weeded; they could be faculty, as when a college library's regular collection is being weeded; they could be other authorities. Faculty often are very jealous of the library's collections and suspicious of librarians' managing of it. Few, however, will oppose weeding when the project is carefully conceived with clear purpose and criteria in line with the collection development policy and with fail-safe procedures allowing them to review and comment on librarians' selections. Librarians in turn must make sure that their purposes, criteria, and procedures are appropriate and clear and must allow their work to be reviewed or even reversed. They should, in fact, be happy to receive faculty opinion for it usually will corroborate their own opinion, and when it does not it should help them refine their criteria and weed even more effectively in the future (not to mention improve their original selection decisions). Most public libraries follow long-established procedures that ensure the participation of knowledgeable librarians and the application of appropriate criteria, but generally do not have an easily identifiable group of expert users whom they consult. One simple way to consult users is to set out weeded books for sale.

The disposal of weeded items is as much a part of the politics as the practicalities of weeding. Disregarding those situations where legal constraints prevent discard of public or donated materials, the discarded items can either be dumped (in ecologially sound ways, of course) or transferred to other collections, as when sold to the public, sent to an exchange program, or moved into cooperative storage facilities managed within the library's network(s). Some money may be realized from sales, but probably the real gain is goodwill and the sale's concrete evidence of the existence of a weeding program; it will give the public confidence that the library is managing its collections effectively (although even here there are exceptions, as when librarians are accused of being philistines or worse by a public who misunderstood the project). As a member of networks and consortia, the library has an obligation, possibly a written agreement, to dispose of its materials in ways that recognize its responsibilities to other members. Presumably the network or agreements were set up to coordinate the management of collections that can in some way be considered composite.

Weeding for discard should be a specific program within the library's overall collection management program. Besides its benefits in improving access and availability and in providing for more cost-effective storage, it also affects the librarians doing the selection, the catalog department, users, branches, and networks. This impact can be managed better and its unpleasant aspects reduced if weeding is worked into regular routines and attitudes and is treated specifically as part of cooperative collection management arrangements. Also implicit is the assumption that weeding for discard proceeds simultaneously with weeding for storage and preservation.

Weeding for Storage. Weeding for storage assumes the existence of a storage system of some type, so that decisions about what to store can truly be thought of in a positive sense. Rather than thinking of this as "relegating" items to storage, we should think of it as selecting for storage, on a fairly rational basis according to predetermined purposes, criteria, and procedures. We are not removing materials from primary space but moving materials to the place most appropriate for them in light of considerations about cost effective storage, accessibility and availability, and retrieval costs. Storage alternatives include the kind of shelving (regular library shelving or varieties of compact shelving), the distance from most users, the kind and frequency of retrieval arrangements, and the provision for direct user access. The purposes for sending materials to alternative storage facilities include the need for space in the main library, the need to put certain materials into more protected storage, the desirablility of separating less-used materials from the more used, and the possibililty of creating certain kinds of special, coherent collections in a separate storage facility. The criteria for moving items from one storage to another include the amount and kind of use they receive, the value of their contents, their physical condition (needing the protection of reduced accessibility), and their current or likely future monetary value. The procedure for selecting them is the same as when weeding for discard.

It is not inconceivable that we may soon build separate storage facilities for materials published during the past century and a half where they can be kept under rigorous climate controls, touched only when retrieved for use, and possibly combined with a local or network-wide long-term program of steady replacement or conversion to other formats. While still available for use, these materials would not suffer the daily stress of typical building environments, excessive handling, and unnecessary use. In some ways this idea is simply a reversion to the earlier pattern of reading rooms and central storage stacks. Selection for this kind of storage is certainly not relegation but really a conscious decision that materials—and users—will best be served with a more protective storage than now is provided.

It is also possible to set up special collections of materials that might in some situations have to be discarded but with a sensible storage system can be kept. For instance, every academic library over the years develops quite a collection of textbooks, books on teaching methods, and professional materials; frequently, these are discarded during weeding projects, but with proper storage available they could be combined to provide a rich source of primary materials for historians, cultural critics, school archivists, and students of educational methods. The Center for Research Libraries was established on this idea, and has, in addition, proceeded to purchase microform sets, foreign newspapers, and other materials that complement the original collection.[28] A public library could do the same with certain kinds of local history materials, particularly those that do not receve regular heavy use, for example, ephemera. Libraries, then, could create a coherent special collection out of disparate collections through the mechanism of weeding for storage. A sensible storage system allows us to keep under our control and in a cost-effective way those materials that we want to keep, without clogging up prime storage space, and allows us to develop a weeding program that gives options for mending or conservation, alternative storage, and outright discard. With these alternatives, we also can set up a program of regular collection review.

Collection Review

Regular, systematic collection review is the capstone to a collection management program—a means by which we assess our collections' quality and condition, tally its use, identify and address problems in it, and evaluate the quality of our selection work. Collection review includes those operations that have already been discussed: weeding;

---

28. Center for Research Libraries, *Handbook* (Chicago: CRL, 1987).

shelf reading; inventories; selection for maintenance, preservation, or renewal; analysis of use; and the work of assessing a collection prior to drawing up a collection development policy, in addition to the review normally performed as materials return from circulation. While primarily concerned with a physical condition, a review certainly does, and should, cover intellectual quality and relevance as well. Collection review should not be random, and if it is to be productive, it should be conducted with several objects in mind. An effective review program should consist of a purpose, a procedure, and the results.

Several kinds of review are included here:

Inventory.
Shelf reading.
Stack maintenance.
Book maintenance, including repair, rebinding, and replacement of books and other materials.

Selection for transfer, as from reference to circulating, regular to special collections, and for shifts of large blocks of the collection.
Selection for discard or storage.
Selection for conservation treatment.

Monitor quantitative input and output characteristics.
Maintain information about publishing and the composite collection.

Analyze quantity and kind of use, in-house and circulating.
Assess collection levels.
Evaluate quality, such as by list checking or expert's judgment.
Determine cumulative, coherent character of the collection.

Any of these activities involves a review of the collection; I urge that we become more systematic and make, as much as possible, each review do the work of several, and perform that review on a regular schedule. If we do set up programs for weeding, maintenance and preservation, inventories, renewal, use analysis, and assessment of levels, then we also have set up a program of review. The questions then become who does the review, how do we combine or coordinate the various reviews, and when or according to what schedule do we undertake the reviews?

In small collections, including self-contained units within larger libraries, we can imagine proceeding straight through regularly and frequently. With large collections, however, a complete review seems overwhelming. Complete reviews have been done, over a period of several years of course, so obviously they are not impossible. Whether complete A through Z review of a multimillion volume collection is worth the effort is questionable: complete review, however, of parts of that collection is definitely possible and desirable. Studies of shelf reading show that under ideal conditions a trained and motivated staff can cover 550 to 600 volumes per hour, rearranging volumes that are out of order, pulling and setting aside volumes that need special treatment or are candidates for discard.[29] At that rate, we won't get through a six-million-volume collection soon, but perhaps much of a six-million-volume collection is already in storage. Within the six-million-volume collection are several smaller, more manageable collections that can be effectively reviewed.

Shelf reading is one form of review that must be done regularly. Most libraries follow established procedures for shelf reading. If we were to add to the duties of shelf readers several simple, clear guidelines for additional review, then we would turn this regular activity into a more ambitious project. Shelf readers could be trained to examine multiple copies and subsequent editions for evidence of circulation, pull damaged volumes, note where shifting seems necessary to free up shelf space, as well as restoring proper order, straightening books, and replacing bookends. Furthermore, if we were to make the shelvers' supervisor a "Collection Manager," then we would have designated a specific person and specific line of responsibilities. Shelf reading may never be fun, but it can be made more evidently important. This set of procedures and responsibilities makes up a basic program of collection review. Maintained over several years it should produce clear results—statistics for withdrawn volumes, volumes moved to storage, multiple copies added, volumes mended, rebound, or replaced, volumes or linear feet shelf read—and it should have passed through much of the collection that receives regular use.

What one might call the inductive or exploratory review should be carried out by the librarian responsible for the collection, whether covering the entire library or only a part of it. Even in small collections, complete collection review can be an overwhelming prospect, if what is meant is an item-by-item survey. Sampling, however, provides an alternative. We can review a sample of the collection and

29. James H. Sweetland, "Time Required for Shelf Reading: A Case Study," *College & Research Libraries* 49 (1988): 75–78.

learn much from this. Most simply, we can go and look at every fifth shelf, for example, trying to find patterns—need for mending, added copies, shelf reading, more space, cleaning, or also possibly a need for more intensive review of the quality. Assuming that the librarian who is responsible for the collection, or part of it, is familiar with the subject and the kind of use materials in it are likely to have, then exploratory review quickly becomes a review of the collection's quality. If this is the case, a more purposeful sampling, such as will be described, might be worthwhile.

A simple sampling review that can be accomplished with student assistants, a modest amount of time, and a greater or lesser degree of sophistication, involves the shelf list and the materials on the shelves. By taking every twentieth card in the shelf list, for example, we can find information about subjects, age, accession date, balance among subjects, language and imprint, primary or secondary literature, formats, and average number of copies or volumes per title. A student can do this. The information can be easily computerized and run through the Statistical Package for the Social Sciences (SPSS) to provide averages, means, and other statistically informative relationships. Using every twentieth card provides a valid sample, although in small collections or small segments of a collection the sample size may not provide convincing information.

Once the sample is drawn, one then can go to the shelves and look at the corresponding books for information about use and physical condition. Depending on how circulation is recorded, we can learn the latest date of circulation, total times circulated, and number of circulations within particular time periods. This data, too, can be processed with the SPSS. Whether one goes beyond shelf list to the shelf, we still can gain a useful overview of our collection, one that should help us spot areas that need attention to any number of actions, such as duplicate copies, increased mending or preservation, decreased (or increased) purchasing in certain subject areas or of certain formats or types of materials. Whatever the range of results, working with a sample can be an effective way to review the collection. Other ways to conduct sampling reviews include selecting books randomly, sampling circulation records, or sampling smaller segments of the collection but doing so more intensively.

Although sampling is a practical way to learn much about our collection's character, it cannot tell us all we need to know. We must recognize the coherent, cumulative value of the collection, which probing its particularities can help reveal; we also must step back to see it whole. We must determine how it fits in with the total possible collection. Collection review, then, should provide each collection management librarian with information about neighboring collections, about relevant publishing output, and about national trends in collections and publishing.

One very important result of regular collection review, especially the exploratory kind, is that it takes librarians into the collection, to the shelves, into contact with the materials where we actually can see the evidence of use, deterioration, and space problems, as well as see the books we have selected sitting on the shelves in their library context. There is a great deal of sensual pleasure in working with books, periodicals, and the other materials, and this does not come from vendor slips or book reviews or even computer files. We should indulge ourselves in book handling. More to the point of this book, however, is that we must see what we have. Statistics on shelf space mean more when we see books crammed onto seven high stacks; brittle books crumbling in our own hands mean more than brittle books listed on a printout; page after page of highlighted text or gap after gap of ripped out articles tell us of a mutilation problem. On the positive side, to see that books that we doubted ever would be used have actually circulated tells us much about the reality of our collections that we need to know. Collection management ultimately deals with this reality.

That there are different kinds of reviews, that they proceed at different speeds, that they need to be conducted at different times, that they must be combined with different other operations, and yet that all are important are reasons to set up a review program. By identifying the different reviews and their purposes, we are more likely to keep ahead of the problems reviews themselves identify, more able to achieve goals we set for reviews, especially the goal of getting through as much of the collection as we want to. We gain control through our reviews of our collections; we become able to monitor their development and slow their deterioration, assess their quality and measure their use, and evaluate their suitability or appropriateness. Reviewing collections does not itself make them better, but it is the one way we have of finding out how good they are. A collection management program must include a well-thought-out review component.

Chapter 9

Personnel, Administration, and the Profession

A collection management program depends on people, on the effective coordination and support of these people's work, and on the interactions among individuals and among libraries: librarians, library administrations, and the library profession. This chapter examines the questions of the kinds and number of staff needed for collection management, the administration of their work in the library, and the profession's contribution to collection management. Management consists of setting goals and objectives, devising and carrying out strategic plans for meeting these goals and objectives, and then providing an accounting of the success, cost, and value of having worked toward these goals and objectives. In the collection management program this definition of management applies at both operational and administrative levels. There seems to be little agreement among libraries about how this management is organized and carried out; no "best way" has been established. Our understanding of the management of collection management is rudimentary. We do, however, know what considerations must be thought about, and it is these that I will cover in this chapter.

Collection Management Librarians

The collection management program encompasses a number of activities, all carried out by individuals. In any particular library the number of librarians, the range of activities being carried out and the activities each is responsible for, the relationships among these librarians and between them and other librarians, and a host of other variables form unique configurations. The individual who manages all or part of a collection must be able to answer three broad questions: What must one know? What must one be able to do? What personal qualities must one have? In many, if not most, libraries, however, the various collection management activities are distributed among several people, so that it is the collective staff whom we must ask, What must they know? What can they do? What personal strengths do they bring?

Knowledge. Anyone who works in collection management must understand the nature of subjects, users, and the ways that materials and information in a subject are typically used. One also must understand publishing in the specific fields and the nature and character of collections and libraries. The first set is perhaps more abstract or intellectual, while the last three are more practical and physical; all, however, are important.

To understand the subjects we must know their history, their current emphases, and the structure of information and publication in each. Subjects cannot, of course, be separated from the people who are interested in them, so in addition to the subject we must try to understand, as appropriate to our situation, academic disciplines, user categories, user needs, and typical user demands. Charles Osburn calls this the "sociology of recorded human expression and communication."[1] Knowledge of this "sociology of expression and communication" is, additionally, as essential for reference and information service, library use instruction, and liaison and public relations activities as it is for collection management.

Using English or American literature as an example, we can see that the collection management librarian must know the history of these literatures—that is, the authors and works, literary movements or schools, common genres, themes, and styles—and also must know, in the public library, what local users' interests are and, in academic libraries, the fairly complex nature of the discipline of literary study. Ironically, many librarians who studied literature themselves in college lack sympathy with popular reading tastes or with academic literary study. Sound collection management, however, depends on

---

    1. Charles B. Osburn, "Education for Collection Development," *Collection Development in Libraries: A Treatise,* ed. Robert D. Stueart and George B. Miller, Jr. (Greenwich, Conn.: JAI Press, 1980), p. 569.

a sympathetic understanding of users as well as subjects, thus Osburn's "sociology."

This kind of knowledge is especially important in selection, but collection management is much more than selection or development. We also must understand the materials. We must know what kinds of publications are common in a subject, what use is made of them, and what varieties of information are needed in the discipline. The relative importance of serial literature in various fields of scholarship, of audiovisual materials in primary and secondary education, of special-interest magazines for popular reading, and the power of current information in public life are examples. We must know reader interests and needs. At the same time we must, as managers, understand these materials as commodities. We must thus understand the quantity of publication, the pricing patterns, the nature of publishing and distribution, and the nature of contemporary manufacturing processes, all of which affect what we can buy, how we must process, shelve, and protect it, and the problems we will have in keeping it accessible and available. While we might not be experts in all the subjects that we are responsible for, we should be expert in identifying and evaluating publications in the subject fields.

Materials are combined into collections, and collections into libraries. Collections are dynamic. They have their own natures and, in specific libraries, they have specific characters. They are almost living systems. We must look at the whole, therefore, not just the parts and not just the users. All libraries have their own use patterns, housing and shelving arrangements, administrations and personnel, policies and procedures, their own set(s) of users, as well as their own collections: no two are the same. The collection manager must understand and work within the limits imposed by each library's character. The library's character is revealed in its mission, its collection development policy, and its selection plans, all of which guide the library's short- and long-term efforts to meet its users' needs.

Activities. With this knowledge of community, of subjects, users, and users' needs, of materials, and of collections and libraries, the collection manager must act—that is, must carry out the work of collection management. Specific tasks in addition to general activities are common to all kinds of management work conducted within organizations. The specific tasks include acquiring the kinds of knowledge previously described and then the activities of community analysis and liaison, selection, use analysis, and collection review. "Tasks" is not the right word, because these are not simple skills that can be mechanically carried out; they require knowledge and training, experience and aptitude, and the ability to work effectively in an organization.

Skills, then, must be managed, and managing involves setting goals and objectives, devising strategies or plans for achieving them, and then judging or accounting for one's work. At the level of the individual collection management librarian, the ability to devise and carry out plans or strategies is particularly important. While there is considerable routine—better yet, a wide range of activities that one must carry on continuously (such as scanning book reviews)—there is also a wide range of project activities. Selection plans, as discussed in chapter six, are an example: the librarian must develop plans for spending desiderata money, for canceling or adding periodical subscriptions, for developing a neglected subject area or user interest, or for solving a collection-related problem, such as underuse. With goals and strategies also comes accountability. Evaluations of collection strengths, collection use, and users' satisfaction must be carried out; in addition, the individual librarian must monitor the collection that he or she is responsible for. To ascertain the growth and use of our collections and to judge their continuing relevance to our users, we must gather and analyze information about publishing in our fields, expenditures for materials and volumes added, circulation and in-house use data, renewal and preservation needs, and applicable community or institutional conditions. With this input and output data, we can provide accountability and demonstrate, if not justify, the effort we have invested in our collections.

Individual librarians do their work within an organization, and this organization—or library—itself plays a role that will be discussed later. As a member of an organization, one is responsible for learning and following policies and procedures, for helping to revise these as necessary, and for contributing to the smooth operation of the system. This work almost always requires supervising other people. Even the newly hired librarian will oversee student assistants or will use secretarial help for typing book requests, preorder searching, and checking bibliographies. In collection management, perhaps more than in any other aspect of library work, librarians must interact with each other for the work of an individual directly impacts on the work of others. We must consider the long-term and wider effects of our own work, communicate and negotiate with those who will be affected, alter or compromise in response to others' needs, and manage our projects efficiently, expeditiously, and smoothly.

Selection affects the work of the Acquisitions and Serials Departments directly; weeding directly affects the Catalog Department; the Reference Department depends on up-to-date reference and circulating collections. A project may cause disruptive effects elsewhere. If we receive a multithousand dollar grant for new materials in a neglected subject, but then use that money to order countless individual titles, we may burden the Acquisitions Department with an unexpectedly large additional work load, particularly if that money must be spent by a close deadline. If we had included a request for additional project personnel in our grant proposal, acquisitions librarians could process orders in the normal course of work. Similarly, a major weeding and withdrawal project to free up shelving space will impose extra work on the Catalog Department; weeding conducted regularly over a long period of time can achieve this end without inconveniencing catalogers.

Personal and Intellectual Characteristics. The collection management librarian must be a professional, capable of working independently but in cooperation with others. He or she must be a self-starter who initiates projects and a goal-oriented manager who completes them. This person must be a generalist in subject fields, that is, a person who knows the history of the subject and the ways it has been, or could be, studied and enjoyed. As far as publications and other media, this person must be a bibliographic specialist, with a knowledge of the kinds, uses, and library life of publications.

At the same time, the collection management librarian must be able to analyze and understand how materials are used, what users' needs are, and how users are succeeding in the manager's own library. The librarian must combine features of the social scientist, who is capable of analyzing users' behavior and who is comfortable with statistical methods, with features of the humanist, who is knowledgeable in history and aware of the complex nature of human records. Above all, the collection management librarian must be sympathetic with the library's users. In simple terms, we must not let our own subject interests dictate what we select or how we maintain it; conversely, we must realize the complex richness of human curiosity and the deep satisfaction that reading can provide. In between the simple and the complex is a range of interests and needs that are, or are not, satisfied by the information we collect in our libraries. An old complaint contends that librarians are not bibliophiles and collectors, but that complaint shows no understanding of our profession. Although we deal with many books, we are not collecting books but rather building and maintaining collections of materials and their contents that will provide library users with information, knowledge, and solace. Truly, in Jesse Shera's words, it is knowledge of people and knowledge of books (and, he added, computers, too) that we manage.

Miscellaneous Issues. Who exactly are these librarians? As mentioned previously, although I am using the word *librarians* I actually am discussing knowledge and activities. These activities can be carried on by a single individual in a small library or distributed among several individuals in a large library; these individuals can be professional librarians, skilled and experienced nonprofessionals, or even relatively unskilled, part-time, temporary staff. Even the knowledge can be distributed among a number of people and inhere in the group if not in a single person.

How many librarians should there be? Probably the major factor to consider is the activity in the collection. Size by itself is significant, but even more so are the volumes and units added, the amount of transferring, weeding, preservation, and renewal, or the amount of time necessary to carry out various activities. Item-by-item selection takes more time than selecting with an approval plan. The collection affects staff needs more than the size of the community does; the collection exists, in this sense, independent of enrollment or population, and the larger the collection, the more complex is its management. In seeking an answer, we must at least look in the right place, and that place is in the nature of collection management work in the individual library. Once we know what the collection needs, then we can determine how many librarians are needed.

What problems do collection managers regularly encounter? These problems are time, attention, money, and organizational support. Seldom do collection managers have enough time (particularly when, as is often the case, they are simultaneously reference librarians or acquisition personnel), seldom can they devote sufficiently concentrated attention, and seldom do they have enough money. Furthermore, they seldom receive sufficient support in the form of education, training, in-house information, and administrative effectiveness. (Even administrators, ironically, are unhappy with their library's administration and management of the collection.[2]) Two examples of excellent institutional support are the *Bibliographer's Manual* (University of

---

2. Jean Sohn, "Collection Development Organizational Patterns in ARL Libraries," *Library Resources & Technical Services* 31 (1987): 123–34.

Texas, Austin) and *Guide to Collection Development and Management* (University of California, Berkeley).[3] Besides describing the qualifications for collection management librarians, they provide considerable detail about functions and activities, including priorities among and within these, and descriptions of the operation and administration of the complete collection management program. These publications are, incidentally, part of a series produced in the libraries designed to support the work of librarians in the system but are also of considerable use to librarians elsewhere.

Administration

Library administrations must ease these problems as well as effectively manage the activities of collection managers. Good administration recognizes what problems need solving. Management consists of setting goals and objectives, devising strategies for achieving these, and accounting for their degree of success. Different situations call for different administrative models; some are effective in one situation, while others are effective in different circumstances. Administration can do little without the active participation of collection management librarians. These librarians know their collections and users, understand publishing and the materials in their fields, and develop their own selection plans. Administration must coordinate these plans, and on occasion choose among them, but it should draw from these people and their plans—that is, it should set goals based on the collection as collection managers understand it.

Goals and Objectives. The library administration is responsible for setting overall goals and objectives for its collection and within these goals each individual librarian with more specific responsibility must in turn set more specific objectives. While the administration and the individual librarian must interact considerably, so that, for example, librarians can suggest possible or prevent impossible goals, it is the administration's responsibility to define the library's role in the institution's or community's mission. Institutions usually do have missions, while communities do not; yet a progressive civic community will acknowledge its citizens' need for the kind of information,

---

3. *Bibliographer's Manual: A Guide to the General Libraries Collection Development Program* (Austin: The General Libraries, The University of Texas, 1982), and James H. Spohner, Dorothy A. Koenig, and Sheila T. Dowd, *Guide to Collection Development and Management at the University of California, Berkeley* (Berkeley: The General Libraries, University of California, 1986).

recreation, cultural, and personal enrichment that a library provides. Educational institutions often follow written mission statements that define their scope, ambitions, and, less explicitly, resources: libraries then can write their own mission statement to conform. Corporate institutions—businesses, research centers, or professional bodies, such as law firms or hospitals—less often have written missions but usually operate with implicit and quite clear missions. Libraries within these institutions will have no trouble defining their appropriate missions.

The mission statement defines the scope of the community to be served and describes the community's needs that it expects to meet with its collections and services. An academic library serves a community of students and faculty, for example, but it must describe the needs it can meet—and in fairly precise terms. The statement outlines the kinds of services that will be provided, which is a point of great importance because this is the goal that the library must cite to argue for its budget. The mission statement is aimed outward toward the institution's administration, the community's government, or the corporation's management, and it is also aimed inward, giving individual librarians the framework within which they can set their more specific goals and objectives.

Aimed outwardly, the mission statement outlines the services the library will provide and expect to receive an adequate budget for. Aimed inwardly, it defines or sets limits to the subjects, users, and needs to be satisfied. As for collection management, for example, the statement must both identify the broad area and define its main parts: collection development, collection maintenance, provision of access and availability, preservation, weeding, and storage. Accompanying it also is a set of priorities, although these might be negotiable. For example, preservation probably is more important for humanities than science subjects, or periodical subscriptions are more important for graduate than for undergraduate users. If the mission can reflect the institutional mission and define the role and range of services of the library, the specific priorities can be set and altered as circumstances require.

Goals and objectives must grow out of the mission statement. These change as time and circumstances change, as some are met and others are abandoned, as problems arise that need immediate attention. If one part of the mission is to house the collection, a goal could be to provide accessible but less-expensive storage of little-used research materials, and an objective could be to construct a storage facility that uses movable compact shelving.

Strategies. To meet whatever goals and objectives it has set, the library administration must win and allocate the necessary resources, must coordinate and support the work of the people responsible for these resources, and supervise or monitor them, their work, and its results. A library works with several broad kinds of resources. It needs money, materials, people, space, and technological capability—but above all, money. The first strategy in successful management must be to win an adequate budget and a reasonable assurance of that budget's continuation. Success is most likely to occur if we can make a clear and reasonable connection between money requested and results produced. With budget in hand, then we can allocate it, as discussed in chapter six.

Human resources also must be won, or recruited, and then allocated. A library full of reference librarians will not produce much cataloging, while an imbalance between professionals and support staff may well accomplish the wrong things. Effective collection management requires an appropriate staff, which must be large enough to do well what needs doing and must have the knowledge and skills to do it right. We do know that the larger the collection, the larger the staff that is needed to manage it. For example, the attempt to set up a static-capacity library at Westminster College requires *adding* staff in order to weed for discard and storage.[4] Keyes Metcalf, to cite another example, points out that staff needs will continue to grow even after collections have reached maturity and their growth rates have tapered off.[5]

No library operation can continue without proper technological capability, although "proper" must vary from situation to situation. Few libraries nowadays can function effectively without OCLC or other bibliographic utility cataloging technology, interlibrary loan subsystems, and high-powered data processing. A microcomputer is as important to a one-room, one-person library as a complex mainframe-based automated system is to a large library.

With resources at least known, if not actually acquired and in place, the library administration must make sure its operation is coordinated. Coordination is not simply a matter of reducing schedule conflicts but of bringing people and other resources together to the best

---

4. F. E. Smith, "The Static-Capacity Library at Westminster College," *Technicalities* 5 (4) (1985): 10–12.

5. Keyes D. Metcalf, *Planning Academic and Research Library Buildings,* 2nd ed. by Philip D. Leighton and David C. Weber (Chicago: American Library Association, 1986), p. 14.

advantage. This may be the essence of the successful operation of any organization. Issues such as the virtues of decentralization or centralization, participative decision making, and techniques of management (such as matrix, MBO, quality circles) most likely will come to a head at this point.

The administration must provide management support in the form of prompt decisions and feedback, promulgation of policies and procedures along with appropriate in-house documentation of them, continuing education, communication, and motivation. This support is, in fact, coordination. As work continues, its results must be monitored and the information gained must be used to evaluate the quality and effectiveness of the work.

Accountability. The library administration is accountable in several directions. Having employed professional librarians, it must account to them for the value of their professional efforts. To be part of a team of successful collection management librarians is tremendously satisfying, for one knows that the combined efforts apply to the whole collection. The administration is accountable to the community, institution, or corporate body of which it is a part, accountable for funds expended for materials, personnel, space, and support. It must demonstrate that a level of satisfaction has been reached, and that the work is of a quality commensurate with expenditures and is truly a contribution to the overall mission and welfare. It is accountable to its users, who no matter how much they personally have invested in the library, do expect, and deserve, from it a high level of service. The administration is also in a sense accountable to its peer libraries. At the same time the administration must demand accountability from the librarians and groups of librarians working in it. These people, in turn, demand accountability from vendors and publishers, suppliers and utilities. A considerable degree of responsibility is delegated to librarians and they must produce.

Administrative Models. Although there is no universally accepted model for any library administration, let alone for collection management activities, several models of administration of collection management activities have proved effective, or at least continue to be used. These are easier to identify in larger libraries where, more often, explicit attention is given to collection management. These several models vary in their degree of centralization and their use of staff for single or multiple responsibilities. The models do seem to agree that a hierarchy of responsibility exists. While the library administration is ultimately responsible for the collection management program, including a collection development policy, individual librarians must be instrumental in drawing up the policy and then giving the program its actual shape.

Several recent reports show how collection management is administered in research libraries, some focusing on librarians, some on the library. Jean Sohn noted:[6]

> . . . ARL members seem to have almost as many organizational patterns as there are ARL libraries. Apparently each library has determined an organizational pattern that fits its own overall structure given the restrictions of budget, personnel, politics, or innumerable other factors.

She also notes, as do Baatz and Bryant, that collection management administrators are frequently dissatisfied with the administrative models in their libraries.[7]

The most common and troubling problem is that collection management administrators and librarians, whatever their level in the library's hierarchy, do not wield sufficient authority over their work. Librarians themselves often deal with multiple responsibilities, of which collection work is not primary or is not scheduled, unlike duty at the reference desk, and therefore is relegated to a later, often nonexistent free time. The collection management head, even when an assistant director, often does not possess enough authority to command the librarians' time, time needed not only for doing the full range of collection work but also for meeting with each other, and learning and thinking about their work. That collection management librarians work under a variety of deadlines and pressures (some implicit, some explicit) adds, Bryant observes, stresses to this work that other librarians do not experience.[8] Acquisitions, serials, audiovisual, microforms, and MRDFs, not to mention reference and library use instruction, still are separate operations and often are outside of the direct control or even outside of the direct relationship with collection management. Collection management may have picked up the new programs, such as preservation, but the old programs still retain their separateness.

---

6. Sohn, p. 131.
7. Wilmer H. Baatz, "Collection Development in 19 Libraries of the Association of Research Libraries," *Library Acquisitions: Practice and Theory* 2 (1978): 85–121, and Bonita Bryant, "The Organizational Structure of Collection Development," *Library Resources & Technical Services* 31 (1987): 111–22.
8. Bryant, p. 119.

Sohn found that the majority of the ARL libraries she surveyed were planning to make administrative changes in hopes of improving collection management work, but neither she, Baatz, nor Bryant discovered any confidence that an ideal administrative model exists to adopt. We still are groping. James Cogswell produced a useful analysis of the relative effectiveness of six different administrative models in dealing with the various functions in a collection management program.[9] None is perfect, by any means, but his analysis suggests that at the very least it is necessary to employ an assistant or associate director for collection development of equal rank with ADs for public and technical services, with a separate (or partially so) staff of collection management librarians. While this is not surprising, neither is it reassuring, for, as he observes, none of the existing models "is properly equipped to handle the substantial and growing concerns of preservation, storage, and weeding decisions."[10] At least in university libraries we still know what must be accomplished even though we may not know how best to do this.

Other types of libraries show greater consistency, although this consistency applies more in selection than in the rest of the management program. The size of the library is a major factor, which is an obvious point, perhaps, but one with implications. Administrative arrangements usually are developed with the people on hand rather than the other way around; seldom are people brought in to staff a newly conceived administrative model. We work with strengths of the existing staff; one result of this ad-hoc model is that we set priorities willy-nilly, and in the range of collection management activities, selection is almost always the first priority. Maintenance, access and availability, weeding, storage, and renewal receive less than adequate attention.

College libraries frequently rely on faculty to select materials, based on the necessary assumption that the collection must directly relate to curricula and syllabi. What varies from college to college is the degree to which the library retains control over the budget, vetoes or prioritizes faculty selections, and makes selection decisions of its own. The more clearly there exists a total collection management program, the more likely the librarians are to possess the necessary degree of control and authority and the more likely they are to consult

---

9. James A. Cogswell, "The Organization of Collection Management Functions in Academic Libraries," *Journal of Academic Librarianship* 13 (1987): 268–76.
10. Cogswell, p. 275.

with faculty in selection decisions, as well as in decisions about maintenance, weeding, and storage. A strong library authority allows us to build balanced collections that serve all programs equitably, to negotiate resource sharing and cooperative agreements, to select appropriate information and bibliographic technologies, and to carry out essential management functions of setting goals, devising strategies, and proving our accountability.

Public libraries have enjoyed more autonomy than academic or special librairies when developing collections. In addition to a centralized control of selection, there is a tradition of weeding and maintenance, as well as of librarians' participation in selection decisions. As in other types of libraries, the exact administrative model varies from library to library, depending in part on size and in part on local history.

The Profession

If separate collection management administrations are relatively new, then equally new is the problem of adequate professional training and support for collection management. Professional education, continuing education, publications, compilation of information, setting standards and standard procedures, and sponsored research are all areas in which the profession as a whole should be and has been involved. We are involved with journals and conferences, committees and projects, standards and guidelines, and a growing pool of information and knowledge. We are weak, however, in providing adequate beginning education, and we did not, until recently, identify collection management as a whole, coherent professional area of activity.

Education. Is collection management education provided? The easy answer is, No. Library schools have not offered courses in collection management. They have taught related subjects and activities, but without clearly identifying collection management as a coherent subject. Selection, reference, literature of the humanities or sciences or business, and so on, library administration, and types of libraries—all these were regularly taught and contained components of collection management. They seldom dealt with information, knowledge, research, and user needs in a way that instilled in students an understanding of the nature of collections.[11] The result is that beginning

---

11. Frederick J. Stielow and Helen R. Tibbo, "Collection Analysis and the Humanities: A Practicum with the RLG Conspectus," *Journal of Education for Library and Information Science* 27 (1987): 148–58.

librarians arrive on their first jobs with some understanding of developing collections, but with no sense of the whole collection management program.

Recent books about library education provide little encouragement. David Kohl's bibliographic handbook, *Library Education and Professional Issues,* does not contain a separate section for collection development or management, although it does provide sections for reference, cataloging, and acquisitions;[12] Herbert White's selection of essays on *Education for Professional Librarians* arranges the topic by types of libraries;[13] even Evelyn Daniel's chapter on "New Curriculum Areas" in *Education of Library and Information Professionals* reveals very little that is new (or even old) in teaching collection management.[14] The easy answer is, thus, a hard one: professional education is not preparing collection management librarians.

An educational program that provides more insight into collections is needed, but what is the nature of such a program? Charles Osburn suggests a "core program concentrating on the sociology of recorded human expression and communication," a proposal similar, as he acknowledges, to Jesse Shera's in *Foundations of Education for Librarianship.*[15] I fear, though, that when trying to equate collection development (or even management) with all librarianship, we may neglect the specifics of that very specific set of functions. We could teach everything only to discover we had taught nothing.

We do not need to offer many new and different courses. We must, however, teach our courses differently. All library-school courses must be concerned primarily with what is initially outside of the library—materials and user needs. If we can adequately understand user needs, then we can teach more pertinent reference courses and make these reference courses directly relevant to collection courses. If in reference courses students learn, for example, what kinds of language information people want and need, then they can under-

12. David F. Kohl, *Library Education and Professional Issues* (Santa Barbara, Calif.: ABC Clio, 1986).

13. *Education for Professional Librarians,* ed. Herbert S. White (White Plains, N.Y.: Knowledge Industry, 1986).

14. Evelyn Daniel, "New Curriculum Areas," in *Education of Library and Information Professionals: Present and Future Prospects,* ed. Richard K. Gardner (Littleton, Colo.: Libraries Unlimited, 1987), pp. 53–70.

15. Charles Osburn, "Education for Collection Development," in *Collection Development in Libraries: A Treatise,* ed. Robert D. Stueart and George B. Miller, Jr. (Greenwich, Conn.: JAI, 1980), p. 569, and Jesse Shera, *The Foundations of Education for Librarianship* (New York: Becker and Hayes, 1972).

stand the kinds of language questions they will ask, can understand how dictionaries and other language resources can (and cannot) answer those questions, and—the point—can understand what a suitable collection of language materials must consist of. This is not a new course, but an old course newly conceived.

A collection management course must be taught, however, and its status must equal that of traditional required reference and cataloging courses. Its contents must be far broader than simply "selection of library materials," and the course must not be subordinated to more specialized ones, such as courses on preservation or selection or scholarly and scientific communication. These latter specialties could, of course, be taught, just as online searching or OCLC cataloging is taught, but the first and strongest emphasis, here as elsewhere in the curriculum, must be on understanding, not just on techniques. Techniques change; understanding enables us to make the right changes.

Professional Support.   One good view of the profession's work as a whole appears in Frederick C. Lynden's annual surveys in the *ALA Yearbook* (entitled "Collection Development" in the 1978 and 1979 volumes, "Collection Management" since then, and preceded by a briefer survey by Jean C. Boyer in 1976 and 1977).[16] Lynden describes current developments, trends, and projects in technology, resource sharing, finances, and management. Individual libraries, consortia, and networks; associations and organizations; individuals and publications; state and federal governments; and foundations and research centers all contribute to our better understanding and operation. We now work with "access (resource sharing); . . . with acquisition, but also with collection maintenance and preservation; . . . with budgeting, but also with fund raising; . . . with collection evaluation, but also with the politics of use; . . . with weeding, but also with storage alternatives."[17]

Library organizations are active and effective. Not only the American Library Association but also the Association of Research Libraries, American Theological Libraries, Music Library, Law Library, Medical Library, and Special Library Associations all offer programs, some very strong, to educate and inform their members about collection management. The ARL's Office of Management Studies, research funded and published by the Council of Library Resources,

---

16. Frederick C. Lynden, "Collection Management," *ALA Yearbook of Library and Information Services* (Chicago: American Library Association, 1980–   ).
17. Lynden, 1980, p. 117.

publications from ALA divisions, and workshops and continuing-education programs sponsored by these bodies (such as the Collection Development and Management Institutes held periodically by the Resources and Technical Services Division) have produced a tremendously beneficial effect on our knowledge and practice of collection management.

A New Paradigm? How a profession thinks about its activities is a kind of paradigm, loosely similar to paradigms as defined by Thomas Kuhn in his *Structure of Scientific Revolutions*.[18] We now may be in the midst of a paradigm shift. Professional thinking has, on the one hand, emphasized specific operations and tasks, such as acquisitions, cataloging, reference, selection, weeding and preservation, and, on the other, been framed by the concept of types of libraries. We deal in administrative units and worker tasks. This is not unreasonable, for we are a profession after all and are concerned primarily with managerial problem solving. This managerial function certainly has been emphasized throughout this book. The flaw may be that we treat these tasks and services as discrete parts of administrative units rather than as integrally related in a process. Our paradigm, then, has been type of library: an administrative model controls our thinking.

If, on the other hand, we were to shift our thinking to the total process of managing collections regardless of the type of library, as I have been trying to do here, then we might better understand the ways in which these collections can and should meet users' needs. In many places this shift has occurred. A new paradigm is appearing, not imposed, but developed, as library educators, administrators, and staff librarians work with and think about library collections. Our collective efforts to better understand and manage these collections produced the idea, and in many libraries, the reality of the collection management program.

In a successful program librarians focus on the process and system, as well as on the specific tasks. They understand that their collections are dynamic yet coherent wholes, each with its own history, needs, and prospects, and each with its own character. They developed and maintained that character explicitly and conscientiously to meet users' needs as identified in their library's mission. The good collection is our best service.

---

18. Thomas S. Kuhn, *The Structure of Scientific Revolutions*, 2nd ed. (Chicago: University of Chicago Press, 1970). For a sound analysis of the uses and misuses of Kuhn's ideas, see Robert J. Connors, "Composition Studies and Science," *College English* 45 (1983): 1–20.

Bibliography

Access to Scholarly Information: Issues & Strategies. Ed. Sul H. Lee. Ann Arbor, Mich.: Pierian, 1985.

The ALA Glossary of Library and Information Science. Ed. Heartsill Young. Chicago: ALA, 1983.

ALA Handbook of Organization 1987/1988 and Membership Directory. Chicago: ALA, 1987.

ALA World Encyclopedia of Library and Information Services. 2nd ed. Ed. Robert Wedgeworth. Chicago: ALA, 1986.

ALA Yearbook of Library and Information Services: A Review of Library Events of [year]. Chicago: ALA, 1976– .

Almony, Robert A., Jr. "The Concept of Systematic Duplication: A Survey of the Literature." *Collection Management* 2 (1978): 153–65.

Alternative Materials in Libraries. Eds. James P. Danky and Elliott Shore. Metuchen, N.J.: Scarecrow, 1982.

Anglo-American Cataloguing Rules. 2nd ed. Eds. Michael Gorman and Paul W. Winkler. Chicago: ALA, 1979.

Atkinson, Hugh. "Atkinson on Networks." *American Libraries* 18 (1987): 430–39.

Atkinson, Ross W. "The Citation As Intertext: Toward a Theory of the Selection Process." *Library Resources & Technical Services* 28 (1984): 109–19.

_____ . "The Language of the Levels: Reflections on the Communication of Collection Development Policy." *College & Research Libraries* 47 (1986): 140–49.

_____ . "Preparation for Privation: The Year's Work in Collection Management." *Library Resources & Technical Services* 32 (1988): 249–62.

_____ . "Selection for Preservation: A Materialistic Approach." *Library Resources & Technical Services* 30 (1986): 341–53.

Austerity Management in Academic Libraries. Eds. John F. Harvey and Peter Spyers-Duran. Metuchen, N.J.: Scarecrow, 1984.

Ballard, Thomas H. *The Failure of Resource Sharing in Public Libraries and Alternative Strategies for Service.* Chicago: ALA, 1986.

Bennett, S. B. "Current Initiatives and Issues in Collection Management." *Journal of Academic Librarianship* 10 (1984): 257–61.

Bibliographer's Manual: A Guide to the General Libraries Collection Development Program. Austin: The General Libraries, The University of Texas at Austin, 1982.

Blasingame, Ralph, and Mary Jo Lynch. "Design for Diversity: Alternatives to Standards for Public Libraries." *Studies in Library Management* 3 (1976): 121–35.

Boll, John J. *Shelf Browsing, Open Access and Storage Capacity in Research Libraries.* Occasional Paper No. 169. Champaign: Graduate School of Library and Information Science, University of Illinois, 1985.

Bone, Larry Earl, ed. "Community Analysis and Libraries." *Library Trends* 24 (1976): 429–643.

Bone, Larry Earl, and Thomas A. Raines. "The Nature of the Urban Main Library: Its Relation to Selection and Collection Building." *Library Trends* 20 (1972): 625–39.

Bowker Annual of Library & Book Trade Information. New York: Bowker, 1965–   .

Branin, Joseph J., David Farrell, and Mariann Tiblin. "The National Shelflist Count: Its History, Limitations, and Usefulness." *Library Resources & Technical Services* 29 (1985): 333–41.

Broadus, Robert N. "Information Needs of Humanities Scholars: A Study of Requests Made at the National Humanities Center." *Library & Information Science Research* 9 (1987): 113–29.

——. *Selecting Materials for Libraries.* 2nd ed. New York: Wilson, 1981.

——. "Use Studies of Library Collections." *Library Resources & Technical Services* 24 (1980): 317–24.

Bryant, Bonita. "Allocation of Human Resources for Collection Development." *Library Resources & Technical Services* 30 (1986): 149–62.

——. "The Organizational Structure of Collection Development." *Library Resources & Technical Services* 31 (1987): 111–22.

Buckland, Michael K. *Book Availability and the Library User.* New York: Pergamon, 1975.

Bulick, Stephen. "Book Use As a Bradford-Zipf Phenomenon." *College & Research Libraries* 39 (1978): 215–19.

The Business of Book Publishing: Papers by Practitioners. Eds. Elizabeth A. Geiser and Arnold Dobin, with Gladys S. Topkis. Boulder, Colo.: Westview, 1985.

Calmes, Alan. "New Confidence in Microfilm." *Library Journal* 111 (September 15, 1986): 38–42.

Capital Provision for University Libraries: Report of a Working Party. Chairman, Richard J. C. Atkinson. London: HMSO, 1976.

Center for Research Libraries. *Handbook.* Chicago: CRL, 1987.

Christiansen, Dorothy E., C. Roger Davis, and Juta Reed-Scott. "Guide to Collection Evaluation through Use and User Studies." *Library Resources & Technical Services* 27 (1983): 432–40.

Ciliberti, Anne C., Mary F. Casserly, Judith L. Hegg, and Eugene S. Mitchell.

"Material Availability: A Study of Academic Library Performance." *College & Research Libraries* 48 (1987): 513–27.

Clapp, Verner W., and Robert T. Jordan. "Quantitative Criteria for Adequacy of Academic Library Collections." *College & Research Libraries* 26 (1965): 371–80.

Cogswell, James A. "The Organization of Collection Management Functions in Academic Libraries." *Journal of Academic Librarianship* 13 (1987): 268–76.

Cole, John Y. "Storehouses and Workshops: American Libraries and the Uses of Knowledge." *The Organization of Knowledge in Modern America, 1860–1920.* Ed. Alexandra Oleson and John Voss. Baltimore: Johns Hopkins University Press, 1979, pp. 364–85.

Collection Development in Libraries: A Treatise. 2v. Eds. Robert D. Stueart and George B. Miller, Jr. Greenwich, Conn.: JAI, 1980.

Collection Management for School Library Media Centers. Ed. Brenda H. White. New York: Haworth, 1986.

Collection Management in Public Libraries. Ed. Judith Serebnick. Chicago: ALA, 1986.

Coordinating Cooperative Collection Development: A National Perspective. Ed. Wilson Luquire. New York: Haworth, 1986.

Coser, Lewis A., Charles Kadushin, and Walter W. Powell. *Books: The Culture and Commerce of Publishing.* New York: Basic Books, 1982.

Crane, Diana. *Invisible Colleges: Diffusion of Knowledge in Scientific Communities.* Chicago: University of Chicago Press, 1972.

Cumulated ARL University Library Statistics. Comp. Kendon Stubbs and David Buxton. Washington, D.C.: Association of Research Libraries, 1981.

Cummings, Martin M. *The Economics of Research Libraries.* Washington, D.C.: Council on Library Resources, 1986.

Cunha, George M., and Dorothy Grant Cunha. *Library and Archives Conservation: 1980 and Beyond.* 2v. Metuchen, N.J.: Scarecrow, 1983.

Curley, Arthur, and Dorothy Broderick. *Building Library Collections.* 6th ed. Metuchen, N.J.: Scarecrow, 1985. Previous editions by Wallace J. Bonk and Rose Mary Magrill.

Danton, J. Periam. *Book Selection and Collections: A Comparison of German and American University Libraries.* New York: Columbia University Press, 1963.

Davies, Roy. "Documents, Information or Knowledge? Choices for Librarians." *Journal of Librarianship* 15 (1983): 47–65.

De Gennaro, Richard. *Libraries, Technology, and the Information Marketplace: Selected Papers.* Boston: G. K. Hall, 1987.

Dennison, Sally. *Alternative Literary Publishing: Five Modern Histories.* Iowa City: University of Iowa Press, 1984.

Derr, Richard L. "A Conceptual Analysis of Information Need." *Information Processing and Management* 19 (1983): 273–78.

Dessauer, John. *Book Publishing: What It Is, What It Does.* 2nd ed. New York: Bowker, 1981.

Dodd, Sue A. *Cataloging Machine-Readable Data Files.* Chicago: ALA, 1982.

Dougherty, Richard M., and Laura L. Blomquist. *Improving Access to Library Resources.* Metuchen, N.J.: Scarecrow, 1974.

Edelman, Hendrik. "The Death of the Farmington Plan." *Library Journal* 98 (1973): 1251–53.

_____. "Selection Methodology in Academic Libraries." *Library Resources & Technical Services* 23 (1979): 33–44.

Education for Professional Librarians. Ed. Herbert S. White. White Plains, N.Y.: Knowledge Industry, 1986.

Education of Library and Information Professionals: Present and Future Prospects. Ed. Richard K. Gardner. Littleton, Colo.: Libraries Unlimited, 1987.

Eisenstein, Elizabeth L. *The Printing Press As an Agent of Change: Communications and Cultural Transformations in Early-Modern Europe.* 2v. Cambridge: Cambridge University Press, 1979.

Encyclopedia of Library and Information Science. 35v. Eds. Allen Kent and Harold Lancour. New York: Dekker, 1968–83.

_____. Supplements, v. 1–   , 1983–   .

English and American Literature: Sources and Strategies for Collection Development. Ed. William McPheron and others. ACRL Publications in Librarianship, No. 45. Chicago: ALA, 1987.

Evans, G. Edward. *Developing Library and Information Center Collections.* 2nd ed. Littleton, Colo.: Libraries Unlimited, 1987.

Facente, Gary. "An Overview of American Publishing for Librarians." *Library Resources & Technical Services* 30 (1986): 57–67.

Farewell to Alexandria: Solutions to Space, Growth, and Performance Problems. Ed. Daniel Gore. Westport, Conn.: Greenwood, 1976.

Fry, Bernard M., and Herbert S. White. *Publishers and Libraries: A Study of Scholarly and Research Journals.* Lexington, Mass.: Lexington Books, 1976.

Fussler, Herman H., and Julian L. Simon. *Patterns in the Use of Books in Large Research Libraries.* Chicago: University of Chicago Press, 1969.

Futas, Elizabeth, ed. *Library Acquisition Policies and Procedures.* Phoenix: Oryx, 1977; 2nd ed., 1984.

Futas, Elizabeth, and Sheila S. Intner, eds. "Collection Evaluation." *Library Trends* 33 (1985): 237–436.

Gapen, D. Kaye, and Sigrid P. Milner. "Obsolescence." *Library Trends* 30 (Summer 1981): 107–24.

Gardner, Richard K. *Library Collections: Their Origin, Selection, and Development.* New York: McGraw-Hill, 1981.

Garvey, William. *Communication: The Essence of Science. Facilitating Information Exchange among Librarians, Scientists, Engineers and Students.* New York: Pergamon, 1979.

Genaway, David C. "PBA: Percentage Based Allocation for Acquisitions." *Library Acquisitions: Practice & Theory* 10 (1986): 287–92.

——. "The Q Formula: The Flexible Formula for Library Acquisitions in Relation to the FTE Driven Formula." *Library Acquisitions: Practice & Theory* 10 (1986): 293–306.

Gilroy, Angele A. "An Economic Analysis of the U.S. Domestic Book Publishing Industry." *Printing and Publishing* 21 (4) (Fall 1980): 8–12.

Godden, Irene P., Karen W. Fachan, Patricia A. Smith, and Sandra Brug. *Collection Development and Acquisitions, 1970-80: An Annotated, Critical Bibliography*. Metuchen, N.J.: Scarecrow, 1982.

Goldstein, Marianne, and Joseph Sedransk. "Using a Sample Technique to Describe Characteristics of a Collection." *College & Research Libraries* 38 (1977): 195–202.

Greene, Robert J. "The Effectiveness of Browsing." *College & Research Libraries* 38 (1977): 313–16.

Greenfield, Jane. *Books: Their Care and Repair*. New York: Wilson, 1983.

Grove, Pearce S., ed. "Library Cooperation." *Library Trends* 24 (1975): 157–423.

Guide for Writing a Bibliographer's Manual. Ed. Carolyn Bucknall. Collection Management and Development Guides, No. 1. Chicago: ALA, 1987.

Guidelines for Collection Development. Ed. David L. Perkins. Chicago: ALA, 1979.

Gwinn, Nancy E., and Paul H. Mosher. "Coordinating Collection Development: The RLG Conspectus." *College & Research Libraries* 44 (1983): 128–40.

Haines, Helen E. *Living with Books: The Art of Book Selection*. 2nd ed. New York: Columbia University Press, 1950.

Haka, Clifford H., and Nancy Stevens. *A Guidebook for Shelf Inventory Procedures in Academic Libraries*. Occasional Paper No. 10. Washington, D.C.: Office of Management Studies, Association of Research Libraries, 1985.

Hall, Blaine H. *Collection Assessment Manual for College and University Libraries*. Phoenix: Oryx, 1985.

Hamaker, Charles. "The Least Reading for the Smallest Number at the Highest Price." *American Libraries* 19 (1988): 764–68.

Harris, Michael, and James Sodt. "Libraries, Users, and Librarians: Continuing Efforts to Define the Nature and Extent of Public Library Use." *Advances in Librarianship* 11 (1981): 109–33.

Hayes, Robert M. "The Distribution of Use of Library Materials: Analysis of Data from the University of Pittsburgh." *Library Research: An International Journal* 3 (1981): 215–60.

Hayes, Robert M., Anne Pollock, and Shirley Nordhaus. "An Application of the Cobb-Douglas Model to the Association of Research Libraries." *Library & Information Science Research* 5 (1983): 204–8.

Hazen, Don C. "Collection Development, Collection Management, and Preservation." *Library Resources & Technical Services* 26 (1982): 3–11.

Heim, Kathleen M., ed. "Data Libraries for the Social Sciences." *Library Trends* 30 (1982): 319–509.

Hindle, Anthony, and Michael K. Buckland. "In-Library Book Usage in Relation to Circulation." *Collection Management* 2 (1978): 265–77.

Hoffmann, Frank W. *Popular Culture and Libraries.* Hamden, Conn.: Shoe String, 1984.

Hokkanen, Dorothy B. "U.S. Book Title Output: A One Hundred Year Overview." Revised by Chandler B. Grannis. In *Bowker Annual of Library and Book Trade Information,* 26th ed. New York: Bowker, 1981, 324–29.

Houghton, Tony. *Bookstock Management in Public Libraries.* Hamden, Conn.: Shoe String, 1985.

Hubbard, William J. *Stack Management: A Practical Guide to Shelving and Maintaining Library Collections.* A revision of W. H. Jesse, *Shelf Work in Libraries,* 1952. Chicago: ALA, 1981.

Hyman, Richard J. *Shelf Access in Libraries.* Studies in Librarianship, No. 9. Chicago: ALA, 1982.

Kantor, Paul B. *Objective Performance Measures for Academic and Research Libraries.* Washington, D.C.: Association of Research Libraries, 1984.

Katz, William A. *Collection Development: The Selection of Materials for Libraries.* New York: Holt, Rinehart and Winston, 1980.

Kent, Allen. *Resource Sharing in Libraries.* New York: Dekker, 1974.

Kent, Allen, and others. *The Use of Library Materials: The University of Pittsburgh Study.* New York: Dekker, 1979.

Kohl, David F. *Acquisitions, Collection Development, and Collection Use: A Handbook for Library Management.* Santa Barbara, Calif.: ABC-Clio, 1985.

_____. *Circulation, Interlibrary Loan, Patron Use, and Collection Maintenance: A Handbook for Library Management.* Santa Barbara, Calif.: ABC-Clio, 1986.

_____. *Library Education and Professional Issues: A Handbook for Library Management.* Santa Barbara, Calif.: ABC-Clio, 1986.

Kosek, Reynold, and Mary Anne Royle. "Library Standards: A Subject Bibliography with Emphasis on Law Libraries." Public Administration Series: Bibliography P. 1316. Monticello, Ill.: Vance Bibliographies, 1983.

Lancaster, F. Wilfrid. "Evaluating Collections by Their Use." *Collection Management* 4 (Spring/Summer 1982): 15–43.

_____. *The Measurement and Evaluation of Library Services.* Washington, D.C.: Information Resources, 1977.

_____. *Toward Paperless Information Systems.* New York: Academic, 1978.

Lee, Marshall. *Bookmaking: The Illustrated Guide to Design/Production/Editing.* 2nd ed. New York: Bowker, 1979.

Library Effectiveness: A State of the Art. Eds. Neal K. Kaske and William G. Jones. Papers from a 1980 ALA Preconference, New York, New York, June 27 and 28, 1980. Chicago: ALA, 1980.

The Library Preservation Program: Models, Priorities, Possibilities. Eds. Jan Merrill-Oldham and Merrily Smith. Chicago: ALA, 1985.

Line, Maurice B., and Alexander Sandison. " 'Obsolescence' and Changes in the Use of Literature with Time." *Journal of Documentation* 30 (1974): 283–350.

Loe, Mary H. "Thor Tax Ruling after 5 Years: Its Effect on Publishing and Libraries." *Library Acquisitions: Practice and Theory* 10 (1986): 203–18.

Loveday, Anthony J. "An Appraisal of the Report of the University Grants Committee Working Party on Capital Provision for University Libraries (The Atkinson Report)." *Journal of Librarianship* 9 (1977): 17–28.

Lucker, Jay K., Kate S. Herzog, and Sydney J. Owens. "Weeding Collections in an Academic Library System: Massachusetts Institute of Technology." *Science & Technology Libraries* 6 (Spring 1986): 11–23.

Lynch, Clifford A., and Edwin B. Brownrigg. "Conservation, Preservation, and Digitalization." *College & Research Libraries* 47 (1986): 379–82.

Lynden, Frederick C. "Collection Management." *ALA Yearbook of Library and Information Services.* Chicago: ALA, 1980– .

Magrill, Rose Mary. "Evaluation by Type of Library." *Library Trends* 33 (1985): 267–95.

Magrill, Rose Mary, and Mona East. "Collection Development in Large University Libraries." *Advances in Librarianship* 8 (1978): 1–54.

Magrill, Rose Mary, and John Corbin. *Acquisitions Management and Collection Development in Libraries.* 2nd ed. Chicago: ALA, 1989.

Makepeace, Chris E. *Ephemera: A Book on Its Collection, Conservation and Use.* Brookfield, Vt.: Gower/Grafton, 1985.

Mansbridge, J. "Availability Studies in Libraries." *Library & Information Science Research* 8 (1986): 299–314.

McClung, Patricia A. "Costs Associated with Preservation Microfilming: Results of the Research Libraries Group Study." *Library Resources & Technical Services* 30 (1986): 363–74.

McClure, Charles R., Douglas L. Zweizig, Nancy A. Van House, and Mary Jo Lynch. "Output Measures: Myths, Realities, and Prospects." *Public Libraries* 25 (Summer 1986): 49–52.

McCrady, Ellen. "Selection for Preservation: A Survey of Approaches." *Abbey Newsletter* 6 (Supplement) (August 1982): 1, 3–4.

McGrath, William E. "An Allocation Formula for Academic and Public Libraries with a Test for Its Effectiveness." *Library Resources & Technical Services* 19 (1975): 356–69.

_____. "Correlating the Subjects of Books Taken Out and of Books Used within an Open-Stack Library." *College & Research Libraries* 32 (1971): 280–85.

Meckler, Alan M. *Micropublishing: A History of Scholarly Micropublishing in America, 1938-80.* Westport, Conn.: Greenwood, 1982.

Metcalf, Keyes D. *Planning Academic and Research Library Buildings.* 2nd ed. by Philip D. Leighton and David C. Weber. Chicago: ALA, 1986.

Metz, Paul. *Landscape of Literatures: Use of Subject Collections in a University Library.* ACRL Publications in Librarianship, No. 43. Chicago: ALA, 1983.

Molyneux, Robert. "Growth of ARL Member Libraries 1962/63 to 1983/84." *Journal of Academic Librarianship* 12 (1986): 211–16.

Moran, Barbara B. *Academic Libraries: The Changing Knowledge Centers of Colleges and Universities.* ASHE-ERIC Higher Education Research Report No. 8. Washington, D.C.: Association for the Study of Higher Education, 1984.

Morris, John. *The Library Disaster Preparedness Handbook.* Chicago: ALA, 1986.

Morrow, Carolyn Clark. *Conservation Treatment Procedures: A Manual of Step-by-Step Procedures for the Maintenance and Repair of Library Materials.* Littleton, Colo.: Libraries Unlimited, 1982.

———. *The Preservation Challenge: A Guide to Conserving Library Materials.* White Plains, N.Y.: Knowledge Industry, 1983.

Mosher, Paul H. "Collection Development to Collection Management: Toward Stewardship of Library Resources." *Collection Management* 4 (4) (Winter 1982): 41–48.

———. "Collection Evaluation in Research Libraries: The Search for Quality, Consistency and System in Collection Development." *Library Resources & Technical Services* 23 (1979): 16–32.

———. "The Nature and Uses of the RLG Verification Studies." *CRL News* 46 (1985): 336–38.

———. "Quality and Library Collections: New Directions in Research and Practice in Collection Evaluation." *Advances in Librarianship* 13 (1984): 211–38.

Mosher, Paul H., and Marcia Pankake. "A Guide to Coordinated and Cooperative Collection Development." *Library Resources & Technical Services* 27 (1983): 411–31.

Murfin, Marjorie E. "The Myth of Accessibility: Frustration and Failure in Retrieving Periodicals." *Journal of Academic Librarianship* 6 (1980): 16–19.

Nemeyer, Carol A. *Scholarly Reprint Publishing in the United States.* New York: Bowker, 1972.

1984 "100 Libraries" Statistical Survey. Chicago: ALA, 1985.

Nonbook Media: Collection Management and User Services. Eds. John W. Ellison and Patricia Ann Coty. Chicago: ALA, 1987.

Nonprint Media in Academic Libraries. Ed. Pearce S. Grove. ACRL Publications in Librarianship, No. 34. Chicago: ALA, 1975.

Novak, Gloria. *Running Out of Space: What Are the Alternatives?* Chicago: ALA, 1978.

One Book Five Ways: The Publishing Procedure of Five University Presses. Los Altos, Calif.: William Kaufmann, 1977.

Ortopan, LeRoy D. "National Shelflist Count: A Historical Introduction." *Library Resources & Technical Services* 29 (1985): 328–32.

Osborn, Andrew D. *Serial Publications: Their Place and Treatment in Libraries.* 3rd ed. Chicago: ALA, 1980.

Osburn, Charles B. *Academic Research and Library Resources: Changing Patterns in America.* Westport, Conn.: Greenwood, 1979.

———. "New Directions in Collection Development." *Technicalities* 2 (2) (February 1982):1, 3–4.

———. "The Place of the Journal in the Scholarly Communication System." *Library Resources & Technical Services* 28 (1984): 315–24.

———. "Toward a Reconceptualization of Collection Development." *Advances in Library Administration and Organization: A Research Annual* 2 (1983): 175–90.

Output Measures for Public Libraries: A Manual of Standardized Procedures. 2nd ed. Eds. Nancy A. Van House, Mary Jo Lynch, Charles R. McClure, Douglas L. Zweizig, and Eleanor J. Rodger. Chicago: ALA, 1987.

Pankake, Marcia. "From Book Selection to Collection Management: Continuity and Advance in an Unending Work." *Advances in Librarianship* 31 (1984): 185–210.

———. "Technical Services in 1984 and 1985: Resources." *Library Resources & Technical Services* 30 (1986): 218–37.

Perrault, Anna H. "Humanities Collection Management: An Impressionistic/Realistic/Optimistic Appraisal of the State of the Art." *Collection Management* 5 (3-4) (1983): 1–23.

Potter, William Gray. "Studies of Collection Overlap: A Literature Review." *Library Research: An International Journal* 4 (1982): 3–21.

Powell, Walter W. *Getting into Print: The Decision-Making Process in Scholarly Publishing.* Chicago: University of Chicago Press, 1985.

Preservation Microfilming: A Guide for Librarians and Archivists. Ed. Nancy E. Gwinn. Chicago: ALA, 1987.

Preservation Planning Manual. Washington, D.C.: Association of Research Libraries, 1982.

Prostano, Emmanuel T., and Joyce S. Prostano. *The School Library Media Center.* 3rd ed. Littleton, Colo.: Libraries Unlimited, 1982.

Publishers and Librarians: A Foundation for Dialogue. Ed. Mary Biggs. Proceedings of the Forty-Second Conference of the Graduate Library School, May 13–15, 1983. Chicago: University of Chicago Press, 1984.

Rawlinson, Nora. "Give 'Em What They Want!" *Library Journal* 106 (1981): 2188–90.

Reed-Scott, Jutta. *Manual for the North American Inventory of Research Library Collections.* Washington, D.C.: Association of Research Libraries, 1985.

"Report on the Library of Congress DEZ Project." *Association of Research Libraries. Minutes of the 109th Meeting. October 22–23, 1986.*

Washington, D.C. Washington, D.C.: Association of Research Libraries, 1987, pp. 81–88.

Rider, Fremont. *The Scholar and the Future of the Research Library: A Problem and Its Solution.* New York: Hadham, 1944.

RLG Preservation Manual. Stanford, Calif.: Research Libraries Group, 1983.

Rohlf, Robert H. "Standards for Public Libraries." *Library Trends* 31 (Summer 1982): 65–76..

Rosenberg, Betty. *Genreflecting: A Guide to Reading Interests in Genre Fiction.* 2nd ed. Littleton, Colo.: Libraries Unlimited, 1986.

Rubin, Richard. *In-House Use of Materials in Public Libraries.* Champaign: Graduate School of Library and Information Science, University of Illinois, 1986.

Rudd, Joel, and Mary Jo Rudd. "Coping with Information Load: User Strategies and Implications for Libraries." *College & Research Libraries* 47 (1986): 315–22.

Saracevic, T., W. H. Shaw, Jr., and Paul B. Kantor. "Causes and Dynamics of User Frustration in an Academic Library." *College & Research Libraries* 38 (1977): 7–18.

Scholarly Communication: The Report of the National Enquiry. Baltimore: Johns Hopkins University Press, 1979.

Security for Libraries: People, Buildings, Collections. Ed. Marvine Brand. Chicago: ALA, 1984.

Segal, Joseph P. *Evaluating and Weeding Collections in Small and Medium-Sized Public Libraries: The CREW Method.* Chicago: ALA, 1980.

Selection of Library Materials in Applied and Interdisciplinary Fields. Eds. Beth J. Shapiro and John Whaley. Chicago: ALA, 1987.

Selection of Library Materials in the Humanities, Social Sciences, and Sciences. Ed. Patricia A. McClung. Chicago: ALA, 1985.

Shaping Library Collections for the 1980s. Eds. Peter Spyers-Duran and Thomas Mann, Jr. Phoenix: Oryx, 1980.

Shatzkin, Leonard. *In Cold Type: Overcoming the Book Crisis.* Boston: Houghton Mifflin, 1982.

Shera, Jesse. *The Foundations of Education for Librarianship.* New York: Becker and Hayes, 1972.

———. *Knowing Books and Men; Knowing Computers, Too.* Littleton, Colo.: Libraries Unlimited, 1973.

Slote, Stanley J. *Weeding Library Collections—II.* 2nd ed. Littleton, Colo.: Libraries Unlimited, 1982.

Smith, Richard D. "Mass Deacidification: The Wei T'o Way." *College & Research Libraries News* 45 (1984): 588–93.

Sohn, Jean. "Collection Development Organizational Patterns in ARL Libraries." *Library Resources & Technical Services* 31 (1987): 123–34.

Spiller, David. *Book Selection.* 5th ed. Chicago: ALA, 1988.

Spohner, James H., Dorothy A. Koenig, and Sheila T. Dowd. *Guide to Collection Development and Management at the University of California,*

Berkeley. Berkeley: The General Libraries, University of California, 1986.

Stam, David H. "Collaborative Collection Development: Progress, Problems, and Potential." *Collection Building* 7 (3) (1986): 3–9.

Stayner, Richard A., and Valerie E. Richardson. *The Cost-Effectiveness of Alternative Storage Programs.* Clayton, Victoria, Australia: Graduate School of Librarianship, Monash University, 1983.

Stevens, Rolland E. *Characteristics of Subject Literatures.* ACRL Monographs No. 6. Chicago: ALA, 1953.

Strategies for Meeting the Information Needs of Society in the Year 2000. Ed. Martha Boaz. Littleton, Colo.: Libraries Unlimited, 1981.

Stubbs, Kendon. *Quantitative Criteria for Academic Research Libraries.* Chicago: ALA, 1984.

———. "University Libraries: Standards and Statistics." *College & Research Libraries* 42 (1981): 527–38.

Taylor, David C. *Managing the Serials Explosion: The Issues for Publishers and Libraries.* White Plains, N.Y.: Knowledge Industry, 1982.

Tough, Allen. *Intentional Changes: A Fresh Approach to Helping People Change.* Chicago: Follett, 1982.

Trueswell, Richard D. "Some Behavioral Patterns of Library Users: The 80/20 Rule." *Wilson Library Bulletin* 43 (1969): 458–61.

Tuttle, Marcia, with Luke Swindler and Nancy I. White. *Introduction to Serials Management.* Greenwich, Conn.: JAI, 1983.

Van Orden, Phyllis J. *The Collection Program in Elementary and Middle Schools: Concepts, Practices, and Information Sources.* Littleton, Colo.: Libraries Unlimited, 1982.

———. *The Collection Program in High School Libraries: Concepts, Practices, and Information Sources.* Littleton, Colo.: Libraries Unlimited, 1985.

Varner, Carroll. "Journal Mutilation in Academic Libraries." *Library & Archival Security* 5 (4) (Winter 1983): 19–29.

Voigt, Melvin J. "Acquisition Rates in University Libraries." *College & Research Libraries* 36 (1975): 263–71.

Waldhart, Thomas J. "The Growth of Interlibrary Loan Among ARL University Libraries." *Journal of Academic Librarianship* 10 (1984): 204–08.

Walker, Gay. "Library Binding As a Conservation Measure." *Collection Management* 4 (1-2) (Spring/Summer 1982): 55–71; reprinted in *New Library Scene* 3 (April 1984): 1, 4–9, 15.

———. "The Yale Survey: A Large-Scale Study of Book Deterioration in the Yale University Library." *College & Research Libraries* 46 (1985): 111–32.

Webb, T. D. "A Hierarchy of Public Library User Types." *Library Journal* 111 (September 15, 1986): 47–50.

Weber, David C. "Brittle Books in Our Nation's Libraries." *College & Research Libraries News* 48 (1987): 238–44.

_____. "A Century of Cooperative Programs Among Academic Libraries." *College & Research Libraries* 37 (1976): 205–21.

Westbrook, Lynn. "Developing an In-House Preservation Program: A Survey of Experts." *Library & Archival Security* 7 (3–4) (Fall/Winter 1985): 1–21.

Whatmore, Geoffrey. *The Modern News Library.* Syracuse, N.Y.: Gaylord, 1978.

Wilson, Pauline. *A Community Elite and the Public Library: The Uses of Information in Leadership.* Westport, Conn.: Greenwood, 1977.

Wortman, William A. "Collection Management, 1986." *Library Resources & Technical Services* 31 (1987): 287–305.

Zweizig, Douglas, and Brenda Dervin. "Public Library Use, Users, Uses: Advances in Knowledge of the Characteristics and Needs of the Adult Clientele in American Public Libraries." *Advances in Librarianship* 7 (1977): 231–55.

Index

Access (Bibliographic), 147–53; cataloging, 149; classification, 149–50; indexing and bibliographies, 150–151; to other collections, 151–52

Access (Physical), 147–48, 153–62; branch libraries 160–162; browsing, 158–60; building types and capacity, 153–57; collection growth, 156–58; facilities management, 153; shelf arrangement, 158–60. *See also* Preservation program, Storage systems

Acquisitions. *See* Selection of new materials

Administration, 217–23; accountability, 220; administrative models, 220–23 (dissatisfaction with, 216, 221); allocations, 132–34; budget, 131–32; goals and objectives, 217–18; preservation, 194–96; responsibility for collection management, 12; stack management, 174–76; strategies, 219–20; support of collection management librarians, 216–217

Allocations, 132–34; formulas, 134, procedures, 133–34. *See also* Budget

Alternatives to ownership. *See* Cooperation

Analysis of collections, 102; of community, 83–85; of use, 109–14. *See also* Use

Arena, library as, 6–7

Availability, 148, 167–78; circulation and regulation of borrowing, 171–73; document delivery, 178; duplicate copies, 173; factors affecting, 168–71; interlibrary loan, 176–77; reserve collections, 174; reshelving, 174–75; selection for storage, 176; stack management, 174–76. *See also* Access (Bibliographic), Preservation program, Storage systems, Use, Weeding

Bibliographic control. *See* Access (Bibliographic)

Bibliographic utilities, 152. *See also* Access (Bibliographic)

Bibliographies. *See* Access (Bibliographic)

Binding, 191–94. *See also* Preservation program

Book reviewing, 66–67

Books, costs in publishing, 63–64; defined, 21–22; differentials by price, quantity, and subject, 49–52; prices, 45–47 (by subject, 49–52); quantity produced, 40–42 (by subject, 49–52); small-press output, 57–58; variety of formats and contents, 21. *See also* Periodicals, Preservation program, Print, Publishers, Publishing

Branch libraries, 160–62. *See also* Access (Physical), Storage systems, Supportiveness

Brittle paper. *See* Deterioration of library materials
Browsing, 158–60, 162–63. *See also* Access (Physical), Shelf arrangement
Budget, 131–32. *See also* Allocations
Buildings. *See* Access (Physical), Preservation, Storage systems

Cataloging. *See* Access (Bibliographic)
CD-ROMs, 35–36. *See also* Computer media
Center for Research Libraries, 127, 136–37, 163–65, 206
Circulation (regulation of borrowing), 111–12, 171–73. *See also* Availability, Use, Weeding
Classification. *See* Access (Bibliographic)
Climate control, 187–88. *See also* Preservation program
Collection analysis, 102; CLR Collection Analysis Projects, 12. *See also* Use
Collection development policies (CDP), 124–29; academic libraries, 126–27; cooperation, 127; public libraries; 125–26; writing the CDP, 127–29. *See also* Conspectus, Selection plans
Collection management (collection development, collection maintenance): defined, 2–3; elements of, 10–11; personal example, 7–10; textbooks and treatises, 3–5
Collection Management and Development Institutes, RTSD, 12
Collection Management Program (CMP), 2–3, 10–11, 13–14; access, 147–53; administration, 217–23; availability, 167–68; collection development policies, 124–29; cooperation and alternatives to ownership, 135–40; evaluation, 103–9; librarians, 211–17; materials, *see* Print, Nonprint, Computer media; preservation and maintenance, 179–98; publishing, 52–70; renewal, 198–99; review, 206–10; selection, 123–24, 140–46; selection plans, 129–31; storage systems, 162–67; use, 109–21; users, 76–83; weeding, 199–206
Collections, 5–7, 15–17, 38; categories of materials (print, 17–29; nonprint, 29–32; computer media,

32–37); character, 122–23; coherent whole, 6; conceived broadly, 5–6; differentials within, *see* Differentials by price, quantity, and subject; dynamic, 6; growth, 47–49, 155–58; levels, 105–7; living system, 157; nature of, 114–22 (composite, 115–16; core, 116–17; obsolescence, 117–18; overlap, 115; subject, 121–22; supportiveness, 118–19). *See also* broad categories and specific kinds of materials, such as Print, Books
Common reader. *See* User types
Communities, 83–87; community analysis, 83–85; place and interest communities, 83; user communities, 85–86. *See also* User types
"Composite collection," 71, 115–16, 138, 153, 167, 197. *See also* Access (Bibliographic), Storage systems
Computer media, 16, 32–37; CD-ROMs, 35–36; experimental period, 32–34; fees, 34–35; Machine-Readable Data Files (MRDF), 36–37; Online Public Access Catalogs (OPAC), 37; software in collections, 37. *See also* Publishing
Concerned citizen. *See* User types
Conservation, 191–94. *See also* Preservation program
Conspectus, 105–7, 126–29
Cooperation, 127, 135–40; access, 135–36; alternatives to ownership, 135–36; coordinated collection management, 136; costs, 139; examples, 136–39 (Center for Research Libraries, 136–37; California Shared Purchase Program, 137; Research Triangle Libraries, 137–38; LCS, 138–39); Interlibrary loan, 176–77; multitype, 138–39; preservation program, 196–98; storage systems, 164–67. *See also* Access (Bibliographic)
Core collections, 116–117; and weeding, 201–2
Coser, Lewis A., 58–65
Costs, of books, 63–64; cooperation, 139; periodicals, 45–47, 68; preservation, 195–96; storage, 165
Crane, Diana, 89–92

Cultural media, 31–32. *See also* Nonprint

Demand. *See* Need and demand for library information and materials
Dependency. *See* Supportiveness, dependency, ethnicity
Deterioration of library materials, 180–84; effect on availability, 169–70. *See also* Preservation program
Detroit Public Library, Reader Interest Classification, 160
Differentials by price, quantity, and subject, 49–52
Disaster plan, 188–89. *See also* Preservation program
Discard. *See* Weeding
Document delivery, 178; from storage, 165
Dowd, Sheila, 127–29
Dynamic nature of collections, 6

Education for collection management, 212, 223–25; in preservation program, 189
Educational media, 31. *See also* Nonprint
Eisenstein, Elizabeth, 19–21
Ephemera. *See* Popular culture materials
Ethnicity. *See* Supportiveness, dependency, ethnicity
Evaluation of collections, 101–2, 103–9. *See also* Review of collections, Use

Farmington Plan, 139
Fees. *See* Computer media
Formulas. *See* Allocations
Fragmentation in theory and practice of collection management, 3

Garvey, William, 88–92
Genre readers. *See* User types
Growth of collections, 47–49, 155–57

Indexing. *See* Access (Bibliographic)
Information industry. *See* Publishing
Information purpose, 74
Input and output data, 105, 107–8
Interlibrary loan, 176–77. *See also* Availability, Cooperation, Library Computer System
Invisible college, 89–91

Journals: defined, 24–26; "journal-centered" collections, 24; prices, 46–47, 68; role in scientific and scholarly communication, 25, 90–91. *See also* Magazines, Periodicals
Juvenile. *See* User types

Kadushin, Charles. *See* Coser, Lewis A.
Kent, Allen, 103, 119–121

Leighton, Philip D. *See* Metcalf, Keyes D.
Levels of collections, 105–7, 127–29. *See also* Conspectus
Librarians, 211–17; activities, 213–15; administrative support, 217–23; education, 223–25; individual responsibility, 12–13; institutional setting, 216–17; knowledge, 212–13; number needed, 219; personal and intellectual characteristics, 215–16; professional organizations, 225–26. *See also* Collection development policies, Selection of new materials
Library Computer System (LCS) (Illinois), 138–39, 152–53

Machine-Readable Data Files (MRDFs), 36–37. *See also* Computer media
Magazines: defined, 24–26; special interest, 26; ranked, 25–26. *See also* Journals
Maintenance, 189–94. *See also* Preservation program
Materials. *See* Print, Nonprint, Computer media
Media. *See* Print, Nonprint, Computer media
Mending, 191–94. *See also* Preservation program
Metcalf, Keyes, D., 155–58, 162–63, 188, 219
Metz, Paul, 86–87, 112, 118–19, 161
Microforms, 29–31; research collections, 29–31. *See also* Nonprint, Preservation microfilming
Mission, 97–100
Mosher, Paul, 7, 105–7, 115–16, 139–40
Multitype corporation, 127, 138–39
Mutilation, 183–84

National Collection Inventory Project, 106, 126
Need and demand for library information and materials, 73–76. *See also* User types
Newsletters, 27
Newspapers, 26–27
No-growth collections, 157–58. *See also* Access (Physical)
Nonprint: defined, 16, 29–32; cultural media, 31–32; educational media, 31; preservation and research media, 29–31; microforms, 29–31

Obsolescence, 117–18
One Book/Five Ways: The Publishing Procedure of Five University Presses, 60–65
Online Public Access Catalog (OPAC), 37, 149. *See also* Computer media
Osburn, Charles, 24, 94–97, 126, 212, 224
Overlap, 115

Paperless library, 15–16
Paradigm, 226
Periodicals: defined, 24–26; prices, 45–47, 68 (scholarly journals, 46–47; commercial publishers, 68); quantity, 42–45 (articles versus volumes, 44–45; in libraries, 50–51). *See also* Books, Journals, Magazines, Publishing
Pittsburgh Study, 119–21
Popular culture materials, 28–29
Powell, Walter W., 61–62. *See also* Coser, Lewis A.
Preservation, 179–98. *See also* Preservation program
Preservation and research media, 29–31. *See also* Nonprint
Preservation microfilming, 29–31, 192–94. *See also* Preservation program
Preservation program, 184–98; administration, 194–96; causes of deterioration, 180–84; costs, 195–96; cooperation, 196–97; magnitude of problems, 185–86; maintenance, 189–94 (selection, 189–90; shelf-reading, 190–91; stack management, 190–91; mending,

binding, and conservation, 190–94); prevention, 187–89 (climate and environment control, 187–88; disaster plan, 188–89; education, 189). *See also* Renewal of collections, Review of collections, Storage systems, Weeding
Prices of publications, 45–57. *See* Books, Periodicals
Print: defined, 16, 17–29; Eisenstein's analysis of, 19–21
Profession, 223–26; education, 223–25; organizations, programs, and publications, 12, 225–26
Professional. *See* User types
Publishers, 55–60. *See also* Publishing
Publishing, 52–70; distribution, 65–67; gatekeeping, 55–56; industry, 52–55; information industry, 69–70; librarians' concerns about, 54–55; library's position as part of, 54, 70–71; "operating behavior," 60; periodical publishing, 68; process, 60–67 (selection, 60–62; editing, 62–63; production, 62–63; costs, 63–64; promotion, 64–66); risk, 56, 61–62; Thor Power Tool ruling, 65. *See also* Books, Periodicals, Publishers

Quality: extrinsic, 108; intrinsic, 103–8; levels, 105–7; quantitative profiles, 107–8; standards, 104–5
Quantitative profiles of collections, 107–8
Quantity of publications, 40–45. *See also* Books, Periodicals

Renewal of collections, 198–99
Research Triangle Libraries, 137–38
Reserve collections. *See* Availability
Reshelving, 174–75
Review of collections, 206–10; kinds of review, 207–8; procedures, 208–10

Sampling, 208–10
Scientific and scholarly communication, 87–97; changing patterns, 94–97; process, 87–92; research different from scholarship, 82, 95–97; system, 92–94

Scholars and researchers, 82, 95–97. *See also* User types

Scholarly Communication: The Report of the National Enquiry, 92–94

Selection, for preservation, 189–90; storage, 176, 205–6; weeding, 200–205

Selection of new materials, 123–24; acquisition systems, 144–46; selection process, 140–46 (relevant, 141–42; pertinent, 142–43; purchase, 143–44); textbooks, 141–43

Selection plans, 125, 129–31. *See also* Collection development policies

Serials: defined, 23–27; quantity, 42–45. *See also* Newspapers, Newsletters, Periodicals, Journals, Magazines, Selection

Shared Purchase Program (California), 137, 165

Shelf arrangement, 158–60. *See also* Access (Physical), Browsing, Storage systems

Shelf reading, 175, 190–91, 208

Software in collections, 37. *See also* Computer media

Stack management, 174–76, 190–91, 208. *See also* Availability, Review of collections

Standards, 104–5

Statistical Package for the Social Sciences, 107, 209

Storage systems, 162–67; alternatives to new buildings, 163; costs, 165; necessity for, 162–63; selection for, 176, 205–6; three models, 163–67. *See also* Access (Physical), Core collections, Preservation program, Weeding

Subject collections, nature of, 121–22

Supportiveness, dependency, ethnicity, 112, 118–19, 161

Theft, 184

Thor Power Tool ruling, 65

Tough, Allen, 78–80

Trueswell, Richard D., 110; "80/20 Rule," 116–17

Types of libraries, 98–99

Union catalogs, 151–52. *See also* Access (Bibliographic)

Use: analysis, 109–14 (in light of circulation, 111–12; in-house use, 112–13; kinds of materials, 113–14; location, 111; noncirculating materials, 112–13; users, 114); defined, 110–11; extending use, 151; factors affecting, 114; Pittsburgh Study, 119–21; weeding, 201–2. *See also* Availability, Scientific and scholarly communication

User fees. *See* Computer media

User types, 76–83; juvenile, 77; genre reader, 77–78; student, 78–80; common reader, 80–81; concerned citizen, 81–82; scholars and researchers, 82; professional, 82–83. *See also* Communities, Need and demand for library information and materials, Use

User surveys, 108–9

Vendors, 66–67

Videocassettes, 31–32

Weber, David C., 195. *See also* Metcalf, Keyes D.

Weeding, 199–206; criteria, 200–203; discard, 200–205; procedures, 203–5; storage, 205–6

Westminster College (Pennsylvania), 158, 219

William A. Wortman is the humanities librarian at Miami University, Ohio. He is a member of the American Library Association, Association of Library Collections and Technical Services, and Association of College and Research Libraries. Wortman is the author of a recent article in *Library Resources & Technical Services* entitled "Collection Management." Wortman has a M.S. in library science from Columbia University and a Ph.D. in English from Case Western Reserve University.